International Series on Consumer Scie

Series Editor:
Jing Jian Xiao, University of Rhode Island

For further volumes:
http://www.springer.com/series/8358

Chan Kwok-bun · Chan Wai-wan

Mobile Chinese Entrepreneurs

Springer

Chan Kwok-bun
Chan Institute of Social Studies (CISS)
4th Fl. Yau Fung Bldg.
93 Lai Chi Kok Rd.
Kowloon, Hong Kong
ckb@ci-ss.org

Chan Wai-wan
Chan Institute of Social Studies (CISS)
4th Fl. Yau Fung Bldg.
93 Lai Chi Kok Rd.
Kowloon, Hong Kong
vivien@ci-ss.org

ISSN 2191-5660 e-ISSN 2191-5679
ISBN 978-1-4419-9642-8 e-ISBN 978-1-4419-9643-5
DOI 10.1007/978-1-4419-9643-5
Springer New York Dordrecht Heidelberg London

Library of Congress Control Number: 2011928242

Printed on acid-free paper

Springer is part of Springer Science+Business Media (www.springer.com)

The authors would like to thank two members of the Sociology Alumni Association, Hong Kong Baptist University, Miss Teresa Ip and Mr Herman Lau, the Department of Sociology, Hong Kong Baptist University, and Lie Jianxi for so generously contributing funds and intellectual efforts to the production and translation, without which this book would not have been possible.

Preface

This is an age of hypermobility. Migrants have travelled to all ends of the Earth.

To and fro, back and forth, they linger between the complexities of life in a strange land and their ingrained memories of their native homes, hovering between the urge to move on and their desire to go back. It is precisely in such lingering that life manifests itself in all its intricacies and paradoxes.

The group of immigrant entrepreneurs that make up the subject of this study speak eloquently for this age of mobility. They shuttle from city to city, place to place, between time zones. Part of their life is always packed up, ready to move. Looking ahead, tickets in hand, they have no idea what their next destination will be. In business, it is their most glamorous time. In daily life, however, they are just ordinary people, frustrated, torn between their loves and hates, struggling between flesh and soul, as they seek the best out of life. Yet existing studies generally focus on the entrepreneur's 'business behavior' while largely ignoring their 'human' side. Why, in fact, does the immigrant entrepreneur 'linger'? How do they linger, and how do they resolve their various emotional entanglements?

It is by no means the economist's monopoly to study man's economic behavior, since sociologists have long been working in the area. From Georg Simmel's observations on the symbolic meanings of money to Max Weber's exposition of the intrinsic links between protestant ethic and the spirit of capitalism, from Mark S. Granovetter's discussions of the utilitarian impact of interpersonal ties on economic development to the theoretical studies of social capital and social networks that have prospered since the 1980s, sociology has actively engaged itself in understanding man's economic behavior. Along the same lines and building upon theories of sociology, the present study situates the individuals within the global landscape of their time and, by so doing, not only seeks to reconsider the underlying functions of cultural factors, but also probes the most secret crannies of the individual's *emotional terrain*. In this way, the dual perspectives of economic sociology and social psychology provide us with certain fairly startling insights.

Entrepreneurship has always been an important lifeline for this commercial city of Hong Kong. Yet, to sustain the territory's vital spirit of entrepreneurship in the face of globalization, we need imaginative and creative powers that are at once transnational and unconventional. 'Mobility' turns out to be the most powerful dynamo of such imaginative and creative energies. A 'mobile sociology' is therefore urgently needed, not only to understand the nature of 'mobility' but also to look into the individual's 'human' joys and woes in the very midst of mobility, thus necessarily evoking a 'sociology of emotions'. Mobility has brought about change and innovation as well as impact. In the 'Cover Notes' to the 1 April 2007 issue of the *Yazhou zhoukan* (Asia Weekly), Qiu Liben had this to say: 'Talents around the globe refuse to yield to adversity, they will not believe in tears. They are creators of life's miracles. They are creators of national miracles'. Much as they refuse to submit or yield to adversity, tears, however, are no strangers to the travelling entrepreneurs. Tears as such flow *within*, turn invisible and run dry, amidst unknown pains and frustrations. This does not concern the economist, and the sociologist is not sufficiently sensitive either. The present study makes a fresh start. It seeks to explore the emotionality of these travelers, hoping to fill these gaps in sociological work.

Hong Kong entrepreneurship has had its glory days, when early Chinese immigrants settled in the territory and started their own businesses, when booming ethnic entrepreneurship constituted the motor of the city's sparkling vivacity. It was a time of numerous individual legends, the legends of this new metropolis of Hong Kong. Yet research of ethnic entrepreneurship in this international immigrant city has generally betrayed serious ethnocentric tendencies. Besides studies of ethnic Chinese enterprises (e.g., Wong Siu-lun's survey of Hong Kong textile industrialists), we have hardly touched upon other ethnic businesses (Indian, Pakistani, Nepalese, Indonesian, Thai, Vietnamese, Philippine, etc.) that have flourished in the territory. Indeed, for Hong Hong's entrepreneurship to go through another period of prosperity, it needs to 'walk on both legs': as much as transnational corporations are welcomed, ethnic businesses that are rooted in the territory, hidden in all corners of the city, and charged with creative vigor, are also needed. While this book seeks to make a fresh start in the study of Chinese immigrants, we are well aware of the urgency of probing other ethnic immigrant groups.

Migrancy has always been the subject of much critical attention. As time elapses, fundamental changes take place in migrants' social situations, their daily lives, the problems they encounter in corporate management, their dilemmas, and so on. The entrepreneurs in this study are mostly small-to-medium enterprise owners who, once highly valued by local governments when they entered the mainland Chinese market in the 1980s, are now put on the back burner, as the local governments are more attracted to transnational corporations and syndicates. Being increasingly 'marginalized', these entrepreneurs from Hong Kong may serve as a mirror for the mass of SMEs now operating on the mainland of China. Challenged by the changes in the state of affairs without government participation or assistance, these people can only unite to protect themselves on the mainland. But such small unions are hardly powerful enough to be effective. What the Hong Kong government must do at this point is work closely with local mainland governments and begin to think about developing measures, policies, and institutions to help and support them.

From knowledge comes prevision, and from now comes the future. Our exercise in economic sociology has the promise of insights which have far-reaching implications, not only for our knowledge of society, but for the formulation of public policies that will help migrant/ethnic entrepreneurship out of its predicament. Good sociology must be an applied sociology, an action sociology, a public sociology.

In 'lingering,' one 'vacillates,' not only between different spatial configurations, but between different times, wistfully desiring the past and ardently anticipating the future. Chan Kwok-bun, a co-author of this study, has written two previous books on Chinese migration, *Smoke and Fire: The Chinese in Montreal* when teaching in Canada and *Stepping Out: The Making of Chinese Entrepreneurs*, while teaching in Singapore. The current book adds a third volume to the trilogy – though the experiences, people, locations, and times are different, all three books mull over the eternal processes of 'hoping, hunting, waiting, and transforming', with or without regrets in life.

Sociological studies operate on the double tracks of retrospect and anticipation, theory and practice, fiction and reality, imagination and fact. From life it comes, and to life it has to return in order to improve it. As Marx put it so precisely, "The philosophies have only interpreted the world, in various ways; the point is to change it." To the sixteen entrepreneurs who shared with us their life experiences, we extend our heartfelt gratitude. This project could never have been possible without their stories, their candidness and their enthusiasm.

Hong Kong

Chan Kwok-bun
Chan Wai-wan

Contents

Shuttling Nomads in Mobile Times

An Age of Mobilities

"Where there is the sea, there are Chinese people."[1] Desire for mobility seems to stand out conspicuously as a characteristic of the Chinese character today. Faced with the waves of globalization, we are undergoing startling changes and transformations. Advances in science, technology and mass transportation appear to have diminished the physical distance between peoples, societies and countries, casting us adrift in a state of unprecedented mobility that is at once frequent and geographically diverse. Social resources move backwards and forwards between the global and the local, bound together in a dynamic set of cross-boundary, circular relationships.[2] This is, in the words of John Urry, a world of "typical mobile, roaming hybrids",[3] where every day we consume foreign goods and services and meet people from all around the globe.

These are the most mobile of times. If, in country life, human activity was once confined within a given endogenous social structure, it is now rather marked by an intermittent circularity of comings and goings, a sense of being both here and there at the same time. What this circularity displays is not a simple back-and-forth pattern of spatial-temporal movement, in which the individual's self-consciousness and self-identity are reduced to a less solid state amidst the instabilities of such maneuvers. One's self-consciousness is kept shuttling among the triple axes of space, time, and social culture, as his or her self-identity criss-crosses past and present, here and there,

[1] This idea derives from Chan Kwok-bun, *Smoke and Fire: The Chinese in Montreal* (Hong Kong: The Chinese University Press, 1991). The original sentence reads, "Where there are smoke and fire, there is a Chinese". Historically, the Chinese diaspora has been a story of sea-faring Chinese migrants, who found themselves wherever the sea had carried them. The sea's mobility speaks vividly to the "ever-in-flux" status of our immigrant entrepreneurs' lives.

[2] John Urry, "Mobile Sociology". *The British Journal of Sociology*, 51, No. 1 (January/March 2000), p. 199.

[3] Ibid., 196.

Chan Kwok-bun and Chan Wai-wan, *Mobile Chinese Entrepreneurs*,
International Series on Consumer Science, DOI 10.1007/978-1-4419-9643-5_1,

the real and the virtual/imaginary – this is a life full of ambiguities and indeterminacies.[4] In addition to the complexity of self-identity, the individual's social networks too have become increasingly complicated and multifarious, so much so that every day in and out of various social structures, one lives in a sophisticated fabric of affirmations and negations.[5]

The Shuttling Nomads

Any particular age produces its people of a particular character. This intensely mobile age of ours too is giving birth to its groups of mobile travelers who scurry, like those ancient couriers, from "station" to "station" across different societal borders. We might for now refer to them as "shuttling nomads".

The mobility of the times manifests itself most blatantly through those involved in trading activities. In the context of globalization, cross-national and cross-boundary businesses are becoming more frequent. Since mainland China introduced its open-up policy in 1978, the ethic of profit maximization has driven an increasing number of Hong Kong enterprises northwards from the international trading center. As new branches are set up and entire production lines moved back to the mainland, there is also a large-scale relocation of people, who have moved either with existing or with prospective businesses into the more open market. It has been the trend since the 1990s for Hongkongers to work and invest in the great north. According to a Census and Statistics Department survey report in 2006, the number of Hong Kong residents who work on the mainland has increased more than twofold over the past 10 years as a result of closer economic ties between the two regions. Specifically, the number has grown from 97,300 in 1995 to 176,300 in 2001 and then to 228,900 in 2005.[6] A similar report in 2004 has it that over 15% of these people are employers.[7]

This book studies a particular group of these "shuttling nomads", those who were born on the mainland and immigrated to Hong Kong before they established businesses

---

[4]Chou Ying-hsiung, "Shenfen zhi rentong: cong Lu Xun de liang ge xiaoshuo tuilun" ["Identity Formation: From Two Stories by Lu Xun"] in *Shenfen rentong yu gonggong wenhua: wenhua yanjiu lunwenji* [Identity and Public Culture: Critical Essays in Cultural Studies], ed., Chan Ching-kiu (Hong Kong: Oxford University Press, 1997), p. 321. Chou's original words are a portrayal of the mind's complexities and changes in self-consciousness that accompanied the native-narrator's return in Lu Xun's novella "My Old Home".

[5]Peter Berger, *Invitation to Sociology: A Humanistic Perspective* (Garden City, NY: Doubleday, 1963), p. 101.

[6]The Census and Statistics Department, "Hong Kong Residents Working in the Mainland of China, 1995–2005", *Hong Kong Monthly Digest of Statistics* (January 2006). Here, "Hong Kong residents working in the Mainland" does not include those who went to the mainland only for conducting business negotiations and inspection of business, and/or attending trade fairs, meetings and business-related entertainment. In addition, transport workers commuting between Hong Kong and the Mainland, and fishermen or seaman working within the waters of the Mainland were also excluded.

[7]The Census and Statistics Department, *Social Data Collected via the General Household Survey: Special Topics Report – Report No.38* (Hong Kong: The Census and Statistics Department, 2004).

back in their birthplace. They are what we call "immigrant entrepreneurs" who circuit within the triangle of birthplace (ancestral homes on the mainland), home (Hong Kong) and workplace (mainland China). We give the name "immigrant entrepreneurs" to distinguish them from the "indigenous entrepreneurs" that were born and brought up locally in Hong Kong. Being "immigrants", however, does not mean that they are "new immigrants" who, as the Hong Kong government define it, have not completed seven years of continuous residence in the territory. No government survey, as yet, shows the exact number of such "immigrant entrepreneurs". Active at the frontiers of this mobile society, they operate, maintain, and expand localized social networks as they alternate for work, family visits, or entertainment between China and Hong Kong. In the meantime, they manage to mobilize and integrate local resources, including interpersonal and other, more concrete, economic resources, so that room can be created for their businesses to survive and thrive in this world of tense global competition.

This special mobile group have their unique experience as immigrants. Such an experience does not evidence the single-route of "uprooting" from home and "re-rooting" in a strange land as portrayed in much immigrant literature, but is rather ever in process or emergent. Their mobility has a certain "liquid" nature, formless in space and inconstant in time. Liquidity is resistant to a constant form but is easily adaptable to any given shape. Liquidity is only a transient occupant. As it flows on, it keeps altering its form and thus defies description of it as transitory and impressionistic.[8] Since the object of the present study is a highly "fluid" group, our research was circumscribed by the temporal and spatial dimensions of the object's emergence. To capture this multi-spatial/temporal trajectory within the constraints of the narrative form, we will center on comprehending and relating these entrepreneurs' experiences as immigrants, business starters, and aggressive venturers. We will strive to demonstrate these social mobiles' self-identity and the networks of their "fluid" floating world. It is our hope to reveal the connections and associations between mobilities, identities, and businesses.

As a study of "immigrant entrepreneurs", this book has its focus on the following. First, it seeks to portray the plight and delight and innate intimacies of working within the spatial triangulation among birthplace, home and workplace. Attention will be paid to the way these immigrant entrepreneurs manipulate their differential identities to facilitate the construction of social networks. This will be dealt with in detail in the Chapter, "The Spatial Triangulation of Immigrant Entrepreneurship". Second, it seeks to lay bare the functions of various social organizations in both public and private spheres, i.e., how they serve as intersections of charity and profit, gain and emotionality, in the daily life of these immigrant entrepreneurs as well as in the operation of their enterprises. Third, it serves to remind the readers that such intense mobility is a double-edged sword: the mobility and identity alternation of being a "shuttling nomad" has reduced the entrepreneur to a state of mind that social psychologists would call self-alienation or self-estrangement. The Chapter, "The Double-Edged Sword: Mobility and Entrepreneurship", contextualizes the emotionality of the businessman, and seeks to bring sociological studies back to the examination of the individual as a human being.

[8]Zygmunt Bauman, *Liquid Modernity* (Malden, MA: Blackwell, 2000), p. 3.

Research Methodology

Defining the Subject

There are two aspects of being an "immigrant" here. The first indicates that the entrepreneurs were immigrants. They must have been born on the Chinese mainland, or somewhere outside Hong Kong, before coming to live and start businesses in the city. Although they later moved their businesses back to the mainland and now spend much of their time there, their families, or the core members of their family, still live in Hong Kong. The second aspect is a description of their "nomadic" lifestyle. Because their businesses are not fixed in one place, they have to keep going back and forth among various locations. They will often stay in A for some time before going on to B to take care of their business, then move on to C to visit a client. Their lives are marked by such frequent shuttling movements.

To qualify as an "entrepreneur" in this study, each subject needed to meet two major requirements. In terms of ownership, the entrepreneur had to be one of the stockholders of the enterprise, which could be either self-established or inherited. Second, the entrepreneur, instead of being a mere financial investor, had to be personally involved in managing and operating their business.

In-Depth Interviews

The information this book has gathered comes mainly from in-depth interviews we conducted between February 2004 and April 2005. As well as the interviews, we attempted "field observation" by attending various social functions with some of the entrepreneurs. These functions included anniversary celebrations of former schools, inauguration ceremonies of alumni associations, new office opening parties, signing ceremonies of new projects, and so on. We found such "field observation" very helpful: on the one hand, we were able to develop a substantial understanding of our informants' daily lives; on the other hand, through such engaged observation

Chan Kwok-bun and Chan Wai-wan, *Mobile Chinese Entrepreneurs*,
International Series on Consumer Science, DOI 10.1007/978-1-4419-9643-5_2,

"in the field", we were able to obtain some valuable information that was not readily available from interviews, for example, what type of people they associated with; what their business talk centered on in public social settings; and how they presented their differential identities as situations changed. Such data not only granted us access to the entrepreneurs' interpersonal networks – aspects that were more personalized and truer to life – but also gave us a practical understanding of their self-identities.

Our informants did not come from a random sampling but were "snowballed", i.e., recruited mainly through the authors' family members, acquaintances, former schoolmates, and so on. Of all the immigrant entrepreneurs willing to be interviewed, the majority were from Fujian Province. This sampling approach will inevitably be questioned as "unrepresentative", despite the fact that no research method can be entirely so. In fact, behind each of our immigrant entrepreneur's pioneering projects there was an exceptional and intriguing story. To be of the same origin does not mean they encountered a homogeneous set of problems in life and work. Their managerial experiences are like the individual tiles of a jigsaw puzzle – similar, yet unique. Only when we have put the pieces, be they big or small, back together against a particular historical milieu can we claim to have a more global and accurate understanding of their life stories.

The interviews generally lasted between one and three hours (with most being completed within one and a half hours), and took place in the informants' Hong Kong offices, sometimes in their homes or hotel rooms, in restaurants, eateries, or community organization offices. In some cases, they were carried out in their offices and residences in the mainland. Cantonese was the major interview language, with a few conducted in Hokkien and Putonghua.

While the interviews were open-ended without questionnaires or directive answering requirements, they had central themes. The first theme concerned our informants' experiences as immigrants. The conversations centered on their early days in Hong Kong, the major setbacks they encountered, their social circles, and so on, so that we could probe into the connections between immigrant experience and entrepreneurship. The second theme looked at the specifics of enterprise management, focusing on how our immigrant entrepreneurs got started, their managerial problems and challenges, marketing strategies, and so on. The third theme was about our entrepreneurs' life and work at different business sites. The data collected here shows how they managed to mobilize and integrate the social resources at different locations in order to create room for development. Despite having these main themes as a focus, our interviews did not follow a particular procedure but were adjusted to suit different interviewees and their life courses.

Our Informant's Background

In total, 18 informants were interviewed, 16 of whom were immigrant entrepreneurs (see Table 1), the other two being family members. Of these two, one was in charge of operating the entrepreneur's business and served as a management representative.

Below we outline some of the characteristics our immigrant entrepreneurs displayed in terms of their business operations and personal backgrounds. As regards

Table 1 Interviewees' Personal Information

Interviewees	Age	Education	Place of origin	Year of arrival	Business location(s)	Business nature (past and present)
Mr. Yee	38	University	Fuqing (Fujian)	1986	Shenzhen, Hebei, Zhuhai	Mixer truck fleets, intelligent networking, real estate
Mr. Chiu	36	University	Jinjiang (Fujian)	1986	Hong Kong and Zibo, Weifang, Qingdao of Shandong,	Plush plants, chemical fiber plants, textiles factories, toy manufacturing, clothing, trades
Ms. Siu	43	Master's degree	Xi'an (Shaanxi)	1995	Hong Kong, Shenzhen, Xi'an	Electronic products, fruits trades, salons, health products franchisee
Mr. Kam	31	Master's degree	Shishi (Fujian)	1985	Hong Kong, Fujian	IT and web design
Mr. Lok	35	Master's degree	Beijing	1985	Hong Kong, Shenzhen	Pest control services
Mr. Kei	34	University	Indonesia	1985	Hong Kong, Shenzhen, Indonesia	Electronic products trades
Mr. Shin	54	Junior high	Quanzhou (Fujian)	1961	Hong Kong, Shenzhen, Shanghai, Jiangsu, Fujian	Plastic box manufacturing, 3D film material, laser imaging, laser labels, laser security packaging
Mr. Ngai	31	Master's degree	Quanzhou (Fujian)	1989	Hong Kong, Fujian	Network services, fruits and vegetable exports
Mr. Kwok	36	Senior high	Jinjiang (Fujian)	1996	Shenzhen	Silk screen printing, pad printing, varnish spray, insulating material
Mr. Chuk	36	Senior high	Fuqing (Fujian)	1998	Hong Kong, Shenzhen, Wuhe, Bozhou, Shanghai, Yingtan, Jiujiang	Real estate, bowling centers
Mr. Wing	57	Senior high	Jinjiang (Fujian)	1961	Fujian, Tianjin	Printing plants, chemical plastics factories
Mr. Yue	62	Senior high	Nan'an (Fujian)	1958	Hong Kong, Dongguan	Printing plants
Ms. Lee	43	Senior high	Jilin (Changchun)	2000	Dongguan	Shoes-making
Mr. Yam	43	Master's degree	Ningde (Fujian)	1976	Hong Kong, Shenyang	Marketing, glass manufacturing
Mr. Chun	63	Senior high	Wenzhou (Zhejiang)	1958	Hong Kong, Guangzhou	Petroleum and petroleum products
Ms. Chai	31	Master's degree	Jinjiang (Fujian)	1989	Hong Kong, Fujian	Garment factories

management, their businesses varied in size, with staff numbers ranging from a handful to more than four thousand. Most were small to medium enterprises, each having a crew of one or two hundred people. The nature of their business was just as varied, covering a spectrum of industries: construction materials, transportation fleets, real estate, textile factories, printing plants, garment factories, international trade, fruit and vegetable exports, glass manufacturing, petroleum products, etc. Fourteen out of the 16 businesses had two or more business locations, the most being seven. Nearly all (14 of 16) had Hong Kong offices. About half (seven of 16) had chosen to set up businesses in their place of origin, while the others were converged in Guangdong Province or in areas where the industry was concentrated.

The following four features were identified from the personal backgrounds of our immigrant entrepreneurs. First, with regard to their place of origin, 11 out of the 16 were from Fujian Province (though from different cities, counties, or towns), and none of them knew each other before coming to Hong Kong. The others were from Xi'an in Shaanxi Province, Changchun in Jilin Province, Beijing, Wenzhou in Zhejiang Province, and Bandung, Indonesia. Second, in terms of gender, the majority of the immigrant entrepreneurs we approached were male. Of the 16 entrepreneurs, 13 were male and just three were female. Third, as regards age, our informants fell within a wide age range, between 31 and 63. Fourth, with regard to education level, seven had completed secondary school and the other nine held Bachelor's or Master's degrees. The older informants were generally found to have a lower education level than their younger counterparts. In addition, they arrived in Hong Kong over a period of time spanning more than 40 years. Some of them came to Hong Kong as early as 1958, while the latest arrived as late as 2000. Having lived through different periods of Hong Kong's development, they have been witness to this city's history and have, with their substantive life experiences, painted it in the distinct hues of their times.

Methodology: Difficulties and Limitations

The information for this book came mainly from the spoken word of the immigrant entrepreneurs. In fact our greatest challenge was to find suitable informants who, apart from being "immigrants" themselves, were also running businesses in mainland China. Since no government statistics as yet show the exact number of such people in Hong Kong, we had just two channels through which we could find the right people: through Hong Kong-registered ethnic associations (*tongxiang hui*) and secondary school alumni associations. These secondary schools, mostly founded by early immigrant Chinese businessmen, have had a major enrolment of new immigrants from the mainland and were generally labeled "leftist patriotic schools" before the handover of Hong Kong back to the Chinese government in 1997. There were five major "leftist patriotic schools": Fukien Secondary School, Pui Kiu Middle School, Hon Wah College, Heung To Middle School, and the Workers' Children Secondary School. Statistics from Fukien Secondary School show that before it became government-funded, new immigrants from Fujian made up more than 90% of its enrolment. With the help of organizations closely related to these immigrants, we were able to come up with a preliminary list of suitable informants. The list, however, was only the first step. For most of these bosses, who have to travel around all year long, the interview sessions were a time-consuming chore. As a result, many turned down our requests.

As well as the difficulty of finding suitable informants, there was a general reluctance among our subjects to talk with a "stranger" about matters related to their business, especially because the interviews included accounts of business operations or even of business secrets. So even having found the "right" informants, we still had difficulties conducting successful interviews and obtaining the data needed for our study. Some of the results did not come up to expectations, and in some areas the details provided were, at best, inadequate.

The "interview" as a data collection method of course has inherent limitations. First, our informants live in a state of hyper-mobility and their lives are not anchored to any particular place. To understand their intensely mobile life, we may draw on John Urry's conception of a "mobile sociology".[1] Urry says sociological research must concern itself with the diversities and processes of the mobility of daily life. Thus, as much as its subjects are fluid, its research methods must also be so "fluid" as to avoid fixing the subjects at a specific time and place. Having said this, and our subject being a group of people ever on the move, we sociologists often adopt a rigid research method, extracting, at fixed times and places, information that bespeaks only of a past. Such a fractured method of data collection has rendered us vulnerable to accusations of being partial, subjective, biased, out-dated, even irrelevant.

In addition, an interview dialog is always the result of a particular interaction matrix that involves the personalities of interviewer and interviewee. For various reasons, an interviewee may say different things to different people on different occasions to achieve different effects, thus making objectivity and coherence of personality somewhat irrelevant. Motivated by a particular ideology, the interviewer may sometimes "select, condition, and mould interviewee's responses".[2] He or she may also intervene and interpret differently based on his or her own experiences and assumptions, thus distorting further other's life drama.[3] The data gleaned from the interview may eventually be appropriated for the interviewer's self-fulfillment – as the contents of the conversation are misinterpreted and misrepresented.

At the same time, we have to admit the complexity of personality. During the interviews, we were inevitably confronted with problems arising from the "double

---

[1] John Urry, "Mobile Sociology", *The British Journal of Sociology*, 51, No. 1 (January/March 2000), pp. 185–203.

[2] Anthony Seldon and Joanna Pappworth, *By Word of Mouth: "Elite" Oral History* (New York: Methuen, 1983), p. 18.

[3] Chan Kwok-bun and Claire Chiang, *Stepping Out: The Making of Chinese Entrepreneurs* (Singapore: Prentice Hall, 1994), p. 21.

psychological spheres" of the human psyche, which is divided between a public sphere and a private, secret sphere, thus resulting in a further divide of a personality between the public persona and the private persona.[4] This may be a prevalent psychological phenomenon in interviews, since the interviewees may be inclined to their own ways of reconstructing their lives and histories, giving out, as it happens, "truths", "half-truths", "untruths", or a salad of the three. They may have two separate systems of expression (*huayu tixi*) for their own use, one for talking in public, the other for talking with their friends.[5] In narrating their personal experiences, they may highlight certain truths and downplay others; their utterances, before reaching the interviewer's ears, may have already been modified or even partially dramatized. The process of storytelling is, therefore, always haunted by the storyteller's cautious attention to his or her own image.[6] We had to decide which system of expression the interviewee used, how much of his or her narration was truthful portrayal, and how much else was deliberate exaggeration. This was a daunting task.

Any sociological research method is bound to be handicapped in one way or another. Any discipline that involves the collection of personal data, that attempts to reconstruct people's lives and histories, is necessarily confronted with problems of subjective tailoring, cultural manipulation, ideological prejudices, and so on. It does not follow, however, that the information gleaned from an interview is innately short of value: while a narration may have been cautiously selective, there is "no more factually correct picture of a 'real' person than the one created by the subject himself".[7] Denied access to the absolute truth, the interviewer is at least given a partial and yet unique path into the subject's emotions, ideas, personality, reflections and interpretations of events, anxieties and aspirations – all via the subject's own words which, being at once individual and true to life, can never be copied or reproduced. Contextualizing these partial truths within the unique historical contingencies in which they are uttered, we can in one way or another obtain fragments of historical significance that will contribute to our understanding of the interaction between the self and society. When necessary, of course, we may use associative interpretations and inferences in a cautious and disciplined way and, with a bit of sociological imagination, even luck, seek to deepen our analyses.

---

[4] Li Qiang, "'Xinli erchong quyu' yu zhongguo de wenjuan diaocha" ["'Double Psychological Spheres' and Opinion Surveys in China"], *Shehuixue Yanjiu* [Sociological Research], No. 1, 2000, p. 40.

[5] Ibid., p. 41.

[6] Chan and Chiang, *Stepping Out*, p. 25.

[7] Ibid., p. 24.

Identity, Interpersonal Networking and Enterprise Management

Some Notes on Identity

Identity as a dynamic emergence

Identity refers to the way people position themselves and engage with others. It represents the extent to which people construct their status, image and role in society as well as their relationship with others.[1] As a product of socialization, personal identity is socially bestowed, socially sustained and socially transformed, changing as society changes.[2] It is, therefore, a complex, ambiguous and shifting concept that is neither constant nor composed of mere histories or pasts.

With the internationalization of the mass media, the advances in mass transport, the intense mobility of people, as well as the accompanying compression of space and time, personal identity in today's globalized world has come to be marked by multiplicity, hybridity and instability. In this modern world of ours, identity has become a "moveable feast", in continuous formation and transformation in relation to the ways we are represented or addressed in our cultural systems and social structures.[3] Immigrant identity in particular has displayed a kind of heterogeneous "multiples rootedness": manifold, multiple, and never singular.[4] All in all, identity

---

[1] Wang Ning, "Xiaofei yu rentong: dui xiaofei shehuixue de yige fenxi kuangjia de tansuo" ["Consumption and Identity: A Conceptual Framework for the Sociology of Consumption"] in *Shehuixue Yanjiu* [Sociological Studies] No. 1 (2001), p. 7.

[2] Peter L. Berger, *Invitation to Sociology: A Humanistic Perspective* (Garden City, New York: Doubleday & Company, 1963), p. 98–99.

[3] Stuart Hall, "The Question of Cultural Identity", in *Modernity and its Future*, eds. Stuart Hall, David Held, and Tony McGraw (Cambridge: Polity Press, in association with the Open University, 1992), p. 277.

[4] Chan Kwok-bun, "A Family Affair: Migration, Dispersal, and the Emergent Identity of the Chinese Cosmopolitanism", *Diaspora*, 6, No. 2 (1997), p. 207. Chan Kwok-bun, *Chinese Identities, Ethnicity and Cosmopolitanism* (London: Routledge, 2005).

Chan Kwok-bun and Chan Wai-wan, *Mobile Chinese Entrepreneurs*,
International Series on Consumer Science, DOI 10.1007/978-1-4419-9643-5_3,

is a dynamic process in which identifications are continuously being shifted about,[5] always in progress and incomplete – a matter of "becoming".[6]

Identity as the result of power and negotiation

Identity is not altogether a subjective choice. The individual moves within society inside carefully defined systems of power and prestige. To be located in society means to be at the intersection point of specific social forces.[7] Identity in this sociological perception bridges the gap between the "inside" and the "outside" – between the personal and the public worlds.[8] An individual can never sustain any kind of identity all on his own, since a person's self-image can be maintained only in a social context against which others are willing to recognize him in this identity.[9] In fact, the pursuit of self-identity originates from a deep-rooted human desire to be accepted. In order to be accepted, the individual needs to assimilate and internalize the various cultural demands, value orientation, and social norms of the society in which he belongs. Self-identity is exactly what enables him to make these social demands part of himself: it is quite often about how one is viewed by, and related to, the "others" in society. Man, as one scholar observes, is born to look and be looked at.[10] In other words, as he communicates and interacts with others in society, the individual always seeks to place them, or is being placed by them, in the "appropriate" social locations on the social map according to a certain taxonomy or category. In order to secure an advantageous place on the social map, one gets entangled in a power relationship between the "categorizers" and the "categorized".[11] To a certain extent, we may say the formation of an individual's or a group's identity is the outcome of a negotiation between the individual and society, between specific groups and the social milieu.[12]

Identity as similarity and difference

Self-identity has twin connotations: similarity and difference. "Similarity" stresses the "sameness" of people, allowing members of a group to believe that they have certain features in common with others – thus creating a sense of belonging to the group. Such "similarity", however, always coexists with the group's "difference" from others, and it is only through the recognition of such a difference that similarity can be maintained. Similarity and difference, in other words, are distinct but coexisting

[5] Stuart Hall, "The Question of Cultural Identity", p. 277.

[6] Stuart Hall, "Cultural Identity and Diaspora", in *Identity: Community, Culture, Difference*, ed., Jonathan Rutherford (London: Lawrence and Wishart, 1990), p. 222, 225.

[7] Peter L. Berger, *Invitation to Sociology*, p. 67.

[8] Stuart Hall, "The Question of Cultural Identity", p. 276.

[9] Peter L. Berger, *Invitation to Sociology*, p. 100.

[10] Chou Ying-hsiung, "Shenfen zhi rentong: cong Lu Xun de liang ge xiaoshuo tuilun" ["Identity Formation: From Two Stories by Lu Xun"] in *Shenfen rentong yu gonggong wenhua: wenhua yanjiu lunwenji* [Identity and Public Culture: Critical Essays in Cultural Studies], ed. Chan Ching-kiu (Hong Kong: Oxford University Press, 1997), p. 316.

[11] Richard Jenkins, *Social Identity* (London: Routledge, 1996), p. 25.

[12] Stuart Hall, "Cultural Identity and Diaspora", p. 305.

dimensions of self-identity.[13] An individual, just as he can position himself according to his similarity to his group members, can establish his unique identity according to his difference from members of other social groups. These two dimensions, of course, are not dichotomous, but are inextricably interwoven among various contradictions, tensions, and conflicts.[14]

Individuals who have more diversified identities may be less devastated by stressful experiences in life, because they will have relatively more social resources on which to fall back in the face of challenges and stresses.[15] Yet an individual cannot infinitely transform his identity, for such transformations not only depend on the social networks he is in, but also on how comfortable he has been with his previous identity. There are times, as Berger observes, "when an individual becomes so habituated to certain identities that, even when his social situation changes, he has difficulty keeping up with the expectations newly directed toward him[16]".

Immigrant identity as a utilitarian need for life

Research into immigrant identities has reflected that self-identification among immigrants is more often than not the result of a utilitarian need for life. Immigrant identity is hybrid in nature and displays a high degree of flexibility.[17] The mobility of immigrants allows them to travel between different social structures. This, in contrast to the experience of the immobile, serves to pluralize the social situations in which immigrants reside, and requires that they assume a kaleidoscope of roles. As an individual moves from one place to another, he faces resistance and constraints in the place he lives, and loses what he previously depended on for life. Under such circumstances, individuals must, on the one hand, strive to be in the tightest possible cohesion, forming a supra-individual unity so as to deal with the sense of isolation and lack of support that they encounter.[18] Thus, an individual living in mobility has a more imminent and acute desire and quest for self-identity than those who stay in a familiar social space, for "birds of the same feather flock together, not as luxury but as necessity".[19] On the other hand, compared to immobiles, mobiles generally have a more flexible and pluralized sense of identity, as they need to display different cultural identities as the situation changes and their objects of interaction vary. Their identity is always in transformation, switching

---

[13] Richard Jenkins, *Social Identity*, p. 3–4, 80–87.

[14] Chou Ying-hsiung, "Shenfen zhi rentong", p. 320.

[15] Peggy A. Thoits, "On Merging Identity Theory and Stress Research", *Social Psychology Quarterly*, 54, no. 2 (1991), p. 108.

[16] Peter L. Berger, *Invitation to Sociology*, p. 106.

[17] Chan Kwok-bun, "From Multiculturalism to Hybridity: The Chinese in Canada", in *Governance in Multicultural Societies*, eds. John Rex and Gurharpal Singh (Aldershot: Ashgate, 2004), p. 227–244; Chan Kwok-bun, *Chinese Identities, Ethnicity and Cosmopolitanism* (London: Routledge, 2005); Stuart Hall, "Culture, Identity and Diaspora".

[18] David Frisby and Mike Featherstone eds., *Simmel on Culture: Selected Writings* (London: Sage, 1997), p. 160–165.

[19] Peter L. Berger, *Invitation to Sociology*, p. 102.

from persona to persona. Such alternate identities are analogous to the art of a Chinese mask-changer, who has different faces to display at different times and places.[20] The self-identity of immigrant is closely related to their experience as social mobiles. Their identity is no longer fixed in a given land and its culture, but is embedded in their mobile nature, being constantly re-shaped as they travel.[21]

Research into the identities of overseas Chinese has focused on the identification with "insiders" (*ziji ren*). This is a kind of place-based identity. In the context of globalization, as China comes into closer contact with other countries, emigrated Chinese people more frequently travel between their birth place and their home overseas. The sense of identity that originates from geographical relations, far from weakening in this to and fro movement, has nevertheless intensified as these emigrants, upon the improvement of their financial conditions overseas, become keen organizers of "native place association" (*tongxiang hui*) activities in their place of migration, or return to their place of origin to sponsor local cultural projects such as rebuilding temples, ancestral halls, and schools.[22] At the same time, these charity projects are also conducive to establishing new, cross-boundary businesses based on existing "native place" relations and family networks.[23]

Personal Identity and Interpersonal Networks

Intrinsic and extrinsic attractions: identity and social networking

Personal identity is the result of an individual's interactions with other people; it is what bridges the individual and the public. Since identity can only be socially sustained, it may be said that specific social or interpersonal networks give rise to specific personal identities which in turn prompt those involved to construct specific interpersonal networks. There is, as we can see, a closely interactive relationship between the personal identity and his social network.

---

[20] Tong Chee Kiong and Chan Kwok-bun eds., *Alternate Identities: The Chinese of Contemporary Thailand* (Singapore: Times Academic Press, 2001); Chan Kwok-bun, *Chinese Identities, Ethnicity and Cosmopolitan*; Chan Kwok-bun, "Quanqiuhua beijing xia de wenhua chongtu he ronghe" ["Cultural Conflict and Hybridization in the Context of Globalization"] in *Zhejiang Xuekan* [Zhejiang Academic Journal], No. 2 (2005), p. 153–159.

[21] D. Lowenthal, "Mobility and Identity in the Island Pacific: A Critique", *Pacific Viewpoint*, 26 (1985), p. 280–315; Rachel Silvery and Victorial Lawson, "Placing the Migrant", *Annals of the Association of American Geographers*, 89, No. 1 (1999), p. 121–132.

[22] Frank N. Pieke, et al., *Transnational Chinese: Fujianese Migrants in Europe* (Stanford, California: Stanford University Press, 2004).

[23] C.K. Leung, "Personal Contacts, Subcontracting Linkage, and Development in the Hong Kong-Zhujiang Delta Region", *Annals of the Association of American Geographers*, 42, No. 4 (1993), p. 403–421; Liu Xin, "Space, Mobility, and Flexibility: Chinese Villagers and Scholars Negotiation Power at Home and Abroad", in *Underground Empires: The Cultural Politics of Modern Chinese Transnationalism*, eds. Aihwa Ong and Donald M. Nonini (New York: Routledge, 1997), p. 91–114.

Since identity involves how people position themselves as well as others, there involves a very intimate relationship between the construction of interpersonal networks and people's recognition of each other. Since Chinese interpersonal relations are based on a "differential mode of association" (*chaxu geju*), people take different approaches to others according to their different relationships.[24] Therefore, in order to establish strong and effective interpersonal networks, the individual must engage in mutual recognition and identification with other people; and in order to secure a beneficial place for himself in this interactive process of identification, the individual has to affect, by all means, the way "owner of resources" will judge him. The most common methods or means to construct interpersonal networks are "pulling strings" (*la guanxi*) and "evoking personal feelings" (*pan renqing*).[25] Through these means, the individual can then tie his objects down to a network of roles related to himself, so as to turn an originally rather general relationship with the "owner of resources" into something special, hybrid in nature, that involves factors of sentiment as well as usefulness. By tying the objects down to this network of roles, the individual binds them to the "rules of personal feelings" so that they will allot their resources in a way advantageous to himself. One's capability of pulling *guanxi* strings depends on how "related" he is to the one he is "pulling".[26] The more "traits of relatedness" (*guishu xing tezheng*) they have in common, the more likely they are to identify with each other; and only in this way can the individual manage to "pull the *guanxi* strings" for the best possible allocation of resources for the individual's fulfillment of himself.[27]

The construction of interpersonal networks is also dependent on the type of social bonds between individuals. Social bonds are built upon two fundamental processes, that is, intrinsic attraction and extrinsic attraction.[28] Intrinsic attraction refers to the pleasure that arises from the discovery of similar intrinsic traits within the two parties in an interaction. Such attractions occur only in the process of an individual's contact with someone similar to himself. Extrinsic attraction rests on a complementary relationship regarding material resources. The two parties enter and maintain a social relationship mainly for the reciprocal exchange of extrinsic benefits. This again translates into the twin dimensions of personal identities, "similarity" and "difference": *similarity* creates pleasure and closeness, thus shortening the psychological distance between individuals; *difference* points to the fact that each is in possession of certain material resources that the other wishes to obtain – the

[24] Fei Xiaotong, *Xiaotu Zhongguo* [From the Soil: The Foundations of Chinese Society] (Beijing: Sanlian Shudian, 1985).

[25] Y.C. King, *Zhongguo shehui yu wenhua* [Chinese Society and Culture] (Hong Kong: Oxford University Press, 1992); K.K. Huang, *Zhishi yu xingdong: Zhonghua wenhua chuantong de shehui xinli quanshi* [Knowledge and Action: A Socio-psychological Interpretation of the Chinese Cultural Tradition] (Taipei: Psychological Publishing, 1995).

[26] K.K. Huang, "Renqing yu mianzi: Zhongguoren de quanli youxi" ["Feelings and Faces: Power Games Among the Chinese"], in *Zhongguoren de xinli* [The Chinese Psychology], ed. K.S. Yang (Taipei: Laureate, 1989), p. 289–317.

[27] Y.C. King, *Zhongguo shehui yu wenhua.*

[28] Peter M. Blau, *Exhange and Power in Social Life* (New York: John Wiley, 1964).

possession of such resources represents a kind of social power that affects others. As we can see, at the earlier stages, the sense of identification has a reasonable role to play in constructing a relationship, but once the relationship is established, emergent properties like trust and commitment will be formed from the two parties' mutually-dependent actions, which makes the relationship more stable and adaptable.

Building from the outside: Ethnic identity and regional associations

Studies have shown that overseas Chinese as immigrants are often dubbed "outsiders" by the local people, for whom ethnicity and skin color are evident tags. Living in an environment that is fraught with discrimination and prejudice against "outsiders", overseas Chinese people are quite often excluded from the mainstream job market. With their employment channels blocked, they can only engage in "dirty" work that the local people are unwilling to take up. Feeling insecure in the new environment and from enduring the looks of discrimination and derision, the immigrants usually seek comfort from those they know, or those from a similar social background. With these "insiders", quite often immigrants themselves, they will develop a sense of identity. This, as a poet famously said, is how "fellow sufferers sympathize with each other". The external force of exclusion, as we have seen, only serves to enhance the ethnic bonds among immigrants. In order to survive and to find an emotional anchor in a land of loneliness, immigrants can quite often manage to build highly homogeneous and trustworthy social networks. Either by living in a compact community or by setting up associations, immigrants seek to improve the ethnic group's negotiating power, and resist the host society's unfriendly or unfair treatment.[29] The emergence of Chinatowns, for instance, has been the result of such utilitarian and sentimental needs.[30] Similarly in Hong Kong, Fujianese immigrants are converged around the North Point area and Hakka immigrants in the New Territories, while San Diu people are spread around Kwun Tong and Kowloon City.[31] Such ethnic distribution is closely related to their place-based identity.

Apart from the convergence of inhabitation areas, institutionalized organizations also help to foster the new immigrants' collective power. These are usually unofficial

---

[29] Peter S. Li, "Ethnic Business among Chinese in the US", *Journal of Ethnic Studies*, 4 (1976), p. 35–41; Peter S. Li, *The Chinese in Canada* (Toronto: Oxford University Press, 1988); Chan Kwok-bun, *Smoke and Fire: The Chinese in Montreal* (Hong Kong: Chinese University Press, 1991); Chan Kwok-bun, "Ethnic Resources, Opportunity Structure and Coping Strategies: Chinese Business in Canada", *Revue Europeanne des Migrations Internationales*, 8, No. 3 (1992), p. 117–137; Chan Kwok-bun ed., *Chinese Business Networks: State, Economy and Culture* (Singapore: Prentice Hall, 2000); Chan Kwok-bun, *Migration, Ethnicity and Chinese Business* (London: Routledge, 2005); Chan Kwok-bun and Ong Jin Hui, "The Many Faces of Immigrant Entrepreneurship", in *The Cambridge Survey of World Migration*, ed. Robin Cohen (Cambridge: Cambridge University Press, 1995), p. 523–531.

[30] Chan Kwok-bun, "Ethnic Resources, Opportunity Structure and Coping Strategies: Chinese Business in Canada".

[31] George C.S. Lin, "Identity, Mobility, and the Making of the Chinese Diasporic Landscape in Hong Kong", in *The Chinese Diaspora: Space, Place, Mobility, and Identity*, eds. Laurence J.C. Ma and Carolyn Cartier (Lanham: Rowman & Littlefield Publishers Inc., 2003), p. 141–161.

community organizations based on blood relations or geographical relations, e.g., "clan associations" (*zongqin hui*) based on a common surname, or "native place associations" based on the same place of origin or a common dialect, etc. They are quite often founded by established business entrepreneurs who were born on the Chinese mainland and later migrated to this new place. Regional associations, "native place associations" in particular, allow people who share a common native dialect to sit together, exchanging information (about their native place or their new home), recollecting their pasts, and chattering about their lives – all these casual gatherings have not only fostered the emotional bonds among the *laoxiang* ("people from the same place of origin"), but also enhanced a sense of identity that has developed out of their blood relations or geographical relations.[32] These associations will also organize traditional cultural activities such as reconstructing temples and ancestral halls, holding traditional festivities (the "lantern dance" during the Moon Festival and the "lion dance" during the Spring Festival, for example), and sponsoring performances by mainland circuses (generally referred to as "song and dance troupes"), etc.[33] Through these activities and commemorations, together with the vivid line-up of various totems, the immigrants' ethnic qualities are being constantly re-presented and magnified, thus sharpening their blood- or geography-bound sense of identity,[34] whose enhancement in turn sustains the life of these associations and fosters the emotional bonds as well as the highly homogeneous social networks among the members.

Mobility and cross-boundary interpersonal networks

Interpersonal networks are like a set of interconnected nodes: it is a dynamic open structure in which the nodal interactions are inextricably linked.[35] Personal identity is constantly being reconstructed and reshaped as people move. Mobility enables people to re-integrate social resources so as to expand their individual space of activity.[36] Thus, the higher people's degree of mobility, the broader their social network will become, and the more extensive the nodal interactions within that network will be. In business management, a broad network plays an important role in attracting capital and creating opportunities. As business managers travel to different places, they come into contact with different people, assuming different roles and identities, so that they are able to establish effective localized networks. Studies of Chinese

---

[32] Richard J. Coughlin, *Double Identity: The Chinese in Modern Thailand* (Hong Kong: Hong Kong University Press, 1960).

[33] Richard J. Coughlin, *Double Identity*. Tung Yuan-chao, "Guding de tianye yu youyi de zhoubian: Yi Daxidi Huaren wei li" ["Stable Fields and Moving Boundaries: The Chinese in Tahiti as an Illustration"], in *Shequn yanjiu de xingsi* [Reflections on Community Studies], eds. W.T. Chen and Y.K. Huang (Taipei: Institute of Ethnology, Academia Sinica, 2002), p. 303–329.

[34] Tung Yuan-chao, "Guding de tianye yu youyi de zhoubian", p. 318.

[35] Manuel Castells, *The Rise of the Network Society* (London: Routledge, 1996), p. 470–471.

[36] Wang Chunguang, *Shehui liu dong he shehui chonggou: Jingcheng Zhejiang Cun yanjiu* [Social Mobility and Social Restructuring: A Study of the Zhejiang Village in Beijing] (Hangzhou: Zhejiang Renmin Chubanshe, 1995), p. 11.

people doing business overseas, or overseas Chinese doing business in mainland China, have shown that localized interpersonal networks play a substantially effective role either in daily business management or in charting future developments.[37]

This is especially the case with immigrant entrepreneurs who return to do business in their birthplace. For these entrepreneurs, the kind of blood- or geography-bound sense of identity that we have talked about is particularly important for establishing economically-effective localized interpersonal networks. Studies of Singapore-Chinese business people setting up factories on the mainland have revealed that the sense of same-rooted-ness (*tonggen gan*) and the sense of responsibility towards the place of origin are decisive factors in looking for a management locale. By strengthening their bonds with the place of origin, they manage to establish local social networks, thus gaining access to local resources. In this way, they are able to fulfill their commitment to their birthplace as individuals coming from the same roots and descending from the same bloodline; at the same time, they obtain tangible economic advantages and benefits as an extension from their "compatriot" status. In such transnational businesses, the entrepreneurs' deliberate engagement in cultural practices and their display of ethnic identities are in effect "transnational strategies" in corporate management.[38]

Interpersonal Networking and Corporate Management

Corporate management and ethnic bonds

There is an interactive relationship between personal identity and interpersonal networks. In corporate management, interpersonal networks have a crucially important role to play. Corporate management is an economic behavior, and as such it is embedded within the social structure.[39] An entrepreneur's methods or strategies in corporate management are largely determined by the business regulations and environment in the business location. In Chinese societies, since business regulations are highly inconsistent, the construction and use of special interpersonal works have become widely accepted and valued business strategies, either in indigenous Chinese societies or in overseas Chinese communities. In the various business activities among the Chinese people, social networks have such a pre-eminent role to play that Chinese business people invariably place a strong emphasis on *guanxi* and

---

[37] Heidi Dahles, "Venturing across Borders: Investment Strategies of Singapore-Chinese Entrepreneurs in Mainland China", *Asian Journal of Social Science*, 32, No. 1 (2004), p. 19–41; Frank N. Pieke et al., *Transnational Chinese*.

[38] Heidi Dahles, "Venturing across Borders: Investment Strategies of Singapore-Chinese Entrepreneurs in Mainland China".

[39] Mark S. Granovetter, "Economic Action and Social Structure: The Problem of Embeddedness", *American Journal of Sociology*, 91 (1985), p. 481–510.

personal feelings. Social networking, in other words, is a key element in managing, sustaining, and advancing corporate development.[40]

Studies of Chinese corporates show that one of the first and most frequently used social networks is the "family-based interpersonal network", or the so-called "ethnic bonds". In other words, ethnic bonds are widely used in business management. This is because in Chinese societies, economic behaviors have always evolved around the "core" of the family. The concept of the "family" is at the heart of one's loyalty,[41] and figures prominently in the Chinese economic life. In traditional Chinese societies, kinship provides one with the most powerful social ties, and the unity of kinsfolk has been one of the most important sources of energy for any Chinese enterprise. The success of one's career is quite often regarded as built upon an indescribable commitment to the family.[42] As a result, the majority of Chinese enterprises are small to medium family businesses that exhibit strong familistic characteristics in their management style.[43] A corporate has to start and develop from essentials such as a good source of capital and a reliable management team. The first source of capital for the Chinese entrepreneur is usually his core family or extended family. In actual management, nepotism is widely practised. Core family members are very often assigned to key, decision-making positions, while other relatives may be positioned at various points along the production line.[44]

The common practice of nepotism is due, on the one hand, to the immense sense of moral commitment among family members and, on the other hand, to the greater trust that comes from being members of the same family. Trust, as a kind of prospective confidence in others' behaviors, can reduce the risks of various uncertainties.[45]

---

[40] Chan Kwok-bun and Ong Jin Hui, "The Many Faces of Immigrant Entrepreneurship"; Bian Yanjie, "Bringing Strong Ties Back in: Indirect Connection, Bridges and Job Search in China", *American Sociological Review*, 62 (1997), p. 266–285; Chan Kwok-bun ed., *Chinese Business Networks: State, Economy and Culture*; Chan Kwok-bun, *Migration, Ethnic Relations and Chinese Business*; Chan Kwok-bun and Claire Chiang, *Stepping Out: The Making of Chinese Entrepreneurs* (Singapore: Prentice Hall, 1994); Liu Jianping, "Wailairen qunti zhong de guanxi yunyong: Yi Shenzhen Pingjiang Cun wei ge'an" ["The Use of *Guanxi* in 'Outsider' Communities: The Case of Pingjiang Village, Shenzhen"], *Zhongguo shehui kexue* [Social Sciences in China], No. 5 (2001), p. 112–123; Li Minghuan, "Qunti xiaoying, shehui ziben yu kuaguo wangluo: 'Ou Hua lianhui' de yunzuo yu gongneng" ["Group Effects, Social Capital and Transnational Networks: The Operation and Functions of the European Association of Chinese Organizations"], *Shehuixue yanjiu* [Sociological Studies], No. 2 (2002), p. 30–39.

[41] Wong Siu Lun (trans. Zhang Xiuli), *Yimin qiyejia: Xianggang de Shanghai gongyejia* [Emigrant Entrepreneurs: Shanghai Industrialists in Hong Kong] (Shanghai: Shanghai guji chubenshe, 2003), p. 121; see also Wong Siu Lun, *Emigrant Entrepreneurs: Shanghai Industrialists in Hong Kong* (Hong Kong: Oxford University Press, 1988).

[42] Maurice Freeman, *Chinese Family and Marriage in Singapore* (New York: Johnson Reprint Corp., 1970).

[43] Donald E. Willmott, *The Chinese of Semarang: A Changing Minority Community in Indonesia* (Ithaca: Cornell University Press, 1960).

[44] Wong Siu Lun, *Emigrant Entrepreneurs: Shanghai Industrialists in Hong Kong*.

[45] Liu Jianping, "Wailairen qunti zhong de guanxi yunyong", p. 120.

In business management, the trust that extends from blood relations can reduce transaction costs to a certain extent and lower the cost of risk. In addition, for small businesses with limited capital, core family members or extended family members provide cheap labor. Surveys of early small businesses in Hong Kong show that only 67% of the companies paid family members as much as other employees. Similar surveys in Singapore also reveal that, in times of economic recession, many small industrial and trading companies survived because the employed family members were willing not only to have the payment of their salaries delayed, but also to work harder for less pay.[46] The employment of family members also eased the resentment that could arise from an adverse working environment. The survival of these businesses, particularly during the pioneering days, relied primarily on the exploitation – low pay and long working hours – of "insiders".[47] From the perspective of "pure" employment, exploitation as such would have caused disobedience and resistance from the employees, but in the case of these small businesses, the relationship between the boss and his men was not purely that of employment; it was mixed with other "insider" (*ziji ren*) relations based on blood, geography or conjugality. Within such a mixed relationship, the hardship at work dwindled, and "We're happy to help out" and "We're a family, aren't we?" became oft-heard refrains from the insiders. Moral commitments as such served to sooth the pain of those who sacrificed and turned otherwise acute employment problems into internal issues within a family. This is exactly what enabled these businesses to survive the hard early days.

But one cannot have one's cake and eat it too. Despite its advantages, a familistic mode of management has its drawbacks. A prominent problem comes with the existence of mediocre employees. Because of the moral responsibilities among family members, unsuitable or even low caliber members are sometimes recruited in order not to violate moral principles. This not only hampers the efficiency of management and production, but also creates a huge fiscal burden for the corporate. For larger corporates, "the recruitment of family members has proven most detrimental".[48] Moreover, studies of family-owned businesses have also shown that office politics can go rampant among family employees. When conflicts occur among family members and evolve into vicious competition, rational corporate pursuits will give way to clique politics – corporate interests being replaced by the interests of specific cliques (branches of the family).[49] The old Chinese adages "wealth never survives more than three generations", "it's tough to set up a business, but even tougher to keep it going" are still written on the wall: when it comes to handing over the business to the next generation, family-owned companies have been vulnerable to failure. Upon the deaths of the first-generation entrepreneurs, the second generation is usually

---

[46] Wong Siu Lun (trans. Zhang Xiuli), *Yimin qiyejia*, p. 130.

[47] Chan Kwok-bun and Ong Jin Hui, "The Many Faces of Immigrant Entrepreneurship"; Chan Kwok-bun, *Migration, Ethnic Relations and Chinese Business*.

[48] Wong Siu Lun (trans. Zhang Xiuli), *Yimin qiyejia*, p. 125.

[49] S. Gordon Redding, *The Spirit of Chinese Capitalism* (Berlin: Walter de Gruyter, 1990), p. 142.

confronted with challenges and problems such as sibling rivalry, jealousy and disharmony, bad management, and so on. Eventually the business is doomed to closure or merger by other corporates.[50]

Corporate management strategies: geographical assistance and opportunity alliances

Apart from the widely practised family nepotism, the bonds that arise from geographical relations have been another important interpersonal relationship valued by Chinese entrepreneurs in general. "Native" networks based on geographical relations not only provide inexpensive labor *sans* resentment, but they also constitute the first source of capital necessary for establishing a business. When it is difficult to get a bank loan through regular channels, especially as a business is not yet on the right track and there is no concrete proof of corporate achievement, the various "chambers" and "foundations", either in the name of an individual or an ethnic group, become an important source of capital.[51] In their study of ethnic immigrants in the United States, Zhou Min and Lin Mingang invented the notion of "ethnic capital" to account for the interactions among financial capital, labor capital and social capital within a given ethnic community. Their research reveals that, confronted with the stark reality of segregation, many immigrants are forced to confine themselves within a community isolated from the mainstream. Isolated, a great number of commercial activities in this community are operated within various social networks based on blood, conjugal, geographical and ethnic relations.[52] Ethnic capital is one of the treasured economic resources in immigrant communities: it provides the starting point for an ethnic economy. By integrating and utilizing their financial, labor, and social capital, immigrants are able to create a highly competitive economic mode: overseas investment in transnational corporate management and local economic development.

The union of ethnic bonds and geographical relations provides a management strategy for small to medium businesses to retain their competitive edge, induce

---

[50] Wong Siu Lun, "The Chinese Family Firm: A Model", *British Journal of Sociology*, 36 No. 1 (1985), p. 58–72; Mary B. Rose, "Beyond Buddenbrooks: The Family Firm and the Management of Succession in Nineteenth-Century Britain", in *Entrepreneurship, Networks and Modern Business*, eds. J. Brown and M.B. Rose (Manchester: Manchester University Press, 1993), p. 127–143; Edmund Terence Gomez and Michael Hsiao Hsin-Huang, "Chinese Business Research in Southeast Asia", in *Chinese Business Research in Southeast Asia: Contesting Cultural Explanations, Researching Entrepreneurship*, eds. Edmund Terence Gomez and Michael Hsiao Hsin-Huang (Surrey, U.K.: Curzon Press, 2001), p. 1–37.

[51] Ivan H. Light, *Ethnic Enterprise in America: Business and Welfare among Chinese, Japanese, and Blacks* (Berkeley: University of California Press, 1972); Chan Kwok-bun, *Smoke and Fire*; Chan Kwok-bun, *Migration, Ethnic Relations and Chinese Business*; Heidi Dahles, "Venturing across Borders: Investment Strategies of Singapore –Chinese Entrepreneurs in Mainland China"; Chan Kwok-bun and Claire Chiang, *Stepping Out: The Making of Chinese Entrepreneurs*.

[52] Zhou Min and Lin Mingang, "Zuyi ziben yu Meiguo Huaren yimin shequ de zhuanxing" ["Ethnic Capital and the Transformation of Immigrant Chinese Communities in the United States"], *Shehuixue Yanjiu* [*Sociological Studies*] No. 3 (2001), p. 36–46.

imperfect competition, or even create blockades. In order to achieve monopoly of economic opportunities, entrepreneurs with similar "traits of relatedness" will form a group to create blocades,[53] which requires many special relations. Among Chinese or overseas Chinese entrepreneurs, one of the most important relations used in competition is that of geography (which by extension overlaps the dialect-based relations), as evidenced in the case of some monopolistic Southeast Asian companies. Hong Kong's textile industry, for instance, was monopolized in its early stages by a group of immigrant entrepreneurs from Shanghai[54]; in Malaysia and Singapore, the banking industry was once manipulated by Fujianese immigrants; and the sales of grain in Thailand were controlled by San Diu people, who also monopolized pepper and areca farming in Malaysia and Singapore.[55]

Institutionalized locality relations and the official-merchant communion

Social networks built upon geographical relations will eventually evolve into institutionalized commerce chambers or community organizations. The sense of identity originally based on sentiments can now be fostered and sustained through organizational institutionalization, which plays a positive role in expanding cross-boundary networks or in establishing future managerial cooperations. Organizational institutionalization provides the fundamental basis of trust for corporate cooperation because it places a trusted third party (TTP) within the cross-boundary networks of Chinese businesses. A "trusted third party" is an entity which facilitates interactions between two parties who both trust the third party. The TTP acts as a mediator and gives both parties the psychological assurance that helps to establish a multi-nexus chain of trust. The emergence of this chain of trust enables interpersonal networks to evolve and expand, making it easy for originally difficult activities to proceed.[56]

Within officially approved and legitimate associations, either local or international, such third-party trust functions prominently. In fact, the main objective in establishing such associations or organizations is to bring together existing but scattered social networks, be they local or transnational, within an institution. The group's interests need to be articulated – the association as a collective, institutional figure has proven much more influential than scattered individuals. Studies of the "European Association of Chinese Organizations" (*ouhua lianhui*) show that, through various activities, the organization has sought to establish virtuous interactions with the European and Chinese authorities so as to enhance the legitimacy of the "Association". The double approval from the Chinese and European governments grants the "Association" specific "resources of authoritativeness" that quickly transform into a kind of cohesive appeal for many small, nongovernment organizations

[53] Wong Siu Lun (trans. Zhang Xiuli), *Yimin qiyejia*, p. 99.

[54] Wong Siu Lun (trans. Zhang Xiuli), *Yimin qiyejia.*

[55] Edmund Terence Gomez and Michael Hsiao Hsin-Huang, "Chinese Business Research in Southeast Asia".

[56] James S. Coleman, *Foundations of Social Theory* (Cambridge, MA: Belknap Press of Harvard University Press, 1990).

to join in order to "elevate" their status. In China and Europe, where "status effects" are still important, such an "elevation" of status is practically very useful, because the higher one's status is, the easier it is for one to develop social relations, and the more powerful one becomes in acquiring resources.[57]

Richard Coughlin's study of Chinese businessmen in Thailand also reveals that their success is largely due, as much in Thailand as in other Southeast Asian countries, to the united and efficient work of Chinese commerce chambers and community associations.[58] On the one hand, the existence of commerce chambers and associations gathered together separate forces, forming a "strangers' league" in a foreign land. This was, in fact, a self-protective league which served to guard against unfair treatment and discrimination from the host society. With their strength thus united and organized, the Chinese entrepreneurs in Thailand were able to expand their power in the country. The union of commerce chambers proved a significant protective strategy, particularly when the local host society set out to exclude Chinese immigrants, or when they set set up various obstacles to put Chinese entrepreneurs in an inferior position.

On the other hand, as Coughlin has pointed out, once they became influential, these commerce chambers and associations would start sorting out the official channels. They have been in frequent communication with the Thai government as representatives of the ethnic Chinese minorities, sometimes acting as mediator in negotiations. In certain special, political settings, for instance, these Chinese chambers and associations acted as messengers or go-between negotiators in communications between governments, thus providing certain business people with opportunities to deal with governments. This means, of course, easier access to official information as well as more abundant business opportunities than ordinary business people could obtain. In addition, these associations, charity organizations in particular, became a platform on which Chinese entrepreneurs could provide outstanding charity work so as to draw favorable attention from the local government. This was conducive to creating a positive corporate image that proved helpful in sorting out "official channels". Studies of Southeast Asian entrepreneurs show that the close relationship between Chinese businessmen and local governments, the local political elite and influential government officials in particular, has been one of the most important factors in the prosperity of these entrepreneurs' businesses.[59]

In the traditional Chinese social structure, social order is built upon moral order. The various formal or informal rules for dealing with interpersonal relationships dictate that the pursuit of personal dignity and values must go hand in hand with that of social harmony. In other words, social relations are always bound with morality in a Chinese society,[60] so much so that for a Chinese businessman, "reputation itself is

[57] Li Minghuan, "Qunti xiaoying, shehui ziben yu kuaguo wangluo".

[58] Richard J. Coughlin, *Double Identity*.

[59] Richard J. Coughlin, *Double Identity*; Edmund Terence Gomez and Michael Hsiao Hsin-Huang, "Chinese Business Research in Southeast Asia."

[60] S. Gordon Redding, *The Spirit of Chinese Capitalism*.

a kind of capital": he wants to be regarded as a "Confucian merchant" (*Ru shang*). It is quite another matter whether the concerns about integrity and reputation are truly from the heart; what is really important is the fact that there is a stress on moral order within the Chinese business circle.[61] Commerce chambers act largely as supervisory organs through which moral conceptions can be turned into restraints on commercial behaviors, so that dishonesty and fraudulence in business can be kept under control.

Some Critical Notes on the Literature

Three disjunct fields of study

Immigrants are not new objects of research. There have been abundant studies of immigrant entrepreneurship overseas, but as people's lives becomes increasingly "mobile", we have to re-examine the values and functions of these "social and economic beings" in different temporal and spatial configurations. This book studies a group of 16 immigrant entrepreneurs who have to travel among different spatial settings. Through their experiences and life stories, we shall probe the spirit of immigrants and entrepreneurship as well as reveal the interactive relationship between identities, interpersonal networks and business management.

In the past, identity, interpersonal networks and corporate management were essentially disconnected fields of study. Studies of personal identity, for instance, have often focused on the manifestations of the subject's "personal feelings". Generally perceived as an expression of emotions or as the pursuit of an ethnic psychology of being an "insider", personal identity is regarded as a criterion for judging whether an immigrant has integrated into the local life. A great number of quantitative studies of interpersonal networks, on the other hand, have stressed the potency of relationships within a network as well as the homogeneity or heterogeneity of a network's constitution, while largely neglecting the connections between a person's sense of identity and the construction of his social networks. In addition, research into Chinese corporates are either concentrated on various relationships and interpersonal networks, or on corporate cultures. Hardly any have offered a head-on analysis of the relationship between personal identity and corporate management.

We are now living in an intensely mobile age. Transnational, cross-boundary communication has become unprecedentedly frequent. As a result, the relationship between people and space has become increasingly "intangible." Personal identity is no longer merely the manifestation of subjective "personal feelings": it may well become part of an individual's props for the "presentation of self" in his brief transit between times and spaces.[62] The boost of mobilities has fundamentally altered our

---

[61] Chan Kwok-bun and Claire Chiang, *Stepping Out*.

[62] Goffman Erving, *The Presentation of Self in Everyday Life* (Garden City, N.Y.: Anchor Book, 1959).

social structure. Sociologists are growing increasingly attentive to the connections between a person's sense of identity and his social networks among the waves of migration, seeking also to provide a theoretical blueprint.[63] Yet there has not been much empirical study of the combined subjects of personal identity, interpersonal networks and corporate management. Moreover, many existing studies of entrepreneurship have displayed two major inadequacies: first, there is a lack of in-depth interviews; second, their objects of research are quite often nationally renowned entrepreneurs and there is little understanding of the multitude of small to medium corporate managers.[64]

Each generation of people has followed a unique track in the trajectory of history. The tremendous compression of spatial and temporal distances today has caused fundamental changes to the relationships between people and societies and between time and space. An attempt to understand entrepreneurship within such a historical context must be accompanied by an understanding of the characteristics of our times: first, the intensity of mobilities; and second, the cross-territory nature of living spaces. If personal identity is the result of the individual's interactions with the "Others" around him, then it inevitably affects the construction of his interpersonal networks, and interpersonal networks in turn are inextricably linked with corporate management. Then emerge the issues that intrigue us: as they circuit between different spaces and come into interaction with different people, how do these shuttling entrepreneurs present their personal identities? How is the variety of their identities related to their interpersonal networks? And how does this relationship affect their management strategies in different places?

"Rationality" over "emotionality"

As well as approaching an entrepreneur and his managerial strategies from the perspective of the social structure of his time, we need also to move inside his heart, to the microcosmic world of his innermost feelings. In other words, as much as we need to develop an understanding of the larger social framework, we also have to look at the entrepreneur as a human being, with all the human characteristics that have been largely neglected in existing literature.

Jean-Paul Sartre once remarked that "all human existence is a passion".[65] Indeed, one of man's existential features is that he has "emotions," and so do entrepreneurs. One of the blind spots in existing literature is its one-sided emphasis on the "business" dimension of a businessman, whereas his emotional needs and perplexities as a

---

[63] Chan Kwok-bun, ed., *Chinese Business Networks*; Chan Kwok-bun and Ong Jin Hui, "The Many Faces of Immigrant Entrepreneurship"; M. Weidenbaum and S. Hughes, *The Bamboo Networks* (New York: The Free Press, 1996); Edmund Terence Gomez and Michael Hsiao Hsin-Huang, "Chinese Business Research in Southeast Asia"; Heidi Dahles, "Venturing across Borders: Investment Strategies of Singapore-Chinese Entrepreneurs in Mainland China."

[64] Edmund Terence Gomez and Michael Hsiao Hsin-Huang, "Chinese Business Research in Southeast Asia", p. 3.

[65] Jean-Paul Sartre (trans. H. E. Barnes), *Being and Nothingness: An Essay on Existential Ontology* (London: Methuen, 1957), p. 623.

"man" are largely ignored. Current studies have scarcely mentioned the emotional worlds of business people, who are often portrayed as determined and dauntless decision-makers. As we explore their managerial strategies and methods, and sing praises for their successes, it seems we must also take note of their human pains, frustrations, loneliness, fears and despair – and joy and delight.

In today's globalized competitive market and within its transnational business cooperation, a businessman needs to travel, in and out of various interpersonal networks in order to operate, sustain and expand his businesses in different places. He can be aptly portrayed as having "one face, many masks".[66] On different stages, he has to face difference audiences, write different scripts, use different props, wear different masks, and speak different languages. He is putting on a variety of plays, but at the same time he can't leave the impression that he is a deceitful, insincere "actor", because in the Chinese tradition, actors are "heartless people". Faced with people's misunderstandings and defence against him, he feels a lot of pressure and fear – pains that make up part of his daily routine. There is currently a vacuum in the research of these areas, because social sciences as a field of study is still too devoted to "science" and unable to rid itself of its excessive worship of "reason". Mainstream studies are mostly concentrated on the level of "rationality" while neglecting the elements of "emotionality": we study human "behavior" but have often remained apathetic to human "feelings". We have "emotional" humans as our objects of study, but we have nevertheless had them dehumanized, objectivized and commodified. This lack of attention to human emotionality represents a serious flaw. Failure to correct it will eventually make social sciences appear "pale" and "indifferent", even irrelevant.

Happiness and sadness

Current studies have displayed, along with the lack of attention to the "human-ness" of business people, a very obvious tendency to "highlight just the good" (*ge gong song de*) about the family's role in corporate management. Just as a coin has two sides, so does the family. In the management of a Chinese corporate, the family as a major support for the entrepreneur, as the first source of capital and as a provider of inexpensive labor, has attracted most of the attention. Its positive role notwithstanding, the family also has its dark and merciless sides, to which existing literature has largely turned a blind eye. There are, for instance, the rivalry and conflicts among family members, which also constitute part of the Chinese entrepreneur's daily life. Research into these areas is regrettably inadequate.

In addition, studies of entrepreneurial mobility have also focused on the positive sides of a mobile status of life, including pluralized ways of thinking and cross-boundary social networks, to name just a few. Yet despite the good it brings, there are apparent and latent constraints which we yet need to explore.

---

[66] Chan Kwok-bun and Tong Chi Keung, "Yizhang liankong, duoge mianju: Xinjiapo Huaren de shenfen renting wenti" ["One Face, Many Masks: Problems of Self-Identity Among the Singapore Chinese"] in *Ming Pao Monthly* (September 1999), p. 20–23.

Human life is complex. People's understanding of themselves is often not as crystal clear as they imagine: sometimes they may even appear stranger to themselves. "People are blinded", as the Chinese would say, "when caught in a move; onlookers see the game better". On the one hand, we wish to have an outsider's view of the realities of our entrepreneurs' world. On the other hand, we realize that completely detached interviews and research are bland and spiritless. It is indeed a herculean task to try and understand the realities of a circuiting entrepreneur's corporate management and emotional world. The constraints of research and the limited information that can be gathered have made it more difficult to gain a comprehensive understanding of his personal identities, the details of his social networks and his actual managerial procedure. We wish, however, to develop an in-depth knowledge of his characteristics as a "businessman" and a "human being" against a larger social backdrop, as he tells his own story and as he reminisces about particular moments in his life.

In this book, we seek to bring together the disjunct fields of "personal identity", "social networking" and "corporate management", to form a tableau against which the relationship between our circuiting entrepreneur's internal feelings and external business behavior, as well as the surprises and frustrations that accompany his intensely mobile life, are dramatized. In addition, we have kept in mind that our entrepreneur, just like the normal human beings that we see in and around us, has his "human" emotions, "passions" and even "griefs." We therefore wish to gain some insight into these least-explored aspects through our informants' very own words. An entrepreneur reveals his emotions partly as a member of a group and partly as an independent figure; his emotionality partly takes shelter under his family's roof, and partly goes adrift on his circuitous journeys. Here in this book, his happiness and pains, his vigor and frustrations, will gradually unfold.

Seven Vignettes

Before embarking on a detailed analysis of the interview contents, we shall unfold the profiles of seven immigrant entrepreneurs. These vignettes or profiles are meant to highlight, by reactivating various biographical fragments and snapshots of life, certain features of entrepreneurial experience or contours of history in the managerial process. While admitting that they are edited records of a number of individuals' life histories, they are by no means arbitrary fragments; nor are they intended to fit individual experience into a pre-determined "frame" of mind. Rather, these profiles, as specimens of life and historical memories, provide us with significant information from our immigrant entrepreneurs' pasts, conveying to us the consciousness of an individual or a group, so that we can make reflexive accounts or diagnoses of this specific group of people. As scholars trained in sociological research, we are aware that we are entitled to no "liberty to invent"[1] in interview-based writing and analysis. Our task is to provide an account or explanation of certain unique historical phenomena through these real life materials.

The 16 immigrant entrepreneurs' experiences make up 16 stories that are at the same time similar and different. The seven profiles are selected for their connections with their own times. Our informants immigrated to Hong Kong during different periods over 40 years, the first arriving as early as 1958, the last in 2000. We wish to establish a certain relationship between the life profiles and different periodic features of history. These people, who came to Hong Kong in different periods of history, have lived through different opportunities and challenges in different social structures. In other words, the different social milieux may have given rise to contrasting *zeitgeists*, and thus contrasting immigrant characteristics. Indeed, a single individual's life experiences can never be entirely representative of his whole generation: what we wish to accomplish with these seven profiles is simply to lay the "brickwork" for the analyses in later chapters.

---

[1]Paul Richard Thompson, *Voice of the Past: Oral History* (New York: Oxford University Press, 2000), p. 172.

Chan Kwok-bun and Chan Wai-wan, *Mobile Chinese Entrepreneurs*,
International Series on Consumer Science, DOI 10.1007/978-1-4419-9643-5_4,

Wing: In the Company of Fujianese People

Businesses: Printing plants; chemical plastics factories
Business locations: Fujian, Tianjin
Place of origin: Jinjiang (Fujian)
Age: 57
Year of arrival: 1961
Arrival age: 11

> The people in my circle are mainly board members in my alumni association who are active in business. There are essentially two groups of them, those doing printing and those doing advertising.

Getting adopted

Wing immigrated to Hong Kong when he was 11, during the Great Famine from 1959 to 1961 on the Chinese mainland. At his Fujian home, he lived a hard childhood – deprived, in fact, at least in material terms. The hardships of life eventually forced Wing's mother to leave in 1961 to seek shelter with relatives in Hong Kong.

For Wing, there was never a father figure in his immigrant life. Like many other village children in the Fujian countryside, Wing was "given" to his father:

> I'm a Philippine Chinese, my father lives in the Philippines. I have no idea when exactly he went to the Philippines. In his twenties I guess. He went with a paternal uncle of mine, who went there first, then took my father along. I wasn't born at the time. He wasn't really my father. He adopted me. Adoption was pretty common in the country then. He left for the Philippines in around 1948 and 1949. Since communications were rather inconvenient at the time, he was not sure when he would be back. Not wishing to leave his wife alone to face the insecurities of life, he adopted me. Country people tended to have more children than they could afford to raise, and it became a common practice to give their children away as gifts. Families with no children would have children bought for them, or given to them. In this case, they would give the benefactors some gifts in return. They said that my adopted father and my own father were sworn brothers. It's probable that my adopted parents had just got married when my adopted father was about to leave, and so I was adopted.

Faced with the uncertainties ahead, many home-leavers were required by their parents to get married before they left. The marriages were arranged, more out of pragmatic reasons than for love. The organisation of a family and the adoption of a child were meant only to keep the home-leaver ethically and financially "attached". The "family", as far away as it was to the "edge of the world", had tremendous control over these home-leavers, creating an ethical bond between them and their families at home, goading them to work ever harder for life.

Refugee days

From 1959 to 1961, the mainland of China went through a great famine. The whole country was starving and poor. The government was forced to take a series of measures to encourage people to migrate to other countries. It was in this context that Wing emigrated to Hong Kong:

> Those three years were a major catastrophe. We were having a hard time in the country. In the face of severe natural disasters, local governments had to encourage 'overseas

> Chinese' ('*huaqiao*') to leave the country. Since my father was in the Philippines, I was regarded as a Philippine Chinese, and so I left for Hong Kong in 1961, a teenage boy still attending the first semester of primary six.

For an 11-year-old, Hong Kong represented hope at the end of a difficult journey. In 1961, Wing left his Fujian home with his mother to seek shelter with an aunt who had come to Hong Kong a year earlier:

> My aunt was in Hong Kong, and we stayed with her after arriving in the territory. She had brought her son with her, and had been in Hong Kong for about a year. Life was difficult at the beginning, when the small room had to house two families, the four of us in two beds. A year or two later we had our own rooms.

During their "refugee" days, Wing and his mother depended entirely on each other. From the time Wing was adopted, during their departure from Fujian and resettlement in Hong Kong, Wing's father remained in the Philippines. For Wing, the only sign of his existence was the financial support from over the sea:

> In our first days in Hong Kong, we were living off the money sent to us from the Philippines. Father didn't come to see us until many years later. Those were the days before telephones, so we had to keep in touch mainly through telegrams and letters. Father would come on family visits which allowed him to stay in Hong Kong for about a month. Then in 1966, Mother gave birth to a son. We were still living in a rented room, the only difference being that my mother was now doing various take-home jobs such as threading beads and assembling plastic flowers.

Teaching

Migration allowed Wing to escape the poverty of Fujian village life, but it never excluded him from the circles of Fujianese people. Instead, their common identity as "sojourners" served to bring Fujianese natives closer together. Among the many "circles" of Fujianese natives was the Fukien Secondary School, which Wing attended as a middle school student and where he worked for 9 years as a primary teacher:

> I completed Form 5 in 1968 at Fukien Secondary School and stayed to teach after graduation. I had other choices, but I decided to stay. In the first year, I was involved in some general administration work and didn't become a primary teacher until the second year. I was the head teacher of one of the Grade 5 classes. I stayed for about nine years, until 1976.

In retrospect, a teacher's life was for Wing simple yet fulfilling. As well as teaching, he and his colleagues organised extra-curricular activities such as National Day and May Day celebrations, student excursions and joint-school sport meets. After school, they would also carry out student counselling and home visits. Being a teacher should have been a respected job, but teachers at a "leftist school" were considered as the contrary:

> As a young man, I had always felt committed to serving the community. But the social climate at the time was rather antagonistic to so-called 'leftist patriotic schools' like Fukien. Society tended to exclude leftist schools, and we were paid far less than other teachers... During the student riots in 1967, or the 'red riots' as they were called, our head teacher was put in jail, taken away when he was on duty in the school. He was locked up in Stanley Prison. I visited him a couple of times. They took him away because he was allegedly involved in making the 'Down with the Hong Kong British Government' banners...

> Our school was one of the objects of exclusion. Many teachers were compelled to quit or emigrate. Most of our teachers were young people from Fujian. Since the school was being excluded and financially it was undergoing a hard time, we couldn't afford to hire senior teachers – nor would any of them dare to teach in our school… Our life was very simple, with our meagre income and narrow sphere of activities. Not having much in the way of entertainment, we would normally go to the theatre, or go on excursions or family visits with other teachers. Life was just like that. The majority of my friends were fellow teachers.

Such exclusion was a major disadvantage to a school's development, but the biases from the outside also helped strengthen the school from within. Having sailed in the same boat in troubled waters, Wing developed a strong emotional attachment to his Fukien Secondary School alumni: there emerged a sense of being an "insider" – call it "friendship" – which continues to play a significant role in his management of his businesses. In a society led by ideologies, the individual's fate is determined by identity labels. Much as Wing hankered to serve the community, the cruelties of life were nonetheless frustrating. Bearing the negative political label and confronted with the government's prejudice, the "leftist schools" could only seek to survive. However noble one's aspirations might be, they would eventually be shoved aside by life's hardships:

> Then I decided to quit, in 1975 or 1976 or thereabouts. Many of us were in our 30s, at the age when we should be having our own families. Quite a number of teachers were already married; others were going pretty steady and planning to get married, which inevitably led to financial considerations. It was already 1975 and I was still paid only $450 a month to cover everything. I had to bring home the bacon. There was my mom and my little brother and the rent, which was a big burden. I couldn't even afford my brother's tuition fees and had to seek help from a former schoolmate. It was so difficult to make ends meet. As teachers, we had only three outfits, while today they have a different one each day. Life was very simple and hard.

Four hundred and $50 a month, to keep an entire family, and furthermore, a plan to marry. Financially this was depressing enough. The political changes back on the mainland forced Wing to contemplate his own future. And so he left, for a better life:

> The fall of the 'Gang of Four' in 1976 led me to feel very negative about politics and the pandemonium it could cause. After 1976, the overall political climate on the mainland didn't appear as tense as it had been. Before, a lot of people would be put into jail once a leader had stepped down. But it was no longer like that after 1976. Things seemed to have relaxed a bit. By that time, over half of the young teachers in our school had changed their jobs. So did those teaching in other schools. That seemed to be the trend of the time. Seeing some of my fellows leave, I finally decided to quit… Young people like to dream about the future, and so I left, too.

Starting a business

On leaving the school, Wing started to work in an insurance firm on the school's director's recommendation. He stayed in the firm for 20 months before quitting, aware that his English wasn't "up to par" for the insurance business. Then he enrolled in an evening programme in jewellery design in the company of a former schoolmate who was equally interested. In 1978, Wing paired up with a Fukien schoolmate and rented a vending stall in Central, where he sold jewellery and his friend sold stationery:

> It was around 1978 or 1979 that I started dealing in medium- and low-rate jewellery. I would get karat gold moulds from local factories. Into these moulds I'd mount Russian-made CZ diamonds. CZ is a mineral that is widely synthesized for use as a diamond simulant, with a specific gravity of about 7.5. I started this business all on my own, with an initial investment of around HK$20-30,000... I set up a stall on Cochrane Street in Central. Nearby, there was a branch of the Ta Hwa Chinese Products, now called Yue Hwa. My stall wasn't fixed. It was set up with wooden planks and had to be locked up for the night. I rented the place with a former school friend, who sold stationery just opposite my booth. He was also one of the committee members of Fukien. We were only fresh starters, so it was better if we could share the stall. He had a photocopier in the stall to provide xeroxing services; I had a counter selling second-hand jewellery; and we ran the stall for two or three years. I didn't make a lot of money, but the jewellery on the counter accumulated because I invested basically all the profit to refresh my stock, which eventually grew from two boxes to five or six. It was a prosperous area, but jewellery wasn't its major attraction. Mine sold for around HK$100-200 a piece, medium-priced, and so didn't sell very well. Fake stuff that sold for a couple of dollars would have fared better.

The jewellery stall was Wing's first business attempt. From a teacher to a businessman, the focus of his life moved from students to the bustling crowds on the street. For Wing, this was a tremendous change that he had yet to adapt to, being fresh to business. The nine years as a teacher seemed to have left an indelible mark on his character:

> I had no idea how to attract a customer. I had no idea how to coax people into buying. As a teacher, I had developed a big ego, but in business you've got to suppress that ego and please others, whether you like it or not. Even today, after twenty years in business, I still find it difficult to suppress that part of me. I'd thought that if you didn't feel like doing something, the worst that could happen was that you would stop doing business with a person. But in reality, even if you don't like someone, you still need to get along with him if he turns out to be a prospective partner. This goes against the self-esteem that you've acquired as a teacher. That's why I still don't feel comfortable when I have to 'lower' myself. It's a teacher's habit just to leave something if he doesn't like it.

Getting conned

The nine years as a teacher were in a way conducive to Wing's confident yet humble way of doing business. At the same time, however, Wing believes that his teacher's character was also what got him "conned" in business:

> I never learned to please others and could be easily cheated. I got 'conned' many times... I guess I was not alert enough, since I was a teacher and teachers are generally more kind-hearted and willing to help. But this characteristic could get you into traps when doing business on the mainland.

It was his secondary schoolmates that had offered help, but it was also his schoolmates that first cheated him. When Wing was still in the jewellery business, a former school friend's husband entered into partnership with him and absconded with all their stock and loans to the Philippines:

> There was this old school friend. Her husband was probably too embarrassed to ask to borrow money, and so he offered to partner me. There were then the three of us, each offering

> HK$10,000, and he was responsible for the new purchases. But once he'd got the new stock, he went straight to the Philippines as if nothing had happened. It then turned out that he hadn't really meant to do business. All he wanted was money and so he did that to us.

He would have to take it "as if nothing had happened". He had no idea what the man had done with their stock, or where the money had gone. His friend would merely say, "The money's been spent and we lost it"; and she was an old friend. Wing decided to let it go "as if nothing had happened".

Alumni-cum-partners

Wing did not stay long in the jewellery business. While it was still trudging along, he joined the advertising company of two Fukien school friends, A and B, by investing cash. When Wing joined, the company was in the red. After two years' work, it started to make some money. When Wing requested to draw a bonus now that the company was making profit, his partners refused and denied him access to all the company accounts. Wing felt that he was not being treated in equal terms as an investor and decided to withdraw in order not to ruin future co-operation if conflicts arose:

> I had no access to the company accounts. The only thing I knew was that we had a deposit of HK$100,000. I knew we'd had our bad days, but now that we were making money, I thought it was time to draw a bonus, especially because the Lunar New Year was approaching. But my partners simply shrugged off my suggestion. I felt I wasn't being treated in equal terms and decided to withdraw… I did that because I didn't want us to end up arguing. We might be partners again in the future, who knows?… In 1994 we paired up again.

After his withdrawal from the advertising firm, Wing met, at an alumni gathering, another former schoolmate, C, who was running a printing plant. He joined the plant and took it over after one or two years when his partner withdrew because the plant was not doing well. After another couple of years, when the plant was still not doing any better, Wing decided to work in C's tourist company, but that was reduced to a shell when the original investors ended up in disagreement and the partnership disintegrated. So Wing returned to A and B's advertising firm as a board member and its mainland general manager, with all the rights to the company's dividends. Two years later, however, the company found a mainland local who they thought was better for the position, and who, more importantly, asked for lower pay. Considering the costs, A and B hoped to relocate Wing and eventually he found himself working as a vice-general manager for one of C's adjunct companies. But things changed again two years later, when A and B invited him back because their mainland businesses had been deteriorating since the new manager's installation. Wing suggested that he run the firm himself, in collaboration with another friend. After some negotiations, A and B agreed to sell their printing plant to Wing in instalments. The plant remains Wing's major business to date.

In his first year running the plant, Wing was cheated again, this time by a good friend's friend who took his loan of several hundred thousand dollars. The friend was a colleague in business, an old schoolmate he had known for decades, and also one of the committee members of his alumni association:

> In 1994 I set up a printing plant in Tianjin. In 1999, I was hoping to expand my business. At this juncture, an old friend of mine introduced a friend of his to me, who told me that

many pharmaceutical factories in Jilin Province were seeking packaging services for their medical compounds. He said he had a contact. At the time I thought he was trustworthy because he was a friend of my friend after all, and I authorised him to sign the contract with the pharmaceutical factory. We worked for about six months, finishing three or four batches that were worth around RMB400,000, but the money never arrived. We waited until June of the following year, that is 1999, but the middleman was nowhere to be found. So we sought help from the friend who introduced him to us, only to discover that the middleman had absconded with the medicines. We approached the pharmaceutical factory, asking why they had taken the goods and refused to pay. The factory showed us a receipt and it turned out that the middleman had already collected RMB60,000 from them, and taken RMB750,000 worth of medical compounds to Fujian. We have no clue how much he eventually managed to sell.

Cheated a second time, Wing felt helpless. He had thought the cheater trustworthy – he was after all also from Fujian and had been introduced by an old friend. The sheer revelation of facts urged Wing to reflect on his own character: the years as a teacher had made him "too kind-hearted, too willing to help, and yet not alert enough". "I had a simple mind", he said, "I tended to trust people. It had become habitual for me". Further, Wing believed "we were both from Fujian, former school friends" and would rather let the issue go "because we might see each other again".

We see in Wing the traditional Chinese man and his desire to "save face" and "retain relations" especially because he believes that his life and businesses will always evolve around Fujianese people.

Back to Fujian

In addition to his printing plant in Tianjin, Wing began an investment project in Fujian in 2003. The return to Fujian was coincidental:

I started going home to Fujian more frequently than before. They were starting a new housing assignment scheme because the older parts of the city were about to be demolished for reconstruction, and my old house was within one of these areas. As compensation they were assigning me a new house and I had to go back to choose one and decorate it. Although no one was going to actually live in it, it needed to be decorated anyway. As I went back more frequently, I came into more frequent contact with the folks back home. My cousin introduced me to two business projects: chemical plastics and TPMS (tyre pressure monitoring system).

Although Wing had emigrated to Hong Kong at the age of eleven, he had retained a very strong emotional attachment to his native place, or "old home", as it is called in Chinese – possibly because he had grown to miss it more and wished to have some "real" estate there. He went home originally to attend to his new house, only to find himself setting up new businesses there, "pushed in" by his cousins:

The plant belonged to my cousin-sister. Then my cousin-brother was pulled in for lack of money. Later on I was also pulled in for a further lack of money. Now there are five of us who own the plant. I have one third of the shares.

For the folks back home, Wing has dual identities. He was on the one hand a "native" with the same roots and on the other, a Hong Kong businessman with abundant capital. For ordinary people, his identity as a "Hong Kong businessman" is perhaps more conspicuous:

At home, they take me as a Hongkonger. Of course, the closer folks and relatives see me as a Fujianese, but my business acquaintances generally regard me as a 'Hongkonger' or a

> 'Hong Kong businessman' – and these labels can be an advantage in business negotiations. When you submit a tender, for instance, you stand a better chance because they normally trust that you have relatively abundant capital and that you're more trustworthy. On the whole, they tend to think that Hong Kong business people have better business ethics and are less liable for late delivery. So they're more willing to work with you, and are less likely to say unpleasant things about you.

Being a "Hongkonger" has been a pleasant experience, and has proven to be more of an advantage on the mainland. But in fact, Wing spends the least time in Hong Kong, so he is less of a Hongkonger than he appears to be:

> Now I spend more time in Fujian and Tianjin. I don't really have much to do in Hong Kong… I will usually be gone for one or two months, sometimes three months. My wife will normally see me in my mainland factory, during summer and winter when school is off.

Wing comes back to Hong Kong normally to carry out two errands: to see his family and to attend to alumni association matters. In Hong Kong, Wing has been an active participant of "native association" and "alumni association" activities and has served as the secretary in various community organisations. Of all the Fujianese people in the territory, he has been one of the most enthusiastic. Now, after many years doing business elsewhere, he feels a little nostalgic about the "old folks" back in Hong Kong:

> We no longer have as much to talk about as we did before…

Shin: Economy Plus Ethics

Businesses: Plastic box manufacturing, 3D film material, laser imaging, laser labels, laser security packaging
Business locations: Hong Kong, Shenzhen, Shanghai, Jiangsu, Fujian
Place of origin: Quanzhou (Fujian)
Age: 54
Year of arrival: 1961
Arrival age: 8

> As a new immigrant, we had to start from the roots. We were bound to endure life's hardships… We started doing manual work, so everything lay in our own hands. As long as you're willing to work, there are opportunities. You earn the opportunities.

Enduring the worst of life

"Hold out or get kicked out"! is what many Fujianese people have as their motto. It's what has motivated Shin throughout his life. The adversities of early life drove home to Shin, more than to many others, the importance of being practical and hardworking.

Like Wing, Shin was also adopted by a man who stayed in the Philippines to work. When Shin was eight, he came to Hong Kong with his adoptive mother. A few years after their arrival, when he was still studying at primary school aged five or six, his father died. Financially trapped, the young Shin had to bear the family's welfare on his own shoulders:

> I grew up in a single-parent family. My mother brought me up on her own, while my father was away in the Philippines. After Father died, I had to bring home the bacon. I had to work while I was still in school. I would do deliveries on my bike after class. I was living in Sai Wan, where my school was. Most of the Fujianese and Teochew immigrants were also living around that area and knew each other. I did deliveries for a Teochew friend who sold biscuits wholesale. For three years I worked as a part-time bicycle delivery boy, and that taught me to persevere.

Living in compact communities is one of the ways new immigrants learn to tackle their difficulties. In the 1960s and 1970s, most Fujianese and Teochew immigrants mainly converged around Sheung Wan and adjacent areas so they could seek help from one another. With the death of his father and the subsequent financial hardship, Shin was in despair, and had to work part-time until he was in Form 3, when he was forced to quit school to make a living for the family. He then started to work for a newspaper, 15 or 16 hours a day.

Shin did not complain about his early problems. He believed he was destined, as a new immigrant, to go through it, but as long as he held out, he would make it in life. This belief motivated him to go on and work harder.

Family craftwork

Two years after he started working for the newspaper, Shin decided to learn to drive a van, hoping this would help improve his life. It appeared to be one of those minor decisions one makes in life, and Shin could never have predicted this simple decision would mark such a great turning point. The new job was to bring him his first business partner, and indirectly put him on the road to entrepreneurship:

> I began doing deliveries for a food factory. They needed a large number of plastic boxes for storing preserved fruits. They got the boxes from a supplier whose supply was later unable to meet their demand. The food factory boss, satisfied with my work and my hardworking character, offered to work with me in the plastic box business. It was around 1978. We started small, a family type of business. Both of us invested HK$20,000, HK$40,000 in total. Machinery wasn't very expensive at the time; we bought our raw material in Hong Kong, batch by batch, so that we didn't have to spend much each time... In the 1970s, family workshops could be found everywhere in Hong Kong. Such workshops didn't need a lot of investment. Once you received an order, you could simply hire some students to work for you after school. I was married by that time, so my wife also helped. We did everything at home, holding out together. We worked very long hours. As soon as we were home after a tiring day of work, we had to start work on the orders. Our daughter was still very little, so we left her in her grandma's care... New immigrants are the most hard-working people. We worked 15, 16 hours a day, all of us. Difficult life.

Shin's business started because of his boss's appreciation for his hardworking character, which in turn had stemmed from his struggles in his new immigrant life. The idea that immigrants had to suffer was character-forming for Shin, and gave him the vigour and fortitude he needed to establish himself. His home workshop was Shin's second shift of the day, but this difficult life, far from intimidating him, served only to boost his confidence. As a result, his business kept expanding and after 20 years it grew from the family workshop to a corporate scale, operating in Shenzhen, Fujian and Jiangsu, with offices in Hong Kong and Shanghai. The Shenzhen factory houses the corporate headquarters and covers more than 200,000 ft^2, with a staff of more than 200.

Now, looking back at how he came from Fujian to start from scratch, Shin thinks it was his perseverance that has brought him to where he is. He "suffered" to make it. "As long as you're willing to work, opportunities will come your way", is his mantra.

Heading North

In 1983, Shin decided to move north, first to Dongguan, then to Shenzhen:

> The factories in Hong Kong were having a bad time, with little space and higher salaries to pay. My factory was originally in Chai Wan. At that time, some of my neighbours in the processing trade had already moved to Dongguan. I was also looking for a new factory location, so I wanted to contact them for some information. That was the trick of the trade: you got to know more about a place through someone who'd already been there. The factory we contacted moved to Dongguan in 1981; we moved in 1983. It's been more than 20 years since, so things may be very different today. But back then, the earlier you entered the Chinese market, the more advantageous it would be for your business. Economic reforms had just begun on the mainland, the workers there were paid a lot less, and the government was far less restrictive [towards foreign investors]. That's how we all managed to expand.

The move to the North was largely due to cost considerations. Information sharing among Hong Kong business people had played a key role in the selection of factory locations. One successfully established business would pass invaluable information onto the latecomers. Thus one factory's move could lead to the move of a mass of factories. This "snowball effect" resulted in the emergence of so-called "centralised areas", convergence areas of ethnic businesses. In Guangdong Province, for instance, the majority of Taiwanese factories are in and around the city of Dongguan. Such centralised ethnic business regions are conducive to the formation of geographical networks for information sharing and cooperation.

Getting back-up

The rules of the game vary from place to place. As one does business in different places, there are different, and usually unwritten, rules peculiar to each place. Now back on the mainland, Shin was starting to realise the importance of *guanxi*, or connections and "relationships":

> It's important to pull the *guanxi* strings. If you're a local, things are easier. There's a Chinese way of doing this, which is not particularly difficult. First you need a friend's introduction. Once introduced, you need to gradually build up a relationship with the new acquaintance. That, of course, is an accumulative process... In business, you need luck, opportunities and certainly *guanxi* – if you get sufficient back-up, you stand a better chance.

The Chinese way, according to Shin, is to "pull the *guanxi* strings", which in itself is not very difficult, provided that you are "introduced by a local". "A mighty tiger", as the saying goes, "is no match for the native serpent". In business, there is also a difference between "insiders" and "outsiders". To become an "insider", Shin said, one not only needs a local's introduction, but also has to be "responsible" and "trustworthy":

> To establish local relationships, you've got to be responsible for each other and have good credit. When a friend is in need, you've got to try your best to help. When they can't make it, you've got to give them a hand.

For the Chinese, the exchange of "personal feelings" (*renqing*) is in essence a type of "social exchange". This requires that whenever you need help, you have to draw those who can help into your *guanxi* network, by such means and through such channels that they feel obliged to help. The ultimate goal of being "responsible" and "trustworthy" is that the other party will do the same in return. With 20 years behind him doing business on the mainland, Shin knows too well that one stands a better chance with sufficient "back-up", which one can receive only by being others' back-up.

Since his move in 1983, Shin has witnessed the changes that took place in Dongguan. The local government's attitude towards Hong Kong business people in particular has gone through a tremendous change:

> When we first arrived in Dongguan, our equipment was far from completed. In those days, if you set out from Hong Kong in the morning, you wouldn't get to Dongguan until about 3 or 4pm. Now it takes just an hour or so. The local government was practical, and our investment was very much appreciated. We hired several dozen people – that number was already fairly large in the area at that time. When we moved into Humen, Dongguan, ours was the fourth factory there. Now the number has grown to about 200, and each is very large.

When Shin first moved back to the mainland, he was immensely appreciated by the local government. Those who are appreciated get good back-up. But now, factories of a similar size can be found everywhere in the region. For various reasons, Shin eventually decided to move, this time to Shenzhen, and he set up his headquarters there.

Back to Fujian

In 1992, Shin decided to extend his business to Fujian. The decision came as a result of Shin's life-long obsession with being Fujianese. While Shin, having left his native home at the age of eight, had only a very vague idea of what Fujian was like, the ideological education he had received from a "leftist school" like Fukien had nevertheless fostered an emotional attachment to his native place and his native country. That's why he always kept himself busy with the activities of his Alumni Association as well as the Fujianese Association after he left school. As various external conditions contribute to constructing and intensifying one's internal sentiments, so Fujian, that vaguely remembered home, stayed crystal clear deep down. Of course while emotionally Shin was geared towards his native home, such sentiments could never have been a decisive factor when it came to a project as big as setting up a new factory. The move, as Shin considered, would enjoy a dual advantage. On the one hand, as a local, as someone who had "come from the same clan", he would be allowed to tap the local resources and social networks. On the other hand, as a "foreign investor", a "Hong Kong businessman", he would enjoy the convenience that the local policies normally granted to "patriotic, home-coming investors helping to advance the economy at home".

Shin pointed out that the trickiest problem facing anyone planning to set up factories on the mainland was how to communicate and negotiate with local governments, especially on issues concerning land and taxes:

> There are always problems when you run a factory on the mainland, because different places have their own requirements. This involves communication and mutual understanding. Quite often, the requirements are a lot more difficult than they seem. You may get into problems if you take them too lightly. In those cases, you've got to be patient in negotiating with local governments. Common problems include land, taxes, preferential treatment, and so on. All of them require a great deal of negotiation. Local policies may vary from place to place. They may try their best to secure your investment, but once you're in, things may turn out to be rather different from what you expected. Then *guanxi*, or influential connections, will help a lot.

To run a business on the mainland, success lies very much in a good relationship with the local government. But things can be much easier in one's home town than elsewhere. "If you come from that place", in Shin's words, "it's very easy to pull the strings, the right strings". Just as there are different rules in different villages, so there are different local rules for establishing *guanxi* and for interpersonal communication. Shin has left his Fujian factory in the charge of his elder brother first because along with the ties of blood comes a stronger sense of trust; and second, it is more convenient for a local manager to tap and mobilise the local interpersonal networks that only "native serpents" can operate, particularly when it comes to dealing with the local government.

Economy plus ethics

In order to establish favourable relations with the local government, Shin not only had to create and parade the mutuality of being an "insider" but also establish his own "ethical enterprise" so as to create a favourable social image. This is because one's economic enterprise and ethical enterprise will ultimately complement and advance each other.

Listed on Shin's name card are 12 public service titles, 11 of which are related to native Fujianese associations in Fujian or Hong Kong. In Fujian, Shin is a member of the "Political Consultative Conference" and a standing director of the "China Overseas Friendship Association". In Hong Kong, he has taken up important positions in a number of native associations (*tongxiang hui*), alumni associations, commercial chambers and association unions. Even when he is very busy with his own businesses, he manages to attend the meetings of various community associations:

> I'm involved in a lot of commercial chambers, native associations and the like. It's very time-consuming, with a lot of meetings and stuff... I think life becomes more meaningful if you spend time on such things... Now I'm a member of the 'Political Consultative Conference' and have meetings to attend every week. It certainly takes a lot of time to travel between Fujian and Hong Kong, but you just feel so fulfilled and successful helping others.

For Shin, his public services are not just morally meaningful, they are economically effective. Society does not measure a businessman's "success" entirely against the material wealth he possesses; they also look at his business ethics and social status.

Acts of moral probity that commercial associations encourage include public servicing, assistance in the construction of community schools and hospitals, and so on. Just like Confucian scholars who tried to prove their "morality" by expounding their ideas in writing, business people have a similar pursuit. The difference is that their "morality" lies in their "achievements" in both economic and moral terms. As a businessman feels fulfilled to a certain extent in his economic pursuits, he normally goes on to engage himself in moral pursuits which, in turn, will indirectly benefit his economic enterprise.

"As long as you're willing to help, there'll be pay-off". Indeed, all human behaviour is to a certain extent "exchange behaviour" that is targeted at some "pay-off", be it profitable or instrumental, economic or emotional. For a businessman, and a highly "mobile" immigrant entrepreneur at that, his "exchange behaviour" is spatially and temporally more pluralized, promising; therefore, there are more "pluralized" pay-offs.

When travelling becomes habitual

Shin's businesses have evolved into a corporate group, with branches in Hong Kong, Shenzhen, Fujian, Shanghai and Jiangsu, each having its own leading products that are mutually compatible. Currently, his Hong Kong office has no substantial function and is mainly used to receive guests, allocate smaller orders and transfer minor supplies. The Shenzhen office houses the group headquarters, occupying a floor area of more than 200,000 ft^2, with a staff of more than 200. When the board needs to meet, it often meets at the Shenzhen headquarters. The Fujian factory, featuring laser labels, is left in the charge of Shin's brother. The Jiangsu factory has been working with a wine factory, working specifically on the wine factory's laser-labelled packages. The Shanghai office is mainly responsible for marketing campaigns. While there is an unambiguous division of labour among the different branches, the management staff are mainly from Hong Kong:

> Our major management staff in the mainland branches are all transferred from Hong Kong. In Shenzhen alone, we have three from Hong Kong, all at manager level. The transferred managers were all hired from the outside. All of them have been working in our company for more than ten years... The Jiangsu branch is managed by two... When we set up the Shanghai branch, I sent two of our staff members and hired another two in Shanghai... My daughter and her husband are currently helping out in the Shenzhen factory to gain some experience. She completed her first degree in Canada, and now she's working on her MBA at City University of Hong Kong. She's going to finish this year.

In managing such diverse businesses in different places, Shin has relied mainly on personnel from Hong Kong, except for the Fujian factory, which is managed by his own brother. For Shin, people trained in places like Hong Kong, where law and order are more respected, are more reliable. He remains sceptical about mainland natives.

It is all too important to have a trustworthy management team when it comes to managing, co-ordinating and supervising such diversely-located businesses and factories. Shin, of course, has to travel a lot himself:

> I spend most of my time in the Shenzhen factory... I normally visit the Quanzhou factory once or twice a month... Those in Jiangsu and Shanghai need frequent inspection as well... In Hong Kong, I'm always busy with my commercial chambers and native associations...

> and there are meetings to attend each week as a member of the 'Political Consultative Conference'. Fujian and Hong Kong take up a large portion of my time.

As a person of multiple identities, Shin has various businesses in different places, and actively participates in public services. About his shuttling life style, Shin simply says, "It's nothing. I'm used to it".

Yam: Survival of the Better Identified

Businesses: Marketing, glass manufacturing
Business locations: Hong Kong, Shenyang, Germany
Place of origin: Born in Indonesia; Returned to Ningde, Fujian, during the Indonesian "pai Hua" (*Getting Rid of the Chinese*) movements
Age: 43
Year of arrival: 1976
Arrival age: 12

> Three years ago I started to 'rehearse' my identities: fortunately I've been proven correct about this... I wanted to organise this exhibition in Germany in the name of their local company, because the [local] faces are much easier for them to accept... we had to cater to their tastes... The 10 years to come will be a time of co-operation, and 'local knowledge will have a crucial role to play.

"I stand a good chance of winning"
Yam was born in Indonesia. At the age of two, he was forced to move back to Ningde in Fujian with his parents because large-scale "pai Hua" movements started to "get rid of the Chinese". In 1976, at the age of twelve, Yam immigrated to Hong Kong with his family and enrolled in the Fukien Secondary School, which normally took new immigrant kids. Because of the differences between the local and mainland Chinese educational systems, Yam was demoted to a lower grade and had to graduate older than the majority of his peers. Moreover, as a new immigrant, Yam was not proficient enough in English so he was limited in entering a university. Throughout his school life, Yam felt he was always the one who lagged behind, which made him uncomfortable:

> Probably I grew up earlier. I was older than my classmates in general because I came from the mainland and was demoted to a lower grade to study and was forced to do this and that... I wasn't one of those who excelled at schoolwork, I never held any particular edge over the others. I almost invariably ranked below 10 in schoolwork in my class. But kids like to compete and I, of course, didn't like lagging behind. So I told myself: alright, I may not be doing as well as you in these 15 years in school, but after this, we have more than 30 years and that's when I'll have my odds. So, I said, I wasn't a smart student and I was a late-comer, but I'll have my own way of surpassing you. I started late – that explains why I lost the game in this initial 15 years. But one day, I'll overtake you all, at work... The education system in Hong Kong as it was designed, with its Advanced Level Examinations and Higher Level Examinations, was pretty much a disadvantage for Chinese school kids. I would not settle for that; I just never understood why the kids from Chinese schools were denied access to, say, Hong Kong University. We could only go to Chinese schools like

> Clementi and then to the Chinese University. It was sad… We could not become professionals, so I decided to go my own way.

In a colonial society like Hong Kong, the social elite were predominantly from top-ranking schools of a higher English level. As a new immigrant student, Yam could only go to the "leftist patriotic schools", which were largely despised by the social mainstream. Over-aged and speaking little English, he was denied access to the elitist Hong Kong University. These were the institutional limitations that new immigrant students had to face. Yam was determined never to settle for this "sure loss" situation and refused to accept that he would never become a professional. He would get his chance, but not in professions dominated by the mainstream elite. And he went into business.

Getting ready

Yam harboured a certain ambition: to start his own business. This idea occurred to him even before he finished secondary school. It haunted him, prompting him to get ready for this enterprise in life:

> I graduated from secondary school in 1983, but the idea of having my own business started well before that… It occurred to me way before I left school, so everything was carefully planned. I began to familiarize myself with the ways and skills of business. I needed some training… I was one of those kids that could be easily reduced to tears, and I was very dependent on my mother. I would not go out without tugging at her blouse. I was afraid of strangers – pretty much an introvert, the total opposite of what I am today. I was aware of the problems in my character, and was determined to improve it – but it needed a bit of honing. So I chose to study business and enrolled in the business programme at Lingnan University. After I completed the programme, I started working as a sales clerk for a car dealer. I stayed there for five years, and came to realise that in dealing with your clients you need to have a thick hide and a lot of techniques… As I got to know more about the skills of communication and coping with strangers, I became aware that I did not know enough about the overall operation of a business. Then I went into banking… and left after one year and enough exposure to the business… Then I realised I needed a more systematic and logical mind, so I became a tutor at Lingnan University. I taught there for four years.

Once an "introvert", Yam was determined to improve his own character and acquire more business skills to prepare for his life career. Yam said everything he did in those early years – enrolling in a business programme, working as a sales clerk and then as a banker to learn more about the overall operation of a business, and subsequent tutoring to train his mind – was all aimed at preparing himself for the ultimate goal: setting up his own business.

First order

In 1997, Yam got married and felt it was time to start his own business. He went into trade with his wife. He chose trade because he had contacts, which is why he received his first order shortly after his company was founded:

> I felt that I'd laid a pretty good foundation for the trading business, because I had many contacts. Many of my former schoolmates were working in banks, and banks need a lot of gifts and souvenirs for their clients. Then I received an order from the Bank of China, shortly after my company was founded. It was two weeks away from the Lunar New Year and no other company was willing to take this order. Well, that was the time of the year

> when factories were about to close for the New Year holidays. Since the Bank was to participate in the Community Chest Walkathon three weeks after the New Year, they needed topcoats for seven of their branches. They came to us because many of the top brands would not take their order with their factories closing so soon. So I took it on, without much thought or fear. It was an order for 69,000 coats.

Yam had prepared for years for this launch, but the real business opportunities would only come with a good social network. His first order came thanks to a banker friend's recommendation. That the order eventually came to Yam, rather than to anyone else within his broader social network, was largely due, Yam believes, to the "inquisitive" character he had developed as a sales clerk:

> The five years as an automobile sales clerk gave me excellent training in communication skills. I learned, for example, how to get straight to the point when communicating with a client. I also forced myself to be 'inquisitive', to gain the best possible overall understanding of the people and things around me. To do that, you've got to put them under 'detailed observation' so to speak... After I launched my company, I kept calling my banker friends to ask if there was anything they needed. I felt that I had to be 'inquisitive', that I had to 'snuffle' around more... There was this secondary schoolmate working for the Bank of China, a close friend. I learned about the job from him and so I got it.

One's social network can be an important source of business information. It is simply a matter of time for a piece of news to turn into an opportunity. Yam's "inquisitiveness" not only strengthened his relationship with his contacts, but also allowed him to obtain useful information in good time. This is also one of the reasons why Yam engaged himself in alumni association activities, serving as one of its board members. Busy as he was with his business, he never failed to stay in frequent contact with his schoolmates and old friends.

Rednecks and Yahoos

After a year or so manufacturing souvenirs for banks, Yam sensed the limitations in the business's development. Since they were not supplying as great a variety as did other companies – which meant, of course, less competitive edge – Yam decided to shift the focus of his business from local manufacturing to international trading:

> In 1998 and 1999, when the European Union lifted its quota restrictions on glass products, I sensed that could be an opportunity in international trade. I had never been in the glass industry, I knew next to nothing about it – neither did anyone else because no one was really doing the glass business in Hong Kong back then. So I talked with my wife. I asked why we didn't shift to international trading. We didn't have any edge over the others in this [souvenir manufacturing business], because we didn't have a variety of products. My wife agreed and said, right, we can give that a try. She was very supportive and eventually we started doing international trade, dealing in glass products.

The changes in international trading situations quite often lead to structural changes in home industries. The European Union's decision to lift the quota restrictions on glass products gave Yam's company an opportunity to transform itself. But the challenges that lay ahead of this newborn glass firm were tremendous:

> Once I started, I felt that probably I was born to have to go through all this, as it turned out that the trade was far from easy. First, all the glass factories in China were in the North, and their products were not machine-processed, but mouth-blown. Second, the glass-makers

> were – sorry to say this –a bunch of rednecks and yahoos that grew up without parental care. How were you supposed to communicate with such uneducated and uncivilized people? Yes, the prospects were fine, but how were you going to train these people so that their work would meet the European standard? I didn't feel totally negative about it, though, because at least I had some real big challenges ahead of me.

As middlemen in international trading, Hong Kong firms had to provide their clients with quality services on the one hand, and maintain a good relationship with the suppliers on the other. Since the Chinese glass factories were all in the North, where "rednecks" and "yahoos" worked, communication became a formidable task for a Southerner like Yam. To continue, individual faith and business skills on the businessman's part would have to play a decisive role. Yam had a strong resistance to giving in, for his immigrant life had instilled in him a drive to win, and this drive became his ultimate motivation to go against all odds. In addition, his experience as an automobile sales clerk had driven home to him the importance of "detailed observation", especially in his cooperation with the supplier. He realised that for cooperation to be successful, it was crucial to understand the ethnic character of the other party:

> To establish relations with the supplier, you've got to be sincere. Sincerity is very important. In China, many factory owners have come from farmer families, and Chinese farmers are generally rather short-sighted. That means what they care most about is real cash. And you need to know this and you need to pay them on time. That's why I never find any excuse to delay their pay when I do business with them... Other than being sincere, you've got to be 'fair' as well. They like working with me because I'm willing to help them improve in different aspects like quality control, production technology, product design, and so on. They eventually learn a lot from me. When they like you, they will help you in their own ways. Sometimes clients ask for quotes from us and from other agents at the same time. When the supplier knows this, they will give the other agents a higher quote and keep us informed. They do this because they like our way of doing business. Now you see the pay-off doesn't always come in hard cash.

In dealing with the Northern glass-workers, Yam realised that "sincerity", "prompt payment" and "fairness" were the best strategies. Business relations are in essence interpersonal relations. Indeed, in business, "relationship precedes judgement" and personal integrity plays a crucial role in affecting supplier-agent relations and cooperation. While deep down Yam had considered the glass-workers a bunch of "rednecks" and "yahoos", he managed to get their help because he had a good understanding of the group character of these people and realised the importance of "prompt payment" to the relationship between them.

Colour strategies and identity deployment

Yam has always stressed the necessity of "detailed observation". The success of a business is largely determined by one's understanding of the overall business environment as well as one's conceptual and perceptual knowledge of the trading partner. In this globalised economy, Yam believes, an important strategy is to utilise different skin colours and deploy different identities according to the mentalities of different clients:

> When dealing with the manufacturers, my yellow skin colour has proved to be an advantage. I've complicated identities but that's not something to whine at. It's something to be enjoyed...

> I've been living in different places, assuming different identities and mastering different languages and dialects – all this has made it easy for me to communicate with different people… My knowledge of different dialects has given me a great competitive edge when I don't have any in other areas, because good relations quite often come with a shared language.

Yam believes that during negotiations, his own skin colour and his mastery of the local dialect helps create between his trading partners a favourable sense of identity that proves to be an "absolute advantage" for him. His Putonghua with a Beijing flavour, accent-free Cantonese and fluent Hokkien have allowed Yam to communicate with such clarity that a kind of tacit understanding is more likely to emerge between him and different suppliers – a kind of understanding that might indirectly lead to business opportunities. Skin colour can be a catalyst not only in establishing favourable relations with the manufacturers, but in seeking overseas clients as well, the only difference being that, in that case, you will need to present yourself using the colour of the local people. During exhibitions abroad, Yam and his Chinese colleagues retreat from the scene and have their local partners on show, as Yam believes that people of the same colour can identify with each other more easily.

In the context of globalisation, China has become the world's factory. With its low production costs, China is manufacturing many of the world's products and has competitively "harmed", and thus caused hostility among, Western manufacturers. Against this background, to gain business opportunities at overseas exhibitions, Chinese companies have to use the local skin colour and conceal their own Chinese identity. In one recent incident, after a Chinese-run shoe factory was burnt down by some local people in Spain, a Chinese exhibitor at a Milan exhibition was attacked after being accused of infringing on a local company's rights. Yam gives the following analysis of the conflicts between Chinese business people and the locals:

> Chinese shoes are inexpensive. This nearly forced the local family shoe businesses into extinction… Would you put up with this if you were the locals? You're virtually left starving to death. Would anyone still care about ethics on the brink of death? He would probably go insane. You may not have expected such irrational, violent solutions to business conflicts in a Western democracy, but now it's matter of life or death… When you have seriously hurt others in competition, when we Chinese continue this kind of competition, this 'either you or me' mentality, then all we get is hatred when we go and exhibit in other countries.

The conflicts between Chinese and Western business people taught Yam the importance of deploying different skin colours on different occasions. Genuine business is on the one hand a display of sincerity and on the other a show that both parties can feel good about.

A trinity of identities

Apart from his skin colour strategies, Yam also stresses deployment of a company's identities. He believes the best possible deployment is for a company to have a trinity of identities, i.e., be a Hong Kong company, have a mainland factory and an establishment in Europe, all at the same time. To achieve these identities, Yam first bought a glass factory in Shenyang and then changed the form of co-operation with his European clients, switching to a seller-buyer relationship to form a closer partnership. When dealing with Western counterparts, Yam uses his European label to avoid foreign competitors' hostility, and at the same time utilises the local identity to pursue business opportunities. When he faces a foreign client, however, Yam will consciously stress his Chinese identity, a symbol of quality and low cost, to gain a competitive edge over his European rivals. When doing business with Chinese mainland suppliers, identity as a Hong Kong company has a certain brand effect. Compared with their mainland counterparts, Hong Kong companies and business people are signifiers of a good business tradition that is synonymous with prestige, affluence and efficiency. Being a Hong Kong businessman, therefore, gives Yam certain advantages over his competitors on the mainland.

It takes a great deal of effort to maintain a company's pluralised identities. Each year, Yam has to spend quite some time abroad, visiting and negotiating with overseas clients. While attending to his business in Hong Kong, he also has to take care of the production and operation of his mainland factory, which requires frequent travelling between Hong Kong and the mainland. As his corporation becomes more pluralised, Yam's life is becoming increasingly mobilised. About this new life style, he says:

> You won't be able to succeed in business until you've managed to experience the local culture and understand the local needs. If you don't understand their life, how are you supposed to establish a long-term relationship with them?... In business, we need to travel to different places and accumulate information about different markets before we can access and utilize the local knowledge. Only in this way can we come to know more about others and learn to be more accommodating and less biased... Our world is like a large garden in which we walk. There are hills and woods, rivers and lakes. It feels great to stroll around it. When you're tired you can sit down to take a break. It's a meaningful activity.

A mobile lifestyle, Yam believes, is one way in which a successful international trader can gain access to various "local knowledges". In order to establish a long-term rapport with someone, we need first of all to understand this person as well as the local culture and the local market. A mobile life, and all the life experience that it brings, is invaluable in this sense. There are times, however, that one feels stressed and perplexed in such a scurrying life. In Yam, we see the more positive side of such intense mobility, because work gives him the "biggest satisfaction" and work, for him, is life. His refusal to give in and his outlook on life have become his ultimate motivation, making his life all the more enjoyable.

Chiu: Do As the Chinese Do

Businesses: Plush plants, chemical fibre plants, textiles factories, toy manufacturing, clothing, trades
Business locations: Hong Kong, Zibo (Shangdong), Weifang (Shangdong), Qingdao (Shandong)
Place of origin: Jinjiang of Fujian
Age: 36
Year of arrival: 1986
Arrival age: 15

> Different businesses are done in different flocks. People in the same business flock together... Each has his own network, which is not something you can join as you wish. You need to be admitted in the first place... When you need help from others, you've got to adapt yourself to their way of business. It's as simple as that, anywhere in the world... Do as the Romans do. In the simplest terms, you've got to follow their rules once you're in their place.

"I didn't really start with nothing"

Chiu started it all with his second elder brother. Headquartered in Hong Kong, they have their production base in Shandong, way back on the mainland. The corporation owns ten companies and factories in three cities in Shandong with a staff of more than 4,000, which makes it a sizable corporation in the area.

Chiu, boasting this achievement in his 30s, does not give all the credit to himself. Rather, he believes he did not really "found" his business because the money he needed all came from his father, who, Chiu believes, practically "gave" him what he has today:

> I didn't start with nothing; I had my father behind me... I wasn't like the generation of early comers: they were the genuine entrepreneurs, because they started everything from scratch.

As early as 1973, Chiu's father had left Fujian and immigrated to Hong Kong, a place that was said to be rich in opportunity. After 10 years' hard work, Old Chiu managed to lick his ironmongery business into its best shape:

> Father tried many things in those early years, ironware, jewellery, garment manufacturing and so on. He made his first fortune as a packaging contractor. Back then, a lot of industries like ironware and garment manufacturing were in urgent need of packaging services. Before that, my father was working in a factory and came to know a lot about the production procedure. His boss found him trustworthy and so outsourced the packaging procedure to him to make the management simpler. Father got many jobs outsourced to him, mostly from home natives, who were introduced to him by relatives, friends, and colleagues... Then my father switched to ironware. Since his factory ran on an automatic production line, he hired just seven or eight people... He stayed in the business for more than ten years. He did not make real profit until the 1980s, when his business was finally on track and began to make big money.

From employer to contractor and finally to boss, Old Chiu's endeavours were what his son would call "genuine entrepreneurship" that starts from nothing. Trust of the boss and help of home natives were the key factors that led to Old Chiu's success. As for Chiu himself, he was born into a business life. After he graduated from university, Chiu joined the company managed by his two elder brothers. Their father's financial support played a crucial role in putting the brothers on track:

> Father's help in our businesses was mainly financial. It played a crucial part, especially during the hard times.

Splitting up

Chiu has four brothers and sisters. In the 1980s, his two elder brothers were doing business together but business disagreements led to their split in 1993:

> My dad then paired up my second elder brother and me, my eldest brother and my elder sister. After my younger sister graduated, she joined me and second brother. Splitting up happens a lot in business. When you don't agree with each other, it's natural to separate...

> After they split up, eldest brother went into plush toys, second brother and I went into textiles and garment manufacturing.

There are pros and cons about a family business. The siblings may see eye to eye about the company's future, but the way they go about it may differ drastically. When siblings disagree and no one will compromise, the only solution is to split up and father has to become the mediator and arbitrator. After the split, Chiu's company occupied an office on the first floor, and eldest brother's company headquartered on the ground floor. Although still neighbours, they would have to go their own way now:

> Eldest brother's office was just beneath us. But now we were two separate companies with our own individual circles, suppliers, and so on. We didn't share our factories and resources on the mainland. We might have the same supplier but we went on separate negotiations. And we were never informed of each other's quotes. These were too trivial and we were just too busy to talk to each other about such things. We'd normally discuss it on the phone if a particularly important matter came up. Otherwise we'd simply concentrate on our own business. We've been two separate companies all along.

Business doesn't come in batches

Though headquartered in Hong Kong, Yam's production base is mainly located in Shandong. After more than 10 years' continuous effort, the company evolved into a sizable corporation. For Chiu, this achievement came with practical work:

> In different markets, you've got to use different ways to market and seek new clients. Back on the mainland, we got our first clients by visiting every prospect with our samples. We started as a cloth manufacturer, and our target clients were toy factories. We first obtained the addresses of toy factories from the local Commercial Management Bureau. Then we went on individual visits to those factories with our cloth samples, door to door, without the help of an agent. Doing business in China was still like the 1970s and 80s in Hong Kong, when you had to pay individual visits to potential clients. On the international market, we do that mainly through expos, or advertising in international magazines, via emails and fax, etc... Once an opportunity comes up, we'll hold on to it and do our best. We go on to expos abroad every year, and we visit our clients as well.

Apart from *guanxi*, luck and opportunity, hard work was also essential in doing successful business. Chiu's clients are not only from the Chinese mainland, but also from Taiwan, South Korea, Japan, Cambodia, Thailand, Vietnam, and Europe, Canada and America. The corporation's achievement has not been accidental, but is the result of years of continuous, practical hard work that involved "door-to-door visits", "expos", "email and fax", "visits to clients" that "made full use of every opportunity". While Chiu, unlike his father, did not start with nothing, he has embodied the spirit of hard work and perseverance that we find in Old Chiu and many a Fujianese person.

Do as the Chinese do

Within China's still developing economic system, in order to establish oneself in the Chinese business arena where interpersonal relations have a crucial role to play, one needs not only to work hard, but to learn to do as the Chinese do – that is, to learn and play by the "rules of the game" of different trades and places. There are written and unwritten rules of conduct peculiar to each. In Chiu's own words, "Different businesses are done in different flocks", and each flock may have features that vary from place to place, trade to trade.

In either Hong Kong or the mainland, Chiu feels, one has to rely on a network to aid one's business, though in very different ways:

> In Hong Kong, we do marketing on expos. You go to expos and people come over. When you both feel like it, you start cooperating. So in Hong Kong, you get to know your clients more in a public setting. There are also expos on the mainland. Guangzhou, for example, holds an international expo twice a year. There are expos in Beijing and Shanghai as well. We go to these expos too. But business practices are not standardised on the mainland, so that personal factors still dominate. Even if you offer quality products for competitive prices, you won't get very far without pulling a few strings and fawning a bit. Yes, your prices are a lot lower and they may know about you, but if you don't have some favourable *guanxi* with the person in charge, you won't get much business with them. You can't rush when doing business on the mainland, because 'personal feelings' are still decisive.

To beat the fierce competition, in Hong Kong one has to rely on "quality" and "service"; on the mainland one resorts to *guanxi*. To extend one's business network, in Hong Kong one has to stand in public to become known; on the mainland one has to "pull a few strings and fawn a bit". Chiu understands that "personal feelings are still decisive" and that he must do as the Chinese do before he can establish himself:

> When you need help from others, you've got to adapt yourself to their way of business. It's as simple as that, anywhere in the world. To survive on the mainland, you've got to do as the mainlanders do.

The establishment and use of *guanxi* is the key to successful business on the Chinese mainland. To build up business *guanxi*, one has to "socialise" profusely:

> Each month I spend about half my time in Hong Kong and the other half in Shandong. My second brother and I take turns to look after our business. While I'm on the mainland, he comes to Hong Kong; when I come back, he goes to the mainland. On the mainland, I have to do a lot of socialising. Most of my clients and partners are men... so we mainly eat or drink.

One "eats" and "drinks" a great deal when doing business on the mainland. Motivated and purposeful, these activities are part of a day's work, and despite frequenting entertainment establishments, Chiu does not consider he receives much entertainment. As a businessman, as a boss, he has times of absolute control, but there are just as many times when he does not have a say. This helplessness is camouflaged under an apparently materially fulfilled life so he never receives sympathy. The apparent is what catches the eye.

Never suspect one you trust; never trust one you suspect

Chiu and his second brother take turns to look after their business on the mainland. With their dozen factories in different places and myriad things to take care of within the limited time of each day, they must rely on a trustworthy management team to effectively coordinate, supervise, manage and develop the corporation's businesses:

> Most of our factories are not wholly owned but joint ventures. Our local partners invariably started as our buyers and later became our partners after some time of cooperation, when

> we felt more comfortable working with each other... At the management level, there are representatives from partner companies and there are hired staff. Most of these hired people are relatives and friends... The relatives we hired previously worked in the same field. For management, you can't have a newcomer to the business or things will became really tough... Quite a few of these people have been promoted to management level. No home-natives have been promoted as yet.

Most of Chiu's factories are joint ventures. For the management team, as well as having partner representatives, he has hired blood and conjugal relatives, a practice he describes as "historically rooted" because they have been working in the factory since the very early days and he wanted to "keep them". Since they were so willing to help despite the initial hardship, Chiu felt obliged to "keep them" even if some of them proved to be unsuitable for the corporation's later development. The solution, Chiu says, is to relocate these "insiders" rather than dismiss them like an "outsider" would be.

Chiu confesses it is a challenge to re-staff the management; it is a matter of "personal feelings" or "business as business". Chiu sticks to his own principles:

> Our principle in managing this corporation is never to suspect those we trust. Once we've hired someone, we never regret using him.

In business, Chinese people are often torn between cool-headed commercial calculation and moral considerations of personal feelings. In these circumstances, Chiu insists on "never suspecting one you trust". Now that these relatives have been hired, they must not be dismissed; if they are unsuitable, relocate them. Chiu's belief is that time will cure the mismatch: historical problems will be solved in time. This is why the "pioneers" must not be dismissed; they will gradually fade out as they retire.

In the early days, "personal feeling management" was crucial because the people at home had been so unfailingly helpful and trustworthy. But as the business developed to a certain scale, "institutionalised" management became the key in bringing together the various companies and factories in different places. To be "institutionalised", however, one has to avoid being "sentimental"; and Chiu, knowing this, has been very cautious in hiring the "folks at home":

> Some folks at home have wanted their kids to work in my company. They've contacted my dad through the elders in the family. My major concern is whether the kids are suitable. I won't even think about it if they're not competent enough. In most cases I'd suggest that they don't come to work for me, because it does not feel good to be away from home and I fear that I can't take care of them. Since my dad passed away, there haven't been any requests. Now I don't have many home natives working in my companies.

The Fukien connection

Although Chiu arrived in Hong Kong in 1986 at the age of 15, he does not feel as strong an emotional tie to his hometown as did his father:

> Nowadays in Hong Kong, people don't feel as close to their place of origin as decades ago. This is mainly because people [of the same origin] are no longer seeing one another as often as my dad's generation. And naturally, when you don't see one another as often, you don't feel as close. I haven't been back to my home town for ten years. My friends in Fujian are mainly my former schoolmates. But since we're not working in the same profession, we don't have much to talk about. They don't understand what I say. Nor do I understand what they talk about.

Chiu may not have returned to his hometown for 10 years, but the world has not stopped. While friends from his first 15 years in Fujian are still there, their lives have followed such different tracks that they no longer have much in common, and a gap has inevitably widened between them. In Hong Kong, most of Chiu's friends were his mates at Fukien Secondary School:

> Most of my friends here in Hong Kong are my Fukien schoolmates, some from higher grades, others from lower grades.

Compared to the land mines in the world of business, one's adolescent relations are safer. Memories of hardworking days in class, hours on the sports field and carefree teenage friendships often last a long time. Socialising madly on the mainland brings Chiu mainly business partners, not true friends, and he finds no fun in doing it. Whereas back in Hong Kong, he loves to be with his school friends, playing mahjong or the finger-guessing game, chatting and drinking.

Home connections and public service

Chiu feels emotionally tied to his secondary schoolmates, just as his father did their native home in Fujian. Although he does not entirely feel the intensity of his father's obsession, Chiu nonetheless shares the old man's commitment to public service:

> After my dad retired, he seldom concerned himself with our business. Rather, he got involved in various public organisations, like native and alumni associations, taking on so many titles and having a lot of public service to attend to... He was most active in matters relating to our native home. He would donate a million dollars or so each year to charities. He occupied positions in alumni and class associations and the Fujian native association but usually you need to donate to get those titles... Now that my dad has passed away, the family request that the second generation keep up the work. That's why I'm getting involved in the activities of the Chiu Clan association. The Fujian Normal University alumni association, of which my dad was the founding president, has also contacted us for donations, offering titles such as Honorary President and the like. My second brother and I have assumed the positions that my dad occupied. My mom cares nothing about these vanities.

Old Chiu committed himself to his native home affairs, making donations of over a million dollars each year. For his wife, at work here may have been the benefactor's social vanity, but for Old Chiu, who had retired from the world of business, that was *the* worthy course to pursue for the rest of his life, the nodal point to which his personal sentiments had clung. For the sons, who do not feel as close to their native home as did their late father, their father's public service must be taken up, partly because of the family "request" and partly out of respect for their father's "life achievements". Had it not been for their father's financial support over the years, Chiu confesses, they would not have come so far today.

Chai: Circuiting and Staying

Businesses: Garment manufacturing
Business locations: Hong Kong, Fujian
Place of origin: Jinjing of Fujian

Age: 32
Year of arrival: 1989
Arrival age: 14

> When I left university, I knew very well what I was going to do. I felt I had to do something for my parents: most of all I wanted to make them happy. But after a period of time, when work came between me and my family, I often felt totally helpless. That was the source of most of our troubles.

Away from mom

Coming from a family of five, Chai is the second child with an elder brother and a younger brother. Chai's father came to Hong Kong in 1978. In 1989, Chai and her mother and younger brother moved over as well. The elder brother had to stay behind in Fujian, prohibited to leave by some mainland policies.

Originally a primary school teacher, Chai's mother had invested in a garment factory with a couple of fellow villagers and became one of its managers:

> The factory started in the name of the school and the village in Fujian. The garments were primarily wholesaled to Tianjin. Many of the villagers clubbed together to get it going. I was still a small kid and can only remember bits of what happened. The first year was a miserable time for them, because the factory was losing money and burdened with lots of debts. Many of the villagers quit [after encountering the first difficulties]. Fortunately my mom and her retailer in Tianjin were determined to carry on. The initial failure, they thought, had taught them an invaluable lesson, and since they had paid for the tuition, there was really no reason to drop out in the middle of the course. They decided to go on. The factory started to do better in 1985.

Chinese farmers in the 1970s were still impoverished after the catastrophic Cultural Revolution. When the villagers clubbed together to get the garment factory started, Mrs. Chai and her fellow managers knew they carried on their shoulders not only the factory's future but the entire village's hopes as well. Mrs. Chai and her partners vowed never to give up and managed to carry on even through the worst of times. The factory finally started to do better in 1985. In 1989, however, Mrs. Chai's application to emigrate was approved and she was immediately caught in a dilemma: to start all anew in Hong Kong or stay with her garment business. Eventually she decided to go to Hong Kong and return to Fujian once everything was settled in Hong Kong. For this reason, the mother figure has virtually been absent from Chai's life in Hong Kong:

> My mom stayed with us just a year before returning to Fujian to continue her business. She had to stay for a year so she could get her 'Home Return Permit'.[2] I was very upset when she left because I had to do a lot of housework. Every day after school, I had to go food shopping and cook for the family. Once mom got her Permit, she spent 80, 90 percent of her time on the mainland, coming back just once in a while.

To look after her business on the mainland, Mrs. Chai had to minimise her time in Hong Kong. Although she and Chai had applied to emigrate to Hong Kong to

[2]Home Return Permit, also referred to as a Home Visit Permit, is the colloquial name for the national identity document officially known as the Mainland Travel Permit for Hong Kong and Macau Residents, issued to Chinese citizens who are residents of Hong Kong and Macau as the entry permit to mainland China.

reunite with the family, the family seldom came together after the application was approved. Husband and wife, mother and daughter lived their own lives. Chai has always felt a "great regret" that, because of their business, she did not have her mother by her side in her teenage years.

Schooling in Britain

For some time, Mrs. Chai returned to Fujian to look after her garment factory, while her husband stayed in Hong Kong working for his boss. Later, as the mainland introduced its opening-up policies and began to encourage foreign investment, Mr. Chai decided to join his wife and invested in her factory as a Hong Kong businessman. Mrs. Chai was stationed in Fujian to manage their business, while her husband stayed in Hong Kong, this time to take care of the local orders. Observing that her parents were working so hard, Chai determined, well before she graduated from University, to live with them and make the best out of the factory:

> When I left university, I knew very well what I was going to do. I felt I had to do something for my parents; most of all, I wanted to make them happy.

So that she could get better prepared to manage the family's garment business, Chai went on to read marketing in Britain after finishing university. She worked for a while in a local garment company:

> I read biology at university. After graduation I went to the UK to study marketing. That year in the UK was extremely fruitful. I got an overall idea of how the market operates; I came to know how to secure clients and look at things from a client's point of view; I came to realise what clients normally look for; and I learned how to communicate with them effectively. This business requires a lot of travelling, visiting clients and inspecting factories. My stay in the UK gave me a lot of confidence and experience. Because I've lived in a Western country, I feel more confident negotiating with Western clients, not just because I know their language but also because I no longer feel insecure in a new environment. I feel I can cope with it. My clients are mainly from Britain, others are from Europe. Because I spent a whole year in Britain, I know the country pretty well.

Schooling in Britain gave Chai plenty of training in professional and language skills as well as exposure to local culture and customs. All this served to elevate her confidence in dealing with Western customers and seeking business opportunities:

> I think it's easier for me to deal with my clients now because I lived in their country for some time. I can view things from their perspective, so our cultural differences can be minimised. After I started this business, I came to realise that people from different places can have totally different views of a product. Take a shirt for example. In certain places, people may think it should be worn a certain way, but for those from somewhere else, from mainland China for instance, it may never have occurred to them to wear it that way. Just as you're not aware of local dress codes, you may be entirely ignorant of local life. As I lived there, it's easier for me to understand what they really are talking about so that I can avoid misunderstandings. I'm conscious of many culture-related things that cannot be easily conveyed in words, like food, their leisure activities, their social structure, what they need and what they wear, etc. In Britain, unlike us, each company normally has its own uniforms. Some of them are pretty well-known corporations, but may be less well-known to people from Hong Kong or the mainland. But when you have lived there, they are immediately recognisable to you once you see their logos. Then you can quickly tell where the client works, or even his position in the company. And such knowledge will help you a lot in communicating with that person.

A stressful life

The Chais have been running the garment business for more than 20 years. The factory at their Fujian home is a medium-sized establishment, currently employing 200 or so workers. They have also set up two adjunct factories. One manufactures cloth, the other embroidery, and they are managed by her elder and younger brothers. Chai is mainly doing marketing and sales in Hong Kong for the garment factory. Her father moved back to Fujian in 2001, tending the factory with her mother. The Chai brothers and sister are in charge of one factory, having their own business to look after while working closely together.

For Chai, the stress of not only sustaining but expanding a business that her parents have spent 20 years of their life developing is immense. Having the company's marketing in her charge, Chai not only has to provide the best service, but also coordinate the production equipment. Eventually she found herself at the forefront of the family business, a position that she feels stressed to be in:

> It is by nature very different to be employed by someone else and be employed by yourself. Psychologically these are two distinct experiences. Doing your own business, you have plenty of room to get ahead with your ideas. My family has given me a lot of freedom in various things. I can organize whatever kind of exhibitions I like in whatever countries I like. But in running your own business, you have nobody to show you the way. You're all on your own. In making decisions, you have nobody to give you advice. Oh yes, I've got my parents, but they've been in the business for such a long time and things are so different now, with totally different people to deal with. I know this better than others probably because I'm at the front line. And because I'm the only one who knows what's going on, I need to depend on myself at every turn. Consequently I feel pretty pressurized... In those days when I first started, I felt I couldn't bear all this... And I told my dad, I couldn't bear this, I feel stressed...

In the battlefield of business, those at the forefront are just like the fighters at the frontiers of war. With "nobody to show you the way", there is immense pressure to bear. Behind the decent facade of a boss, there looms the incredible burden and pain of a loner.

Family *matters*

Upon completing her studies in the UK, Chai came home and threw herself into the family's business. Dauntless at first, Chai, who had only ever worked for others, was unaware of the hardship in business. Nonetheless, she was prepared to go on this adventure and overcome the difficulties on her own. What troubled and perplexed her most, however, was a series of conflicts she had with her family:

> When work comes between me and my family, I often feel totally helpless.

The conflicts, big and small, that arose between Chai and her family were largely due to disagreement on managerial strategies:

> The foremost challenge in taking up a family business comes from the older generation's mode of thinking. Sometimes the younger generation will come up with new ideas, novel ideas, only to be banned by their parents.

When Chai's father was doing marketing, he was unable to take overseas orders for his lack of English, so his clients were primarily Hong Kong companies. After she took over, Chai, sensing a fall in their Hong Kong business, embarked on a strategic change, shifting their focus to the overseas market. Immensely ambitious, Chai was ready to apply what she had learned in school and the marketing skills acquired in the UK to the actual management of the family's business. But plans don't always fit with reality. Just as Chai was ambitiously launching her strategic shift, she experienced, for the first time, the generational differences and conflicts in managerial ideals.

Because her parents had been managing the company in the old style for more than a decade, they were convinced that the old style, though probably conservative, was more reliable. On the other hand Chai, with her professional training in school and life experience in a multicultural overseas setting, realised there were many new styles to draw on. She knew about them having come into contact with a variety of companies. Chai wished to use some of these new methods which, though by no means new elsewhere in the world, were foreign and risky to her parents. Conflict was inevitable.

Sometimes conflict happens so frequently that Chai feels under stress. Carrying her parents' expectations on her shoulders, she is determined never to let the family's business perish in her hands. It is not simply a matter of sustaining what exists, Chai believes, with a mentality typical of a more educated, enterprising younger generation, but also a matter of pushing further what her parents have achieved. But she feels helpless. Ambitious as she is, Chai finds herself fettered by her parents' insistence on the old managerial practices. In family businesses, such generational conflicts are particularly common, for as long as the parents are alive and healthy, they still have absolute power over the business's operation. Such is the dilemma in which Chai finds herself trapped: she is a boss and at the same time she is a daughter, and consequently she is painfully torn:

> Then it becomes a rather unhappy relationship. Sometimes I can't help wondering why I'm doing all this. Even if I'm making big money, there's no fun to speak of. Absolutely none.

The conflicts have caused tension within the family. Chai feels lost in the confusion of family and business matters. What, she wonders, is she working for? Her hard work not only fails to bring appreciation from her parents but also gives her a great deal of pain. Where she makes good money, she loses her happiness. For Chai, this is a dead end and she has to compromise:

> I had great hopes about our family's business. I wanted to make it prosper. But after these years, given all these obstacles, it seems it would be best just to 'sustain' it.

Mired in such conflicts with her parents, Chai feels frustrated and helpless. She is, of course, far from hopeless in the family's business, but her ambition to push it further daily loses momentum. Now, she simply hopes to sustain what her parents have achieved and look forward to setting up a business of her own, where she can put all her theories into practice.

But before she can set up her own company, Chai still has to be at the front line of the family business, travelling among the mainland factories, the Hong Kong company and overseas clients. She is a "nomad" at the very forefront, living a mobile life that her family knows nothing about, which inevitably distances her from her loved ones. In circuiting and staying, the conflicts of ideas unavoidably occur between generations.

But changes won't come about without conflict. The survival of family businesses, we would assume, considerably relies on resolution of such conflicts, painful as they are among family relations. What remains is hope about what comes next, and that hopeful anticipation will give one the strength to move ahead.

Siu: A Road to Dignity

Businesses: Electronic products, fruit trading, salons, health products franchisee
Business locations: Hong Kong, Shenzhen
Place of origin: Xi'an of Shanxi
Age: 43
Year of arrival: 1995
Arrival age: 31

> I felt neglected and disrespected... My self-respect was considerably hurt... I felt very upset about that. I was not willing to work for anybody, although my husband had introduced me to quite a few companies. I never worked for anyone in Hong Kong. I just wanted to be my own boss.

A very far cry
A martial arts champion, Siu had taught physical education at a Chinese university before she immigrated to Hong Kong. Back home, Siu was a big name, a much-respected figure. She had lived, in her own words, with "a halo over my head". But the move to Hong Kong put all that into the past tense, and as the halo dissipated, Siu became one of the ordinary millions, and a much-despised "new immigrant" at that, in this glamorous cosmopolitan city. The move led Siu to develop a totally different outlook on life.

Because of the differences in their educational systems, Siu's education was not recognised in Hong Kong. After she moved to the territory, she was unable to find a teaching job at the same level and consequently found herself teaching *kung fu* to some local children and *tai chi* to a group of rich housewives. Back on the mainland, being a martial arts champion, she had enjoyed decent social recognition, but the move to Hong Kong changed all that:

> Teachers are respected on the mainland. But the kids here in Hong Kong usually get lost once school is out and they will pretend not to know you when they see you on the street. That is a great insult to your self-respect... Here, you're neglected because of your accent. Mainlanders tend to speak Cantonese with a certain accent that immediately betrays them. Sometimes, as you talk to your acquaintances in Cantonese, you can detect a trace of contempt on their faces. I was once invited to dinner by this acquaintance who told me it was 'sweet potato noodles' when shark's fin soup was being served. I got very mad at that. They tended to see mainlanders as rednecks and yokels. In fact, I had plenty of shark's fins in my refrigerator that I never managed to finish after my friends gave them to me when I was sick. I felt that Hong Kong people were rather disrespectful about us mainlanders. I realised that this was due to our regional differences, differences that are bound to persist. We were not respected here, just as country folks were not respected in the city. It's about our different life styles, city dwellers versus rednecks.

In daily life, Siu felt insulted. The move to Hong Kong made her aware of "regional differences". In order not to appear "rustic" to the *tai chi* housewives, Siu tried to change herself and began to dress like them in "loud colours". But such deliberate imitation, far from boosting Siu's confidence, only served to hide her "true colours" and turn her into a caricature of herself:

> I tried to change myself, and eventually became a caricature figure… I was going after all these expensive labels and stuff and spent a lot of money. It was very stupid but I was feeling totally lost and was desperately trying to look 'better'.

For Siu, Hong Kong had been an imaginary city of high hopes and expectation. But once there, she found it was entirely different from how she had imagined it. Siu was at once frustrated and helpless about the discrimination, particularly as she knew it was "regional differences" at work here, differences that would never disappear. Trapped, Siu was determined to earn some dignity back, and decided the only way was to become her own boss.

Losing "face"

Siu was determined to be her own boss, but there was no royal road to entrepreneurship. As she and a friend pooled to set up their first company, the Chinese government's policy to encourage investment was in full swing. Taking advantage of that and with the help of a friend of her brother, Siu managed to secure a project in a government development district. The project would be her first step on the road to entrepreneurship. As well as the project, Siu began dealing in paintings and calligraphic works in Hong Kong. She had considerable connections in Chinese artistic circles, including with well-known painters and calligraphers. The artists would often let her have their works for little money or even for free, and Siu would then sell them to Hong Kong galleries for fairly high prices, thus securing a substantial middleman margin. This did not last long, because her company closed down after two years. Siu subsequently went into electronic products and fruit trading, but neither fared well. All these setbacks were discouraging:

> We [Siu and her partner] kept failing when we worked together, then I entirely lost hope… He, my business partner, never made it and kept letting me down. In the end, I felt so humiliated I no longer had the heart to introduce him to any new businesses. Things gradually grew hopeless for our company… My friends have always been my invisible capital… But relationships are sustained by contacts. Society changes too rapidly for your memory to catch up. I used to go home in such glory but since I was no longer making good money, I didn't want to see my friends any more. It was a vicious circle. The less I saw them, the worse things turned out.

The defeat was a tremendous blow to Siu's self-confidence. In retrospect, she attributes it to her unwise choice of business partner, through whom she lost all the opportunities that her connections in the government had provided. The repeated failures shocked her, and she lost faith in herself. Thinking she had lost "face" all along, Siu ostracised herself from her friends and destroyed, with her own hands, the social networks she had managed to establish. In a society like China, where *guanxi* plays such a significant role, the loss of contact means the loss of "feelings", which will eventually lead to the loss of one's "source of wealth". Siu felt so humiliated to have failed in Hong Kong that she was afraid even to return to her place of origin. Even when she did go back, she would stay in her house: "I wouldn't see anyone", she recalls. "I was practically locking myself up".

While emotionally she was still mired in these initial setbacks, Siu realised that she did not have much time to lose, especially as she grew older, so she decided to split with her Hong Kong partner. After the break-up, Siu joined an insurance company as a sales agent – partly to make a living and partly to, in her own words, "see more of the world". She fared pretty well at the start, because the insurance policies at the time allowed mainland clients to buy insurance without personally coming to Hong Kong. Most of Siu's clients were from the mainland, since she had more connections back home. But as insurance policies were later revised, Siu lost many of her clients.

The Shenzhen beauty salons

The change of policies "cornered" Siu, making it "virtually impossible for her to survive". Utterly disillusioned about her future in Hong Kong, she decided to return to the mainland, a place closer to her heart.

Upon her return, Siu chose Shenzhen as her foothold and started a new life there by opening a beauty salon:

> I had a beauty salon in Shenzhen in the early days. But I didn't feel comfortable having to be there at one or two o'clock in the morning to collect money. Sometimes you even needed to deal with drunk customers... I found it utterly repulsive when people called me '*Mama-san*'. It sounded as if I were running a whorehouse. So I told my staff to call me '*Da-jie*' (Big Sister), but definitely not '*Mama-san*'. At any rate I never felt comfortable running a salon. Sometimes when people came in for a shampoo session, they picked staff as if they wanted some bloody special service. What did they think we were? That's why my salon didn't do good business. Once there was this guy who kept harassing one of my girls and they ended up fighting. My girl got slapped and her face was swollen. I got really mad. How could he have done that! I felt totally helpless and sad because I wasn't able to protect my girls. All I could do was send the girl to a doctor and pay for everything. The problem is that you really couldn't do anything about those sons of bitches. They would've avenged themselves by throwing a stone or two through your window before disappearing into one of those murky streets. If they came back, we would suffer severe losses. Eventually I closed down my salon because I knew it wouldn't go very far.

There are salons and salons in Shenzhen. Many of them are de facto brothels behind the facade of a beauty salon. Siu had wanted to run a proper salon, only to attract malicious customers. After the attack, Siu felt so disappointed that, once again, she terminated her own business.

Health products franchise and direct sales

Encouraged by a university school friend, Siu became a franchiser of health products, a business that would engage her to date. She has since been mobilising her networks in Hong Kong, Shenzhen and Guangzhou as well as in her hometown to get her products to a broader community. After years of hard work, she managed to set up branches in a number of cities. Last year, an accidental encounter brought her to the attention of a businessman who had made decent profits doing network marketing, and her unique appeal as a "martial arts champion" and a "Hong Kong businesswoman" played a significant role in welding this new partnership:

> I was in Beijing attending this Century Forum. During a luncheon, Tian Hu's (alias of a certain health product) CEO was sitting opposite me. We were all cramped in the hotel's

> restaurant. A lot of people accosted him and asked for his business card only to be turned down. When I saw him, I went over and produced my own business card. During our brief chat I told him that I had actually met him the October before and that I was running a franchise in Hualian with a couple of branches in Shenzhen. Before I left, I mentioned in passing that I had once won a national championship in martial arts. On hearing that, he immediately handed me his card. I had someone from my Hong Kong company standing next to me then. When he introduced himself to the CEO, the CEO, of course, would not offer his business card until I told him that I was from Hong Kong with my delegation. I think I appealed to him because, first of all, being from Hong Kong played a part; second, his South China manager had mentioned me before the Forum and so he already had some idea of who I was; third, I mentioned I was a national martial arts champion. All these factors combined to make me impressive... They had just had a board meeting the day before and they wanted to meet me... My goal is to spread Chinese martial arts overseas with the help of Tian Hu.

In business, Siu has to highlight at the right moments her roles as a "national martial arts champion" and a "Hong Kong businesswoman", because these two roles have a substantial role to play in appealing to her potential partners. Siu is currently busy working out a schedule of co-operation with Tian Hu, in a bid to bring together martial arts and health products. She is hoping to make the best of each other's influence and establish a partnership based on their respective achievements.

The future is always fraught with setbacks and challenges, but Siu is full of confidence when talking about this new partnership:

> I feel like a warrior in this. Tian Hu gave me a stage to perform on. I feel pretty great to be back in Xi'an... and now my cousins and friends are all in it.

Failures and frustrations torture people as much as they train them. Coming out of her failures, Siu believes that her life in Hong Kong has given her all the training she needs for life:

> Now my friends back on the mainland think I'm 'invincible'. If I were, it would have been because of my life, ten years of life, in Hong Kong... I might have had a better life, had I stayed in Xi'an, but then I definitely couldn't have understood so much about this world. Being away from home, I learned to be less proud. I learned to be modest. The ten years in Shenzhen and Hong Kong was a time when I was truly brought down to earth.

Indeed, Siu has mixed feelings about Hong Kong. As new immigrants, some have given in to the psychological shock they experience, while others have overcome it. Siu is one of the latter. Plunged into an unfamiliar social environment, new immigrants need to take considerable pains to re-orient themselves. In the process of such a metamorphosis, pain is quite often accompanied by happiness. As a new immigrant, Siu felt compelled to transform herself in order to attain dignity. Such a yearning has become an important part of entrepreneurial personality: the will to push ahead and the reluctance to give in.

Chuk: Life of a Traveller

Businesses: Real estate, bowling centres
Business locations: Hong Kong, Shenzhen, Wuhe, Bozhou, Shanghai, Yingtan, Jiujiang

Place of origin: Fuqing of Fujian
Age: 36
Year of arrival: 1998
Arrival age: 27

> My friends like to call me a Hongkonger. But I don't feel at home in Hong Kong, because I spend most of my time travelling around.

Chuk does real estate business. He goes wherever real estate projects are under way. Although a permanent Hong Kong resident, he spends most of his time "travelling around", returning briefly to Hong Kong only once in a while. His life, in other words, is in a state of constant shuttling.

From construction site to real estate

Chuk did not start with the real estate business. He started, following his father, as a civil engineer. Upon finishing junior high school, Chuk went on to specialise, possibly under his father's influence, in the study of civil engineering. It was inevitable he would follow his father's profession on graduation, so, at the age of 20, Chuk left his native home in Fujian and began taking up projects in different places. His first project was in Loyang, Henan. For a young man with little money and minimal social connections, the first project came by chance:

> I went to Loyang on a friend's recommendation. A friend of my dad's in fact, back in Fujian. This friend was doing some small business in Loyang, nothing substantial. He got the news from his connections that there was this particular project looking for a construction team. Then he passed the information on to my dad, who was a civil engineer. But my dad was too busy at the time and he sent me instead. I was totally new to this trade and didn't have much capital. My dad was hardly better off, so we borrowed RMB2,000 from an uncle. I bought spades and other tools with the money and got this project that was worth RMB100,000, of which we got RMB30,000. My dad was rather suspicious at the start, because he hadn't inspected the site. I had been to the site and thought the project was manageable. I was younger and more enterprising and wanted to have a go. You can't know what will happen unless you try. My dad went to the site a bit later and thought it was manageable too.

It was Chuk's enterprising spirit that opened the door to success. Young and inexperienced as he was, he took the chance because "you can't know what will happen unless you try". He went from Fujian to Henan, borrowed enough money from his uncle and got all the tools ready that would bring him his "first pot of gold" – not much of a pot, but encouraging enough for a young man to go further. When the first project was over, Chuk returned to Fujian and contracted, with his father's help and recommendation, with the government to build railways:

> I worked for two years in Loyang and then returned to Fujian. My dad then got another project for me, to build railways. It was about 1993, 1994. I worked on the railways for two years until around 1995. Railway construction was not difficult, but the sites were always in the countryside and life was not easy. But we never got the money. When the project was completed, they didn't even settle the accounts and so we never got the government outlay. They kept delaying it. It was about RMB1,000,000. The government owned the railways. When the government plays the deadbeat, you can do nothing about it. Many companies have encountered such problems. We were not alone. It was because different companies had their own share of the same railway. There was really nothing we could do about it.

Chuk survived the two difficult, lonely years in the barren countryside only to find himself confronted with the most powerful deadbeat ever, the government, who owed him over RMB1,000,000 of construction fees. There was nothing he could do about it. After this incident, Chuk felt that doing construction projects meant he had less control. He wanted to play a more active role, so he shifted his business to cash-based real estate transaction.

Connections are important

From construction sites to the real estate market, from a meagre initial loan that enabled his first construction project to his first real estate sales event, Chuk went through a great deal and became acutely aware that "everything would have to depend on connections". During Chuk's entrepreneurial adventure, especially during his shift to real estate development, the help from various connections – relatives, former classmates, fellow natives, friends as well as friends of friends – has played a decisive role. In the first few years in particular, Chuk's real estate development projects were all directly or indirectly referred to him by his friends:

(a) Cousin's friend

> I entered the real estate business in the second half of 1995. Negotiation began in Yingtan [Jiangxi Province]. Work started in 1996 and lasted a year. I was in Yingtan on a friend's recommendation, in fact a friend of my cousin's brother. They were both natives of Yingnan, former school friends; both worked in the real estate business, both were foremen. This friend of my cousin was a manager in a water factory. He told me they had a piece of land to develop but they didn't have enough money. He would like to work with us so we could share the cost. In return, we could sell our part of the building. It wasn't a very large piece of land, only about 0.8 acres, and the project used about 10,000 square metres of it. They owned about 30 per cent of the project; we owned the rest.

(b) Friend's brother-in-law

> I got a loan of RMB200,000 from a friend's brother-in-law, with a monthly interest of RMB8,000 to pay. He felt intrigued when he learned about our project and offered the loan, but the interest was still too high. Anyway, I got my company going with this loan. It was pretty straightforward back then. You didn't have to go through registration or make deposits and stuff.

(c) Uncle in Japan

> To get a company going, you only needed to show the government a bankroll proof. I got my bankroll proof from my uncle in Japan, and so became a foreign investor. Foreign investors could take their time and didn't have to register right away. But the regulation was that if you were going to do cross-province business, you'd need to re-register your company in the second province. My company was registered in Loyang so I wasn't allowed to do business in Yingtan. In 1997, I came to Hong Kong to sign the second project in my life, this time again as a Japanese company. I was about to develop a cinema and a business mansion, around 20,000 square metres in total. The situation was similar this time. They gave me the land, I built the houses and kept the rest.

(d) Foreman's friend

> After the project in Yingtan, I moved to the nearby city of Jiujiang in the province of Jiangxi. This was also on the recommendation of a friend, a native of Jiujiang, who was a

construction foreman. We got to know each other in Yingtan. My Jiujiang company started in 1999, then I went to Anhui Province, again on a friend's recommendation. He was a native of Anhui and also a foreman. [He said] they had a piece of land for sale in his hometown. So I went over to negotiate [with the sellers] and the deal was made after six months. It was around October 2002, and a new company was registered in Anhui.

(e) Government connections

As I came to know more of the local people, I got more and more information. Many of my connections are in the government. In the real estate business, you get to know a lot of government people as you go through the various procedures. They know you and you need to take them out from time to time, just to get familiar. You may get together for lunch or for a drink... If you get recognised by society, by the government, then gradually everything will turn out fine for you... It's all like that in mainland. You need good connections. You need friends.

To do real estate business on the mainland, where personal relations have a key role to play, it is essential to have good connections in the trade as well as in the government. Quite a number of Chuk's projects were recommended by his friends in the trade. In cross-province projects, it is particularly important to have connections in the local network in order to obtain the necessary information and get hold of whatever opportunity comes up. Each trade has its intrinsic ways. For Chuk, who is developing real estate in different cities, "friends and connections are tantamount to business". Personal relations, be they friends of relatives, friends of friends, business acquaintances or government connections, lay the foundation for successful business. Relations with government officials in particular are built on a great deal of deliberate socialising:

Chinese bosses need to socialise a lot, because the more you socialise, the more people you get to know. Information comes with friends; opportunities come with friends, too.

There is pretty good pay-off in socialising. One doesn't socialise, in other words, for nothing. For both parties, it is a process of tangible or intangible exchange – not as casual, however, as ordinary dining. Great care has to be taken, with the pleasurable food and numbing alcohol, as one socialises with government officials, because one may unknowingly "choose the wrong words and offend people".

Chuk knew very well that to establish himself on the real estate scene, he had to train himself to be more outgoing and better at socialising. Chuk felt "compelled" to be trained for this.

Being a Fujianese Hong Kong businessman

From the construction site to the real estate business scene, Chuk's business underwent tremendous changes. For him, however, life did not change much and he remained just as "mobile". On his construction team, Chuk had to travel a great deal. In the real estate business he has to follow each one of his projects in various cities. Since 1995, when he got his first real estate project, Chuk has set up companies in Yingtan, Jiujiang, Wuhe, Bozhou, Shanwei, Shenzhen and three provinces as well as in Hong Kong. His companies have different functions, and to keep his business organised, he needs to do "a lot of travelling" between all the various locations.

This kind of mobile, shuttling existence is necessary for the real estate business. Wherever Chuk goes, he will get to know people from the trade and the government, because he finds it important to stay closely connected to the local real estate circles as well as to the government's policy-makers and city-planners. To get into these two circles of people, an agent, who might be a trade-based commercial chamber, a clan-based native association or a government political group, is needed. To be part of these organisations, one may need to perform different identities. Chuk feels that his status as a Hong Kong entrepreneur has been helpful in getting him into these local organisations. In Jiujiang, he joined the Fujian Chamber as a Fujianese, while in Yingtan, in the same province, he became a member of the local "Political Consultative Conference" as a Hong Kong businessman. Chuk has practical reasons for his active participation in these organisations:

> To be in a certain association helps to build local networks.

In the real estate business, it is necessary to deal with government officials. The various activities hosted by these different associations often provide appropriate settings in which Chuk gets to know people and expands his networks. Joining government discussions also allows him to obtain first-hand information about the government's city plans, which are important and even decisive for a real estate dealer.

Home, the folks' home

Since he left his Fujian home, Chuk has set up business branches in seven locations. Now, the adventurous young man that Chuk had found in himself has transformed into a corporate chairman – and the transformation, of course, was never easy. There are many aspects to a real estate business: externally, there is various documentation to be settled, and strings to be pulled with the government; and internally, there are project blueprints, negotiations, the purchase and allocation of construction tools and marketing strategies to be taken care of by a trustworthy management team. In the early days, Chuk had relied on his relatives back home who, for Chuk, were more trustworthy people, though not very well educated. When the company was still operating within the confines of the family's stronghold, these native folks from home were a very important part of his staff. But as the company grew and developed and gradually got on track, these helpers were daily "lagging behind", "growing older and feebler". Then it became a problem as to whether they should be laid off. Chuck believes there are very different ways of handling this problem within the real estate business:

> I don't normally lay off my relatives. Real estate is a very lucrative business. The workers are low-paid, around RMB1,000 a month. Also, there is no way you cannot make use of a person – it all depends on how you use him. So we don't normally fire anyone. In this way, my men will feel secure working for me. They know we won't easily give them up… Now our staff are mainly hired from the outside. A person shows his competence as he does his job. When we spot a really competent person, we'll try to employ him.

Chinese enterprises are known for their "managerial humanism" – where the man stays, feelings will persist, and the *guanxi* will hold out. In this sense, the individual manages his business not so much out of commercial considerations as his concerns with ethical bonds, friendship, gratitude and personal feelings. In the first days of an enterprise's development, one's native friends and relatives and family connections are often the first social resources to be mobilised. This kind of social resource is a mixture of money and sentiment, restriction and trust, dictatorship and democracy.

Once mobilised, these resources will thrust the enterprise into inescapable sentimental and developmental dilemmas. In Chuk's eyes, the real estate business is lucrative and "there is no way you cannot make use of a person". Confronted with such dilemmas, Chuk compromises, that is, "neither fire a person nor trust him with an important position".

After 10 years of business adventures, having experienced a variety of modern urban culture, Chuk still feels a special emotional attachment to his native home:

> I've been travelling to different places these years. Where is my home? My home is in Fuqing, where I grew up. I think people have special feelings towards where they grew up.

Having left, come back and left again, his native home is almost unchanged, Chuk however is acutely aware of the differences between the people back home and himself:

> The economy back home has improved, but the people's minds have not changed.

The move away from home was in fact a move away from a certain way of thinking and a certain attitude to life. Out there, while there is a lot to sigh about, there is equally a lot to marvel at. The mobility of his life allowed Chuk to bring together the different ways of thinking that he has experienced and develop his own outlook on life. Returning to his native place, Chuk feels that although people at home are making more money than they did before, they never realised the importance of "enjoying the best of life". The elderly people, on the other hand, feel Chuk is no longer the country boy they knew because now he looks more like a *nouveau riche* who has come from nowhere. A sense of inferiority has distanced them from Chuk.

For the people at home, emigrants are those who live a *foreign* life; for the emigrants, home is represented in hauntingly beautiful remembered fragments whose colour may change one day or even fade away altogether. There is a tension between the leave takers and the people who stay, between change and non-change; one may come to accept the irreconcilable differences between anticipation and reality, or one leaves again.

Home, sweet home

Chuk lives a multi-regional life, spending his time in various places each month: visiting government officials in city A today, discussing a construction project in city B tomorrow, and settling his bank accounts in Hong Kong the day after... Life's mobility has brought immense stress, but the achievements along the way are a reward. Chuk has learned to make himself at home "where it doesn't really feel like home". The native home, Hong Kong, and the work places all have their respective emotional appeals but none has a draw on Chuk as *the* home. The native homeland now appears so distant because he has been away for so many years. Hong Kong seems to provide, in his constantly shuttling life, a kind of hotel-like convenience; the work places, where Chuk started and prospered, "haven't had much of a grip on my heart". Deep down, he feels solidly "rootless", lonely but it is alright, he says, as long as "my family are doing well". For Chuk, his family and his career are closely tied together:

> The concept of the family has quite some bearing on my business. Or rather I'm mainly concerned about my company's development, and at the same time hoping for a more

> comfortable and stable life for my family. Am I motivated by the idea of a 'better home'? I think I am. But for now, I'm more preoccupied with my company. I need to chart its course. I need to tap its potentials. It's my primary concern at the moment...

Now a corporate chair, Chuk thinks his family has some bearing on his career, for as long as his business prospers, his family will do well. Ten years have passed since he launched into this adventure, and for 10 years he has been "busy, *real* busy". Starting with a meagre loan, his company has developed into a sizable corporation, but Chuk is never ready to take a break, putting the best of his time into his real estate business. But life is tiring, and sometimes painful, out there, especially when one has to deal with those inscrutable government officials. For the sake of the family, however, Chuk thinks that life's hardship is worth every bit of it. His wife, of course, feels the opposite:

> My wife has been complaining, saying I've left them alone too much. She says I don't understand how hard it is to take care of the two kids all on her own. Then I think that she nags too much, that she doesn't understand how hard it is for me either. My daughter is mad at me, too. She says I've never been to any of the parental meetings ['*jiazhang hui*'] of her kindergarten. I wasn't even able to attend her graduation ceremony. She said she was very unhappy.

Chuk does not usually respond to his nagging wife and complaining daughter. He says all he can do now is make sure they live a comfortable and stable life. There is not much else he can do as he is still "travelling around".

Conclusion

Growing from neglected "new immigrants" to recognised business people, immigrant entrepreneurs have become the typical "Hong Kong story" protagonists, whose success has been so much highlighted and even mythicized. Current studies of overseas Chinese entrepreneurs have generally focused on two aspects of their lives: first, their personal character and moral integrity as an important source of capital[3]; and second, the economic functionality of their interpersonal networks and in particular the clans they belong to.[4] Our study in this chapter has

---

[3]S. Gordon Redding, *The Spirit of Chinese Capitalism* (Berlin: Walter de Gruyter, 1990); Chan Kwok-bun and Claire Chiang, *Stepping Out: The Making of Chinese Entrepreneurs* (Singapore: Prentice Hall, 1994).

[4]Richard J. Coughlin, *Double Identity: The Chinese in Modern Thailand* (Hong Kong: Hong Kong University Press, 1960); Ivan H. Light, *Ethnic Enterprise in America: Business and Welfare among Chinese, Japanese, and Blacks* (Berkeley: University of California Press, 1972); Edmund Terence Gomez and Michael Hsiao Hsin-Huang, "Chinese Business Research in Southeast Asia", in *Chinese Business Research in Southeast Asia: Contesting Cultural Explanations, Researching Entrepreneurship*, eds., Edmund Terence Gomez and Michael Hsiao Hsin-Huang (Surrey, U.K.: Curzon Press, 2001), p. 1–37; Heidi Dahles, "Venturing across Borders: Investment Strategies of Singapore-Chinese Entrepreneurs in Mainland China", *Asian Journal of Social Science*, 32, No. 1 (2004), p. 19–41.

sought to delve further into the relationship between our entrepreneurs' personal character and their immigrant experiences. In addition, we find it worth looking into the ways interpersonal networks and clan circles are sustained. The current literature usually concentrates on the practical functionality of such networks and generally ignores how they are sustained and fostered. Apart from their practical use, should we not also examine the non-practical side of them? Or is there a price to pay to be part of these networks?

While these seven profiles have already partly answered these questions, we shall embark on more concrete and in-depth analyses in the next three chapters. What follows is something of a summary-cum-prelude.

In probing the personal character of overseas Chinese entrepreneurs, existing studies have often stressed their diligence and industry as if these were intrinsic merits of the Chinese character. But such stereotypical surveys are simply mistaken, as these entrepreneurs, a successful part as they are of immigrant groups, have actually acquired their industrious habits from their immigrant experiences. Wing, Shin, Yam and Chai, for instance, all went through the pain of scathing discrimination in the early days of their immigrant life. The stigma of being a "new immigrant" completely undermined the opportunity structure of their careers. Largely neglected by mainstream society, they sensed that the pursuit of a brighter future would have to depend on extra hard work and extra sacrifice on their part. Their industrious character, in other words, has been forged from the hardship of life. They needed such a character to survive and maintain their dignity, and they needed a new identity that would be recognised with respect. This inner yearning was what carried them through.

Wing's story opens up a new perspective on how immigrant entrepreneurs' interpersonal networks and clan relations are sustained. Wing's life and work have essentially evolved around Fujianese circles, but the circles of the so-called "insiders" (*ziji ren*) are not always full of goodwill and harmony. They are in fact often fraught with fraudulent and deceptive behaviour. The people Wing trusted most were his old schoolmates and home natives, yet it was these same people who betrayed him in the first place. This being the case, Wing preferred to let it be rather than ruin his own social network. By "saving face and the relationship", Wing only wished to stay connected to the Fujianese circles. Wing's generosity was a helpless compromise concealed. Since his world evolved around such a network, breaking up with an "insider" would not only be emotionally disturbing, but potentially an economic loss. In the guise of an "insider" is in fact a bog of clashes and conflicts.

Each age has its unique business strategies. Our immigrant entrepreneurs, living in intensely mobile times, have employed strategies that fully demonstrate their understanding of the age. The cases of Yam and Chiu stress the importance of "identity deployment" and "local wisdom". Successful business relies not merely on a good grasp of the items in trade but also on knowledge of the people involved. It is all about the understanding of "human nature" and "person-hood". Since the mobility of life pluralises one's trading partners, one deploys different identities when dealing with different people, as a familiar set of signifiers will help create psychological closeness. The mobility of life also dictates that one may be staying in A today before going to work in B tomorrow, only to find himself visiting clients in C the day after. This allows one to acquire a variety of "local wisdoms", a kind of invaluable cultural capital that is capable of turning out business opportunities.

There are indeed pros and cons in a life of intense mobility. The fragmentation of such a shuttling lifestyle not only means mental and physical fatigue, but conflict between those who shuttle and those who stay. The cases of Chai and Chuk are testament to this. Chai, who stands at the frontiers of the family's business, saw her attempts to introduce novel managerial strategies into the family business disapproved of by her parents. Such constant conflicts with her family have consequently distanced her ambitious ideals from reality. Chuk, entirely devoted to his business, has put himself through all the harshness of the trade simply to secure an easy and comfortable life for his family. Yet the pains he has taken are often rewarded with his wife's complaints and his daughter's misunderstanding. There is a price to pay for a life of constant travelling: it will distance him from his family and leave him stranded in emotional solitude. Such are the unspeakable pains of many an accomplished man approaching middle age.

The Spatial Triangulation of Immigrant Entrepreneurship

Forced Construction of "Ethnic Niches"

United in discrimination

All the early immigrants from China left their native homes behind in hopeful anticipation of this city. Our informants were no different. These weary wayfarers had come in search of a more promising future, expecting they might have to work hard at first and not gain immediate prosperity. But the cruelties of life soon drove home to them the huge differences between the realities in Hong Kong and the mythical affluence of a "promised land". There was prevalent discrimination against these newcomers from the mainland. While their lives would materially improve in time, psychologically they were experiencing pain in a way they never had back home:

> I felt so much discrimination in Hong Kong. I arrived in May and started to look for a school. It was a miserable experience. I had been attending Junior 2 in Fujian. In Hong Kong, I wanted to enroll in Primary 6 but was rejected for fear of possible language problems. Then I went for Junior 1 and was rejected again because they were afraid my English wouldn't catch up. Then I sought help from the Education Bureau but they just left us like that and never offered help. It was probably my mom's lousy Cantonese. Or they never really took our case seriously. (Kam)

> I had taught in a university on the mainland and lived a much-respected life. In Hong Kong, I felt totally out of place, so much neglected and not respected... My self-respect was immensely hurt. I think everybody needs to be respected, but in Hong Kong, as a new immigrant, you're simply denied that. You become a nobody merely because of your accent. A nobody!... I felt Hong Kong people in general didn't have much respect for us mainlanders... Now I realised this was due to our regional differences, differences that are bound to persist. (Siu)

Kam was only 14 when he landed in the territory, and Siu arrived at the age of 31. Both encountered language problems. Before the Handover in 1997, the general Hong Kong natives had hardly any Putonghua. In life, a Putonghua speaker – or a speaker of "rustic" Cantonese – was quite often the subject of much ridicule and

Chan Kwok-bun and Chan Wai-wan, *Mobile Chinese Entrepreneurs*,
International Series on Consumer Science, DOI 10.1007/978-1-4419-9643-5_5,

was generally labelled a "new immigrant" who had come from an impoverished Chinese countryside. It was the accent, not the content of what one said, that decided who one was and how one was to be treated. In Hong Kong, accent has become a label of identity that invites contempt and is almost impossible to remove. As a result, to avoid ridicule, contempt or discrimination, many immigrants choose to remain silent in public, thus falling into a vicious circle. The less they speak, the more rusty their Cantonese; the more rusty their Cantonese, the less confidence they have to speak it. New immigrants thus flock together because only among themselves can they speak as they wish, free of the burden of accent.

Immigration is essentially the act of moving from one social structure into another. As people from different places come together and become aware of the differences between themselves, the desire to pursue a sense of identity will become foremost. Once the other is distinguished from the self, new immigrants will be labelled as the "outsider" that is to be ostracised and despised. New immigrants as such will have to live in circles not entirely of their own choice, as the boundaries of social interaction that the mainstream has established for them often restrict the range of their interpersonal networks. Research into Chinese overseas has revealed that, faced with the mainstream resistance to "outsiders", Chinese immigrants are usually forced to include only people of a similar background during the construction of social networks in their new homes.[1] Their livelihoods are often restricted by others to certain professions and trades. To stand up against discrimination and prejudice from the social mainstream and to blaze a road out of the restrictive life they found in Hong Kong, immigrants felt compelled to come together. This convergence of "insiders" intensified their sense of ethnicity. Before their move to Hong Kong, these new immigrants might have been total strangers to one another, living either end of the country. Their early days in the territory were just as troubled by contempt, discrimination and segregation: this shared experience has served to narrow the psychological distance that might have stemmed from previous geographical disparities. Thus they have gradually developed an incommunicable sense of identity with their fellow immigrants. This, as one poet once said, is how "fellow sufferers sympathise with each other". The external force of prejudice and all its negative effects, as we have seen, becomes an internal force that creates strong ethnic bonds among the immigrants, enabling immigrant entrepreneurs to build highly homogeneous, consolidated

[1] Peter S. Li, "Ethnic Business among Chinese in the US", *Journal of Ethnic Studies*, 4 (1976), p. 35–41; Peter S. Li, *The Chinese in Canada* (Toronto: Oxford University Press, 1988); Chan Kwok-bun, *Smoke and Fire: The Chinese in Montreal* (Hong Kong: Chinese University Press, 1991); Chan Kwok-bun, "Ethnic Resources, Opportunity Structure and Coping Strategies: Chinese Business in Canada", *Revue Europeanne des Migrations Internationales*, 8, No. 3 (1992), p. 117–137; Chan Kwok-bun ed., *Chinese Business Networks: State, Economy and Culture* (Singapore: Prentice Hall, 2000); Chan Kwok-bun, *Migration, Ethnicity and Chinese Business* (London: Routledge, 2005); Chan Kwok-bun and Ong Jin Hui, "The Many Faces of Immigrant Entrepreneurship", in *The Cambridge Survey of World Migration*, ed., Robin Cohen (Cambridge: Cambridge University Press, 1995), p. 523–531.

and trustworthy social networks.[2] Birds of the same feather, as Peter Berger observes, "flock together, not as luxury but as necessity".[3]

The history of immigrants is repeating itself. Irrespective of time and space, immigrants, especially those moving from underdeveloped areas to better-off communities, have been helpless "outsiders" who never seem to be capable of breaking away from the shackles of prejudice imposed by the local mainstream. As time progresses, certain societal attributes, including deep-rooted flaws in the individual character, survive the different stages of human civilisation. This explains why in this age of globalisation, discrimination has never been eliminated despite (and sometimes, because of) increasing interaction between different people. In this sense, the self's differentiation from the other is not entirely under the control of individual sentiments: rather, it may be deeply rooted in the social structure. As long as power differences exist, exclusionism and discrimination will persist; and as long as discrimination persists, there will be a drive towards identity and, by extension, a segmentation and subsequent building of social networks.

Leftist schools: An emotional stronghold

Discrimination, as we can see, has undoubtedly intensified the sense of ethnicity. But not all immigrants suffering from discrimination will come together. Even if they do, it might be a temporary union. From the stories of our immigrant entrepreneurs, we can see that the construction of an "ethnic niche" is tightly connected with the first school they attended in Hong Kong. In reality, new immigrants, and those coming from the same provinces, may not necessarily get on well or for long with each other, although they have a common background. In fact, discrimination and hostility are often present among the home natives themselves. Thus the construction of an "ethnic niche" has to depend on some external conditions. From the words of our immigrant entrepreneurs, we have discovered that the unsophisticated rapport and friendship among former schoolmates has been a powerful cohesive force in the establishment of highly homogeneous social networks. The growth of this potentially powerful, unsophisticated, even naïve, rapport has to depend on the interaction between two factors: their age of arrival in Hong Kong and the nature of their schools:

> Most of my friends in Hong Kong are former Fukien schoolmates. Why is it that a secondary school friendship can last so long? I remember reading this survey about the kinds of relationships that last. Family relations top the list. Secondary school friendship follows. Secondary school kids are relatively unsophisticated. So their friendship is simpler. Each year, we organise secondary school gatherings. (Ngai)

> I moved from A's company to B's and finally to C's factory. In and out, I've never left the Fujianese and Fukien circles. (Wing)

---

[2] Chan Kwok-bun, ed., *Chinese Business Networks: State, Economy and Culture*; Chan Kwok-bun, *Migration, Ethnicity and Chinese Business*.

[3] Peter Berger, *Invitation to Sociology* (Garden City, New York: Doubleday & Company, 1963), p. 102.

> My friends in Hong Kong are mostly Fukien schoolmates. Secondary school friendships generally last longer, because we were still simple in school. There was more room to develop a certain rapport. (Chiu)

Ngai and Chiu are about the same age, both coming to Hong Kong in the mid- and late 1980s. They come from a similar educational background, both graduates from the locally well-known Chinese University. Wing is different. He came to Hong Kong more than 25 years earlier. Twenty years their senior, he has had less education. But the three of them have one trait in common: most of their friends in Hong Kong are former secondary schoolmates, who, like them, had also emigrated from the mainland. It is generally understood that it is normal for the older, less-educated generation of immigrants to have compatriots and fellow immigrants of a similar background forming the bulk of their social connections, while people like Ngai and Chiu, the younger generation of "successful" and "outstanding" new immigrants who went to local universities, are thought to have more pluralized social networks. In fact both our younger and elder informants have homogeneous social networks. This is an intriguing phenomenon. Further analysis will show that this has not been accidental: while the three of them came to Hong Kong in different periods, they all arrived at similar ages and went to schools of a similar nature.

One's time of life at emigration quite often has a major influence on one's life in the new home. We tend to neglect the parameter of "timing" when we analyse a person's experiences. Just as the individual's self-identity has an impact on his social network, one's social network itself has an impact on the construction of one's self-identity. As the individual migrates, his original self-identity will be continuously adapted and modified as he moves into different social settings. Berger believes the extent to which one's identity can be modified is dependent on the extent to which one has been used to the original identity, the latter again being dependent on one's age at migration.[4] New immigrants must arrive in time to enrol in local schools or even go to local universities. If they have arrived over the school age, they will most likely be denied access to further education and forced to join the work force. Denied of education in an elitist society where education is highly stressed, immigrants in general have to stay in low-position menial jobs. In other words, if an immigrant has access to local education in his new home, this will phenomenally affect his future life, interpersonal network, and the formation of his sense of identity in the days to come.

Among the immigrant entrepreneurs we interviewed, those who arrived young in Hong Kong normally had access to local education, although they had few choices of school. Before the 1990s, it was by no means easy for immigrant mainland children to enrol in private or government schools as transferred students, because the schools would generally reject the child's application because of problems of "articulation", "language of instruction" and "English level", fearing that the children would become the school's "black sheep" and hamper their university matriculation rankings. Thus, this particular group of new immigrant students, whose English was

---

[4] Ibid.

considered hopeless and whose Cantonese was not proficient enough to carry them through the programme, became a "detested community" in the eyes of mainstream society. Eventually, the only schools willing to take them were those so-called "leftist patriotic schools" that had major enrolment of new immigrants from the mainland. These schools were mostly founded by early Chinese immigrant businessmen who, aware of the educational and social restrictions that immigrant children faced, decided to pave the way for the coming generations by founding schools of their own, taking their rejected children and turning them into talented people. It is precisely for this reason that "ethnic circles" have emerged beyond mainstream society, pulling new immigrants from similar backgrounds into circles of "insiders". Before Hong Kong's handover in 1997, there were five major "leftist patriotic schools", namely Fukien Secondary School, Pui Kiu Middle School, Hon Wah College, Heung To Middle School and the Workers' Children Secondary School. Statistics from Fukien Secondary School show that before it became government-funded, new immigrants from Fujian made up more than 90% of its enrolment. In these schools, not only were most of the students immigrants, most of the teachers were too. These teachers, originally graduates or teachers from famous universities in China, were unable to find teaching jobs in government schools since the government would not recognise degrees from the mainland. So they were forced to work in these private schools. In this way, discrimination and prejudice formed a powerful external binding force that brought together immigrants from similar backgrounds, thus enhancing their ethnicity and creating a strong sense of self-identity. These immigrants formed an intangible and yet substantial community that is similar to what Benedict Anderson calls "imagined community" in his study of nationalism,[5] or what co-author of this book, Chan Kwok-bun, terms "ethnic ghetto" in his study of the Canadian Chinese.[6] In fact, these immigrants might have come from entirely different backgrounds or lived totally differently on the mainland, but once in Hong Kong, they found themselves equally trapped in the marginalised "leftist schools", confronted with the discrimination and contempt from their "common enemies". Consequently, the similarities – their accented Cantonese for instance – between these immigrants took on some imaginative significance that was conducive to their highly homogeneous, consolidated and trustworthy social connections. Once mobilised, these connections turn into effective social capital for corporate management, which is particularly important for a business in its early days to be able to hold out.

Fellow natives in a strange land: Co-operation and division

New immigrants come together with a common pursuit, namely to create, within a larger uncongenial environment, a congenial inner environment for their own survival. For this reason, ethnic networks are very often mobilised. The help provided by

---

[5] Benedict Anderson, *Imagined Communities: Reflections on the Spread of Nationalism* (London: Verso, 1983).

[6] Chan Kwok-bun, *Smoke and Fire: The Chinese in Montreal* (Hong Kong: Chinese University Press, 1991).

"insiders" has a significant role to play, especially during the pioneering days of a business:

> I felt that I'd laid a pretty good foundation for the trading business, because I had many contacts. Many of my former schoolmates were working in banks, and banks need a lot of gifts and souvenirs for their clients. Then I received an order from the Bank of China, shortly after my company was founded... I had quite a few contacts and so I kept asking if they'd got anything to recommend. I'd usually call them up. I felt that I had to be 'inquisitive', that I had to 'snuffle' around more... There was this secondary school friend working for the Bank of China, a close friend. I learned about the job (The Bank needed topcoats for its staff) from him and so I got it. (Yam)

> I wasn't doing particularly well in jewellery and decided to join an advertising company. Two of my friends ran that company. When I joined the business, I bought about 15 per cent of the shares... But we came together and separated a couple of times as we saw fit. (Wing)

As Yam set out on his adventure into the business world, he had his first order referred to him by an old schoolmate. When his own business did not fare well, he joined a company run by some other school friends and managed to shift to a new business. He and these friends had come from a similar background, all being some of the earlier immigrants from mainland China. In Hong Kong, they all attended the leftist schools. To survive in the intense market competition, these fellow natives could only cling together in mutual help. The cases of Yam and Wing have demonstrated to us the important co-operative function that ethnic networks perform in the early days of a business.

However, as George H. Mead has pointed out in analysing the nature of human societies, the individual members are interrelated in a multiplicity of different intricate and complicated ways whereby they all share a number of common social interests – interests in, or for the betterment of, the society – and yet, on the other hand, are more or less in conflict relative to numerous other interests.[7] In highly homogeneous ethnic networks, just as there are good moments of active co-operation and mutual assistance, so there are bad times of conflicts and ruptures. From the perspective of the individual immigrant, their pursuit of benefit can be essentially conflicting, but current studies demonstrate a fundamental lack of attention to this dark side of ethnic networks.

It is a formidable task to probe into the dark sides of ethnic networks. Underlying our problems here is Li Qiang's identification of the human psyche as consisting of "double psychological spheres": a public sphere that tends to reveal what is good, and a private, secret sphere that tends to conceal what is bad.[8] This problem has

---

[7] George Herbert Mead, *Mind, Self, and Society: From the Standpoint of a Social Behaviorist* (Chicago: The University of Chicago Press, 1962), p. 307.

[8] Li Qiang, "'Xinli erchong quyu' yu zhongguo de wenjuan diaocha" ["'Double Psychological Spheres' and Opinion Surveys in China"], *Shehuixue Yanjiu* [Sociological Research], No. 1, 2000, p. 40–44.

revealed itself during our interviews, but some informants did manage to vent their resentment, which at some point even amounted to anger:

> Fujianese people appear united but they actually like to go their own way. It is essentially very difficult for them to work with others, because they like to disagree. There's no way to work together. (Yam)

> We couldn't just come together and go independent – it wouldn't work that way. We had become part of Hong Kong society and Hong Kong life. But the Fujianese part of us was always tenaciously present. There were, of course, good things and bad things about it. One of the bad things was that there's too much of a cliquish flavour to it. Is the cliquish flavour still there? It certainly is. (Yue)

Yam, one of the committee members of his alumni association, is an active participant of alumni activities. The committee members are all from a similar background, mostly being the earlier immigrants to Hong Kong. Yam had his first business referred to him from a school friend: he pulled himself together to start his trading company simply because he felt he had abundant contacts and school friends. But eight years have shown him the ultimate reality: Fujianese people like to go their own ways. Hidden behind the facade of a unified, mutually-beneficial brotherhood is a group in disagreement, a group unable to work together. Yue, an equally enthusiastic participant of community and public services, serves as president or committee member in a number of community organisations in North Point and the Eastern District. North Point is traditionally known as "Fukien Minor" for its large population of Fujianese immigrants. Having spent years in community service in the area, Yue is all-too familiar with the "cliquish flavour" of Fujianese ethnic groups.

Having come together because of discrimination from mainstream society, these immigrants have all experienced the pain and frustration of being marginalised. However, once they have formed their own circles of interaction, they begin to unconsciously repeat what they have abhorred before, namely, marginalising the other and setting up ethnic boundaries. Their circles don't always brim with harmony and altruism, but are conversely often fraught with conflicts and dark secrets. As Mead points out, members of a social group are, on the one hand, brought together by their common social interests, and divided on the other by conflicting interests in many aspects. These fellow natives in a strange land have flocked together in common need only to split up in competition for a limited common good. Co-operation and division have come in a circular process. Immigrants' ethnic niches, too, have followed this pattern of human history in its cycle of unions and separations.

Sameness and Difference: The Return of the Native

Where personal and family networks converge

Our immigrant entrepreneurs have one thing in common. Their business are diversely located. Fourteen of the sixteen informants have two or more business locations, the most being seven. Apart from the diversity of business locations, another prominent feature is that about half of our informants have chosen their native home as one of their bases. Why, then, are immigrant entrepreneurs inclined to set up businesses back in their hometowns? During our interviews, we realised that while quantitative calculations must have had certain reference values for our entrepreneurs, non-quantitative considerations have often played a more significant role. This is particularly the case on the mainland of China, where "personal relations" are highly stressed, where non-quantifiable factors are often decisive in corporate management. These factors need to be carefully weighed before the entrepreneur can gain an understanding of the other side of a relationship. In fact, in the course of corporate management, every decision may be identified as a "negotiation", and in negotiations, the exhibition, even performance of a right kind of self-identity can become an important bargaining tool:

> In the 1990s, the success of your business largely depended on your strength. And your strength came in two forms. The first was the size of your personal network; the second was the power of your financial muscle. (Siu)
>
> It's important to pull some *guanxi* strings... In business, you need luck, opportunities and certainly *guanxi* – then you get sufficient back-up, you stand a better chance. (Shin)
>
> *Guanxi* is particularly important in this trade. Very important... In a place like the mainland, interpersonal relations have a crucial role to play. You need friends. (Chuk)

Siu, Shin and Chuk are in businesses that are entirely different in nature. Once in the trading business, Siu is now a health product franchisee. Shin runs printing factories. Chuk is a real estate dealer. Yet they are all well aware, and have actually insisted on various occasions, that *guanxi* is a matter of dire importance to their management. Since *guanxi* cannot be measured in monetary terms, our entrepreneurs, in determining the next suitable business locations, are primarily concerned with the strength of their local networks or the feasibility of entering the local social structure. Our case studies have shown that the major reason why immigrant entrepreneurs tend to set up businesses in their native places is that they can take advantage of the native social networks that have grown out of geographical and blood relations. Fei Xiaotong has pointed out that in traditional Chinese society, the family is a clan-based "extended entrepreneurial community" that embodies sophisticated political, economic and religious functions.[9] Chinese society traditionally consists of communities that run various enterprises by exploiting kindred ethical bonds. When an immigrant entrepreneur establishes a business in his native place, he comes to mobilise not only his own personal network but also the totality of the family's networks. In the course of corporate management, such a powerful assembly of interpersonal networks has proved to be a kind of highly-efficient social capital that enables a business to confront challenges and settle problems.

[9] Fei Xiaotong, *Xiangtu Zhongguo* [From the Soil: The Foundations of Chinese Society] (Beijing: Sanlian shudian, 1985).

The place that was home

Fear comes with strangeness, security with familiarity. During the interviews, we discovered that one of the reasons why immigrant entrepreneurs tend to set up businesses in their native places is that their familiarity there gives them a sense of security:

> We are planning to start a farm of our own, but it isn't easy to find a piece of land... Now we decide to look beyond [where we live]. There might be something in Zhangzhou in Fujian, where a distant uncle of mine is running his tin factory. He is a local and knows the place well. He's promised to help out... This uncle is not from Hong Kong. He's from the mainland. Before he started his own business he had been working in a state-owned company. But as China started to advocate the separation of government administration and enterprise management, my uncle decided to go his own way. He's a big figure in the local network. It never occurred to me to run my farm outside Fujian, because I'm native here. Elsewhere, it just doesn't feel as good. (Ngai)

Ngai is one of our immigrant entrepreneurs that have chosen to expand their businesses in their native place. He does fresh vegetable exports. His sources vary from season to season: he sources primarily from Fujian during the winter and from Shandong during the rest of the year. He exports mainly to South Korea. While proportionally his vegetables are mainly from Shandong and geographically Shandong is closer to his Korean clients, it never occurred to him to start his farm in Shandong, or anywhere outside Fujian, because he feels he is Fujianese and it would not feel as good to be elsewhere. Ngai identifies himself as a Fujianese chiefly because he has a relatively larger number of connections in Fujian, where he can mobilise more and stronger interpersonal networks to facilitate his management.

Personal identity, as Chou Ying-hsiung observes, is a matter of one's involvement with the "Others" around him or her.[10] People leave home, it is believed, to become "worthless", because an outsider in the local eye is something to be excluded, something threatening in itself. Exclusion stems from a fundamental hierarchy of wealth between the locals and the outsiders; threat largely originates from the sense of a less secure livelihood in the face of a population of more hard-working newcomers. In addition, the immigrants have brought with them new modes of thinking as well as new solutions to problems – to local social paradigms, both are potential shocks. Exclusion is quite often a symptom of such psychological insecurity. Having returned to his familiar home in Fujian, Ngai feels "secure" in the local social network. This sense of security is rooted in the familiarity that comes from an attachment to the native soil as well as in the local people's identification with him as an "insider", as "one of us" – a kind of identification that can only be "felt", an inner experience that is too intangible to be quantified.

---

[10] Chou Ying-hsiung, "Shenfen zhi rentong: cong Lu Xun de liang ge xiaoshuo tuilun" ["Identity Formation: From Two Stories by Lu Xun"] in Chan Ching-kiu, ed., *Shenfen rentong yu gonggong wenhua: wenhua yanjiu lunwenji* [Identity and Public Culture: Critical Essays in Cultural Studies] (Hong Kong: Oxford University Press, 1997), p. 315–324.

Clan-based partnership

"A mighty tiger which has migrated", as the saying goes, "is no match for the native serpent". The return home gives the immigrant entrepreneur not only a stronger sense of security, but also a certain competitive edge and relative convenience as an "insider", as compared with his competitors from the "outside". This has been demonstrated in studies both at home and abroad. A two-decade empirical study of the Italian economy has revealed that the existence of wide-ranging social networks of mutual trust and co-operation in the north has done a great deal to elevate its economic and administrative efficiency way over that of its southern counterpart.[11] This exemplifies the significance of social networks of mutual trust for corporate management. The members of an immigrant entrepreneur's native network are quite often his relatives, either close or distant. In Chinese society, where the extended family still functions as a basic social unit, and where interpersonal relations still operate on a "differential mode of association" (*chaxu geju*),[12] people are less on their guard against those within the core or extended family. Thus, when a new business branch is established, immigrant entrepreneurs usually employ relatives and fellow natives that they find competent in their work force:

> Our [Fujian branch] has just hired a couple of people, and my cousin is helping out as well. She just finished school and so I dragged her in. Though nominally she's not put in any position, she's now our de facto purchasing manager.
>
> My own brother is now in charge of our Fujian branch. I was adopted by another family as a kid. That's why I'm Shin and he's Ng. But who would care about family names today? (Shin)

> As I went back [to my native place] more often, I came into more frequent contact with the folks at home. A cousin brother of mine introduced me to two business projects. One of them was a chemical plastics plant… Production hasn't started at this stage, but the plant is taken care of by five or six people. All of them are our relatives… A cousin sister is managing another factory in Fujian, together with the cousin brother… The factory originally belonged to her. Later on she pulled in my cousin brother and still later pulled me in as well. (Wing)

Ngai was originally doing vegetable exports in Hong Kong with his elder sister. In 2003, they decided to move the business back to Fujian and are now busy starting a farm in their native place. Shin, a plastic box and laser label manufacturer, set up a factory in 1992 in his native home in Fujian, manufacturing laser labels. Wing was originally in the printing business and later joined his cousins' factory. While in different trades, these three immigrant entrepreneurs have entrusted their businesses

[11] Wang Jun, "Shehui ziben yu shengchan fangshi dui jiti yanjin yingxiang: yige guanyu qiye jiqun de fenlei yu yanjin kuangjia de taolun yu yingyong" ["The Influence of Social Capital and Production Organisation on the Evolution of Social Networks: A Theoretical Framework and a Case Study"], *Shehuixue Yanjiu* [Sociological Research], No. 5, 2004, p. 37–47.

[12] "Chaxu geju" is a term introduced by the renowned Chinese sociologist Fei Xiaotong to describe how traditionally the Chinese people have taken different approaches to others according to their social hierarchy and relational distances. Cf. Fei, *Xiangtu Zhongguo*.

mainly to relatives that they trust. Studies have shown that for small to medium enterprises, it is a fairly effective managerial strategy to have a family-based staff.[13] On the one hand, native "insiders" are generally more loyal and trustworthy people due to their ethical bonds. On the other hand, as studies of overseas Chinese business people have shown, hiring home natives helps enterprises overcome the initial difficulties of the earlier days. If a business was not yet on track and did not have a stable group of clients, it was sustained mainly through the ungrudging contribution of the "insiders". While low pay, long working hours, unfavourable working conditions and lack of promotion channels, among others, are all common exploitative features of a family business, "insider" relations based on blood, geography or conjugality greatly diminish the acuity of such issues and ensure a smooth business operation.

Due to the diversity of their business locations, our immigrant entrepreneurs have to rely more on a truly trustworthy staff than does the ordinary businessman. In each location, they need people in whom they have complete confidence to operate, manage and supervise. In his analysis of the business strategies of Ming and Qing businessmen, Yu Ying-shih reflects that it was during the Ming and Qing periods that China's unprecedented *huoji* ("assistant") system came into existence, when mega businesses were prospering throughout the country and business tycoons found themselves in urgent need of "assistants". These assistants, mostly from poor families of a businessman's clan or relatives, were largely trusted due to their blood relations to the boss. In addition, Chinese culture stresses individual "virtue" and "reputation" to such an extent ("The gentleman becomes rich to practise his virtue", so the adage goes) that both the boss and his men ("huiji") know they have to discipline themselves with "virtue" and build up good reputations to secure a brighter future. In this way, business people during the Ming and Qing periods managed to transform original ethnic bonds into a new kind of commercial partnership by utilising traditional cultural resources.[14] Our immigrant entrepreneurs' move back to the native home is to a large extent an extension of the *huoji* system that originated in the Ming and Qing times. Consciously or unconsciously, they have come to tap the apparent or potential value of their interpersonal networks back in the native home.

Sentiment and propaganda

The move back home, of course, is not entirely out of a utilitarian need for efficient social connections, but also out of a deeply felt attachment to the native soil:

> We chose to set up our factory here [in our native place] because this is where we grew up. This is where our home is... My whole family has been living in the same house. If we were to set up our factory somewhere else, we would also have to move away from home, too.

---

[13] Chan Kwok-bun and Ong Jin Hui, "The Many Faces of Immigrant Entrepreneurship"; Chan Kwok-bun, ed., *Chinese Business Networks: State, Economy and Culture*; Chan Kwok-bun, *Migration, Ethnicity and Chinese Business*; Wong Siu Lun, *Emigrant Entrepreneurs: Shanghai Industrialists in Hong Kong* (Hong Kong: Oxford University Press, 1988).

[14] Yu Ying-Shih, *Zhongguo jinshi zongjiao lunli yu shangren jingshen* [Religious Ethic and the Spirit of Merchantry in Modern China] (Taipei: Linking Books), p. 151–154.

> That sense of being 'rooted' here, you know... It's a very sentimental feeling... We wouldn't leave because we bought the land and built the house on our own... Fujianese people won't sell a house they have built for themselves. For us, it is part of the family's 'enterprise'. So you need something substantial there to make your forebears feel proud of you and proud of themselves. This is a very traditional mindset. We didn't even think about selling it, how could we have given it up altogether? The land was ours. The house had been built with our own hands. So was the factory built with our own hands. (Chai)

> The factory in Fujian was set up in 1992. The decision to return to Fujian came to me naturally as a Fujianese. I felt I needed to do something for the economy back home. Fujianese people have been known for centuries as a home-leaving people. So deep in us, there is probably an inherent yearning to go home. I had come to Hong Kong at the age of eight. Little remained in my mind about my old home. But since I went to a 'patriotic school', I developed a strong attachment to the country and to my native place. (Shin)

Chai runs her family's business, while Shin started from nothing in Hong Kong: both, however differently they began, eventually decided to go back to their native place, to where they are emotionally attached. For Chai, the move was a reflection of the family's "root-seeking" tradition: they need to have something "substantial" in the native home so their forebears will feel proud of their descendants as well as themselves. Shin's move, on the other hand, was largely the result of "an inherent yearning to go home", an inner yearning that the finest bards of old times have lamented with charming melancholy. Traditionally, there has been an indissoluble bond between the individual and his native soil. While our immigrant entrepreneurs had been away from home for a fairly long time, in Hong Kong, they had been rejected by the mainstream schools and were forced to go to immigrant-run institutions where they would have a large input of patriotic ideologies. As a result, their attachment to the country and their native place was being constantly moulded and intensified, although many of them had been away from home since they were young children.

Such self-identity, that stems from an attachment to the native soil, has often been exploited by the mainland authorities and made into propaganda slogans to appeal to overseas business people to come home and invest. But paradoxically, when these emigrant entrepreneurs come home to invest, they have to label themselves not as "insiders" but as "outsiders". On their return to the native place, these home-leavers find in themselves a combination of a homely native and a "patriotic, home-coming investor helping to advance the economy at home". A "patriotic home-comer" is an "outsider", an outsider that the local government identifies with and pays much attention to. This is what Richard Jenkins identifies as the Janus-faced nature of our identification mechanism: the co-existence of the contrasting dimensions of similarity and difference.[15] The highlighting of differences under such circumstances means that the emigrant entrepreneur is in possession of certain material resources that the other desires – a kind of "extrinsic attraction" as Peter Blau would have called it.[16] Such an attraction is not to be found in the locals but in the

---

[15] Richard Jenkins, *Social Identity* (London: Routledge, 1996).

[16] Peter Blau, *Exchange and Power in Social Life* (New York: John Wiley, 1964).

home-comers who have made a name for themselves overseas. These home-comers possess the kind of economic resources from abroad that the local government wishes to employ through their "investment promotion" (*zhaoshang yinzi*) policies. Thus, when an emigrant entrepreneur goes home to invest in or set up local branches, he or she will be referred to as a "home-loving patriot". The return of the investing native is something the local government takes pride in, proof of their official achievements and "excellent" governance. In this sense, both the emigrant entrepreneur and the local government will benefit from the return: the former comes to enjoy the favourable state policies and often earliest and most convenient access to business opportunities that come with their fine relationship with the local administration; and the local government can make use of the foreign investment to improve the local economy, thus demonstrating their "excellence" in governance and thereby securing their power status. The return of the emigrant entrepreneur demonstrates fine co-operation between governance and commerce as well as the existence of "interlocking networks" in traditional Chinese culture.[17]

As much a stumbling block as a stepping stone

There are mixed feelings about home. The return to the native place has indeed brought a great deal of psychological and actual advantages. This, in the words of Heidi Dahles, is a kind of "transborder strategy".[18] Local favourable policies, clan-based partnership, trustworthy *huoji* assistants, among others, are all positive factors at the emigrant entrepreneur's disposal. But not all home-comers have ended well:

> Some friends of mine, big bosses [in the Philippines], were made to suffer when they returned to Fujian. They complained that the local people kept feasting at their expense and soon their money was all gone. They said they felt totally awkward there, not about the local [business] culture but about how people would take them for granted. So, in the end, we were determined not to hire our own relatives. In Fujian, we have loads of relatives, aunts and cousins and the like, but we have preferred to hire people from elsewhere. This is essentially because these home folks tend to take everything for granted. This is something unpleasant in their constitution. They never put themselves in your situation. We can't, of course, promise to substantially improve their lives, but we certainly won't exploit them as if they were slaves. But they just refuse to think this way. If anything comes up, they will begrudge and go against you, which causes a lot of trouble to the company. (Yue)

Who could expect these big bosses from the Philippines would be made to suffer so much when they came home to invest? These emigrant business people had expected to take advantage of being "local serpents", only to find themselves and their money at the disposal of their home folks. These otherwise trustworthy people have turned out to be a most dangerous gang, who have not only feasted at the

[17] Chan Kwok-bun and Claire Chiang, *Stepping Out: The Making of Chinese Entrepreneurs* (Singapore: Prentice Hall, 1994), p. 72. The original term was used by the authors to refer to the interactive networks of mutual confidence and close co-operation that exist among Singaporean-Chinese entrepreneurs.

[18] Heidi Dahles, "Venturing across Borders: Investment Strategies of Singapore-Chinese Entrepreneurs in Mainland China", *Asian Journal of Social Science*, 32, No. 1 (2004), p. 19–41.

home-comers' expense, but taken everything for granted. Intent on getting the most out of the home-comers' businesses, they will only "begrudge and go against you" once anything goes wrong.

In real social life, we are, in one way or another, "all impostors".[19] As Goffman sees it, each of us is putting on a show, but not all can identify with the roles they themselves are playing. Rather, there exists, as Goffman goes on to explain, a kind of "role distance", which means playing a role tongue-in-cheek, without really meaning it and with an ulterior purpose. There is therefore a duplicity of life under such circumstances.[20] Each role is carefully played out without the player's internal identification: there is, in other words, an inherent distance between the role-play and the player's consciousness.[21] Not all our immigrant entrepreneurs who come home to invest have been happy, for the folks at home may be "sheep" as much as they may be "wolves". Blood relations may act as some ethical constraint, but that does not always work when money gets in the way. Sometimes, in the eyes of the local people, these "big bosses" who have come home to invest are just not "one of us", born and bred as they were on this land and loyal as they are to its soil. For the native folks, these big bosses, who have come in from the "outside", belong to the handful of the "rich" and are different from the multitudes of "us":

> The economy back home improved, but the people's minds never changed... This is what's bad about the people here in this part of Fujian. They're loners. They won't work with others... Now that you've been away for so many years, the folks at home will think you're unreachable. Some people do think this way. Some of them have been abroad, but most have been working for others and not starting their own businesses. (So they think you're a big boss now?) Sort of, I think. The folks back home tend to look down upon themselves. Resource-wise, they might think they've been put in an inferior situation. (Chuk)

Chuk has peculiar feelings about his native home. Having returned after all these years, he has come to have close contact with the place he deeply loves. The landscape has not changed much, but the local people no longer appear as lovely as he has remembered – their minds have never changed; they "won't work with others"; they feel "inferior"; they think the home-coming entrepreneurs are "unreachable". Emigrant entrepreneurs have come home to find their own self-identity torn between an "insider" and an "outsider". On the fortunate side, they may come across truly helpful friends and relatives. On the unfortunate side, they may encounter "unpleasant" fellow natives and get the enterprise into a difficult situation. Home, for our emigrant entrepreneurs, can be as much a stumbling block as a stepping stone.

---

[19] Peter Berger, *Invitation to Sociology,* p. 135.

[20] Erving Goffman, *The Presentation of Self in Everyday Life* (Garden City, N.Y.: Anchor Book, 1959), p. 135.

[21] Peter Berger, *Invitation to Sociology,* p. 135.

Leaving or Staying: Hong Kong as a Border City

Out of Hong Kong

The "push-pull" model is often applied to explain the migration (city-country migration, in particular) of people. The "push" factor primarily refers to the outward thrust created by the adverse (material as well as institutional) environment in the original place of residence. The "pull" factor refers to the kind of external attraction created by the superior conditions of life (either actual or imaginary) in the new home. Sometimes the two factors coexist. The immigrant entrepreneurs we interviewed have displayed a mode essentially different from the usual city-country migration in that they have not given up a place altogether in favour of another. Rather, they have kept their original business location as they went on to develop other locations. This shows that different locations have different functions to perform but are limited in their own ways. Through a combination of these scattered business locations, the entrepreneur is able to maximise the values of the resources at his or her disposal. The co-ordination of these locations has enabled the enterprise to gain a firmer foothold amidst intense competition.

Hong Kong has been the "first stop" for most immigrant entrepreneurs. Their cramped offices have witnessed all the pains they have gone through. In the early days, with limited money and human and material resources, they tried their best to develop and expand. Today, they still have offices in Hong Kong, but the major management has moved back to the mainland:

> We started small, the family type... The factories in Hong Kong were having a bad time, with little space to use and higher salaries to pay. So we moved back to the mainland in 1983. (Shin)

Shin's factory was originally in Chai Wan. In 1983, he decided to move to Dongguan in Guangdong Province. In Hong Kong, the cost of running a factory was enormous, with very high rent and salaries to pay. By then, China was gradually opening up its market and improving its economic infrastructure. As it went on to introduce favourable policies to appeal to investors from Hong Kong and Macau, many Hong Kong companies felt an urge to leave the territory. The immigrant entrepreneurs we interviewed, like most of the others, moved back to the mainland because of cost considerations.

It wasn't just cost. Another reason for this mass movement out of Hong Kong has remained largely untouched in current research. It was the need to rearrange corporate identities:

> Hong Kong has traditionally been a middleman. When you're doing business with a foreign company and you identity yourself as a Hong Kong company, they'll feel that you're a mere broker and that you're seeking to profit from the pricing differences. (Ngai)

> We're unwilling to do business with Hong Kong brokers, because the profit margin will be very slim. It's difficult nowadays, because the margins are way too narrow. (Chai)

Ngai is a fruit and vegetable exporter, sourcing primarily from Fujian and Shangdong provinces. Ngai partnered his sister and set up a company in Hong Kong in 1997. They decided to move back to the mainland in 2003. Chai manages her family's garment factory in Fujian. Her Hong Kong company is primarily responsible for marketing matters. Most of her clients used to be Hong Kong companies, but as she gradually ceased to do business with her Hong Kong clients, she started having more European and overseas clients. Before the Chinese mainland opened up its market, its economic system was far from perfect and the local companies were far from familiar with the "know-how" of international commerce. Hong Kong, as a transit port, had always acted as a middleman or broker between the factories on the mainland and their overseas clients. In fact, Hong Kong's success can largely be attributed to its role as a middleman. However, with the advances in computer networks, the globalisation of communications and the unprecedented prosperity of international trade, border-crossing has become all the more convenient, while commodity prices have become highly transparent between places. In these circumstances, Hong Kong's status as a middleman has become very much disadvantaged, as many clients now wish to have direct contact with the factories to save agent fees. "Middleman" has since turned into a negative label, a hindrance for the Hong Kong businessman. "Out of Hong Kong" has thus become a survival strategy for the modern Hong Kong enterprise. Indeed, in order to survive and not be eliminated amidst intense competition, an entrepreneur has to employ a variety of strategies as if commanding troops on an ancient battlefield:

> Two years later, after much discussion, we decided to buy this factory. This is because I had come to realise that, whatever excellent service you offer, you won't go very far and you won't be able to pluralize your products if you don't have a good price to offer. Business is just as realistic as that... Three years ago I started to 'rearrange' my identities; fortunately I've been proved right about this. First, I present myself as a European company with Chinese factories... You know what I mean? It's just about catering to what they want. A Ferrari, for instance, for the price of a Honda. (Yam)

Yam is a glass products trader. He used to be a pure trader, sourcing his glass products from Chinese factories and then selling them to his overseas clients, thus profiting from the price differences. But after some time, he came to realise that business was "realistic", that Hong Kong's middleman status was becoming a burden as most overseas clients were now reluctant to pay the extra fees of a middleman. So he bought an entire factory on the mainland and started to "rearrange" his own identities. "All warfare", as the ancient war strategist Sun-tzu observes, "is based on deception".[22] Encapsulated in this is the importance of deception in any kind of rivalry. As entrepreneurs came to realise the negative impact of the once profitable middleman status, they felt an urge to "rearrange" their identities to survive on the battlefield of business.

---

[22] Sun-tzu (trans. Lionel Giles), *The Art of War* [Sunzi Bingfa] (St. Petersburg, Florida: Red and Black Publishers, 2008).

Impression management: The Hong Kong identity

Dealing with overseas clients in international trade, one realises that one's "Hong Kong" identity can turn out to be a disadvantage, while being a "Chinese manufacturer" can be an appeal. In the tug of war of price negotiations, Hong Kong business people have to eliminate the suspicion of trying to cash in as a middleman by labelling themselves as Chinese manufacturers. Ironically, however, while having to conceal their Hong Kong identity in front of overseas clients, they have to be as "Hong Kong" as they can when dealing with mainland factories:

> When we do business with the mainland, we reveal that we're a Hong Kong company. But when dealing with overseas clients, even Southeast Asian clients, we identify ourselves as a mainland company. There are practical advantages with this arrangement. This is what I call 'attitudinal difference'... Mainland companies are most happy to do business with Hong Kong partners while overseas clients tend to believe that you're a broker, as Hong Kong has always been. They'll feel that you're going to ask for more than mainland companies. (Ngai)

> When I contact potential clients I normally stress that we're a Hong Kong company with a branch on the mainland. But back on the mainland, I'll say we're a mainland company with a branch in Hong Kong. If you identify yourself in the right way, you get more trust. At least they won't think it'll be difficult to collect a loan from you. (Kam)

> In negotiations I've always identified myself as a Hongkonger... It's almost a guarantee of quality and punctual delivery. Mainland companies don't stand for such guarantees. (Yue)

Ngai, Kam and Yue are in entirely different businesses: Ngai does exports, Kam is a web services provider, and Yue runs a printing factory. Disparate as their businesses are, they all agree that the use of different identities at different times helps to build up clients' confidence in their companies. Ngai believes that in business one needs to be aware of people's "attitudinal differences". Doing business is in fact a matter of making exchanges. His own experience doing business on the mainland has made him aware that sometimes people will wish to deal with people that are in a way different from themselves – opposites attract; and to win a negotiation, he realises, one needs to understand people's minds. Kam, as he reflects upon his own business experience in both Hong Kong and the mainland, thinks a businessman has to be very clear about what to highlight about himself – and identify himself accordingly. Yue says that identifying himself as a Hong Kong businessman has proved to be a kind of unwritten guarantee for his clients. The label "Hong Kong businessman" has come to stand for good credibility and repute, a promise for quality service. "A Chinese factory", "a Hong Kong company", "a Hong Kong company with a mainland branch" and "a mainland company with a Hong Kong branch" – in fact, all these labels combined represent a kind of "identity rearrangement", or what Goffman would have called "impression management".[23] The entrepreneur is like an actor on a stage, highlighting different aspects of himself according to what the

---

[23] Erving Goffman, *The Presentation of Self in Everyday Life*.

client is looking for. One face, many maskes, as co-author Chan Kwok-bun put it earlier.[24] All this is done, in the words of Jenkins, to better position his enterprise in his interaction with the "other" so as to complete a transaction.

Border city

It is now a trend for modern Hong Kong enterprises to go "out of Hong Kong". At the same time, many of them find it necessary to remain partly stationed in the territory so that on the one hand it will be more convenient to construct dual identities, and on the other they can continue to enjoy the unique advantages that come with Hong Kong's history and geography:

> Things are slow, inefficient and rather inconvenient on the mainland... In Hong Kong, you have quicker access to information. Here, you can be easily updated with the latest information on new products and new production methods. (Chai)

> Our Hong Kong office is mainly for short visits. Much of our business is now done on the mainland. So the office in Hong Kong no longer has much of a practical function... It's practically a lounge for our clients. It's more convenient for them to drop by for a short visit after they get off their plane. (Shin)

Chai's factory is in her hometown in Fujian. It is a sizable factory that employs 200 people. Her Hong Kong office, however, hires only three, whose work is principally to follow orders and keep the factory management updated with the latest information (the current fashion styles abroad, the most appealing display arrangements, etc.). Chai reveals that, compared with her family who work in the mainland factory, she is "walking at the frontier". In Hong Kong, she is able to keep abreast of the international market and get to know the latest development in the fashion business. In contrast, the mainland is a much slower, less efficient and less resourceful place. Shin's business has now expanded to four different provinces. While his Hong Kong office no longer performs a significant practical function, he feels it necessary to keep it for client reception. In fact, many clients like to drop by Hong Kong on their way to the mainland. Compared with its counterparts there, Hong Kong as a developed international metropolis still holds considerable edge in both hotel services and daily consumptions.

Hong Kong has become a border city, with advantages as well as more recent, critical disadvantages. The word "border" as it is used here takes on a dual meaning. First, it refers to a boundary between one country or region and another. The border area between two places is quite often where the two peoples come into most frequent contact: it is the liveliest place in both daily life and commercial trading. The "border people", therefore, are often conversant with the local knowledge of both places – languages, habits, cultural norms – as well as the multitudes of unwritten rules of social interaction.[25] As they stand astride the borders, ready to travel across

[24] Chan Kwok Bun and Tong Chee Kiong, "Yi zhang liankong, duo ge mianju: Xinjiapo huaren de shenfen rentong wenti" ["One Face, Many Masks: Singaporean Chinese Identities"] in *Mingbao Yuekan* [Mingpao Monthly], September (1999), p. 20–23.

[25] The Chinese like to say, "They don't understand our way", meaning each place has its own ways of getting things done and its own rules of behaviour. These "ways" and "rules" cannot be put in words.

different spaces of life, these "border people" help to bridge the different spaces and become "brokers" who feel at ease on both sides. At the same time, the border of a place is also the frontier at which one feels most sensitive about the regional differences, where change and adaptation take place. A border city is often the most creative place.

"Border" takes on its second meaning in relation to the "centre", as the far away, neglected "periphery". Hong Kong, as a "melting pot" of Eastern and Western cultures and as a window on both the mammoth Chinese production base and on the overseas market, has traditionally been a "border city". Those doing business in this "border city" used to be very proud of their role as middlemen. This role, however, as we have seen from our informants' actual managerial strategies, has lost its significance in today's globalised world as trading is increasingly computerised and commodity prices have become highly transparent. In these circumstances, entrepreneurs are consciously concealing their middleman or broker identities and trying to move back to the mainland or invest in Chinese factories to get ready for a rearrangement of identities. This is after all a business strategy akin to what the war strategist Sun-tzu describes: "Water shapes its course according to the nature of the ground over which it flows; the soldier works out his victory in relation to the foe he is facing. Therefore, just as water retains no constant shape, so in warfare there are no constant conditions. He who can modify his tactics in relation to his opponent and thereby succeed in winning, may be called a heaven-born captain".[26] This is how ancient Chinese war strategies have emphasised the proper deployment of one's weak and strong points. Likewise, much as Hong Kong remains a "border city", what she needs is only a mask that will enable her to survive the intense challenges ahead.

Emotional islands

For the sake of their businesses, our immigrant entrepreneurs were forced to leave Hong Kong and start up on the mainland. In emotional terms, however, they have almost unanimously confessed an inclination towards Hong Kong:

> I'm friendless here [in Guangzhou, where my company is]. No friends. We [the local people and I] have different lifestyles. We are polar opposites, culturally and in our ways of thinking. My friends are mainly in Hong Kong. I'll normally contact them when I'm back in Hong Kong, but not very often. But honestly, my daughters are the ones I want to see most each time I go home. I'll eat and talk with them. Then I'll go out with my friends if there's enough time. I normally stay for just one or two days... I really don't have much time for my friends. (Chun)

> Emotionally I'm more dependent on Hong Kong, because I spend at least half of my time here. Most of my friends are here. When I come home, I like to stay with my friends chatting a bit. Business-wise, there's not much to do here, but friends are many. (Ngai)

> I feel that I'm more attached to Hong Kong. I feel more like a Hongkonger because my home is here... I spend most of my time on the mainland, coming home only once a fortnight, mainly to see my family... But when I get into problems, I don't normally talk to my family. I don't want them to worry about me. (Kwok)

---

[26] Sun-tzu (trans. Lionel Giles), *The Art of War*.

Chun's life in Guangzhou, where his company is located, is "friendless", to use his own word. He feels he is too different from the local people, "culturally and in their ways of thinking", to have any genuine friends. Chun's friends are mainly in Hong Kong, but work has kept him on the mainland most of the time. During his short stays at home, his primary concern is to be with his two daughters, so he is spending less time with his friends. In the past, he would play table tennis or football with his friends after work. Now, he spends nearly all his time in Guangzhou tending his business – but he has no friends there to do sports and hang out together after work. This friendless life gives Chun a rather isolated feeling that he can do nothing about.

Ngai spends half of his time in Fujian, the other half in Hong Kong. While business-wise "there's not much to do" in Hong Kong, he feels he belongs here because he has his friends and old schoolmates. Ngai is an active member on the alumni board, enthusiastic about its activities. But in the half-and-half allocation of time, he confesses, half of his life is friendless.

Kwok has two toddlers. His wife works in Hong Kong. Although he feels more attached to Hong Kong, he has to spend most of his time on the mainland. So when problems occur on the mainland, he normally talks with his native friends in the factory rather than with his family, because he does not want to worry his family. In real life, Kwok feels distant from Hong Kong, while emotionally he is more inclined towards it, hoping to find emotional anchorage there. Whenever he comes home to Hong Kong, he tries to hide all the problems at work behind the facade of a caring father and good husband. On the one hand, he does not want his family to worry; on the other, he wishes to show his family, by covering up his problems at work, that he is capable of managing the company.

The life of an immigrant entrepreneur is ever divided in a constant shuttling between Hong Kong and the mainland, life and work. Spatial distances have created in him/her an emotional and psychological void. It is frustrating to have no friends to talk to in one's workplace, but work makes it impossible to come back to meet friends in Hong Kong whenever one wants. Even when they are finally back, they have to make a choice between family and friends. At work, they live behind masks, and this life continues at home because, in order to uphold their own image as the family's mainstay, they have to stick to the persona of a "successful" businessman. As the masquerade of life goes on, it exhausts itself in this internal stress – the emotional price one has to pay as an immigrant entrepreneur.

Conclusion

As Peter Berger has pointed out, "…just as there is no total power in society, there is also no total impotence".[27] Hated and marginalised by mainstream society, immigrants are not ready to take everything nonchalantly. Rather, they try their best to

[27] Peter Berger, *Invitation to Sociology*, p. 129.

fight back within their restricted opportunity structure, hoping to break away some day through continuous hard work. Discrimination stings, but negative external suppression can be transformed into a kind of positive internal power that intensifies the sense of ethnicity among immigrants, pushing them together to form a highly homogeneous network of "insiders". In the first days of an entrepreneur's career, this network has proved valuable. The cases of our immigrant entrepreneurs show that the secondary schools they attended in Hong Kong have been the fountainhead of such an "ethnic niche". As new immigrant students who spoke hardly any English, they were denied access to local government schools and were forced to enrol in the so-called "leftist patriotic schools" funded by Chinese immigrant businessmen. Thanks to their ideological input of patriotism and successful alumni connections, these schools became an emotional asylum for them, thus fostering "insider" circles of immigrants. Confronted with their "common enemies" of hatred and exclusion by the local people, these new immigrants became "native folks" who had come together to create, within a larger uncongenial environment, a congenial inner environment for their own survival. However, as the anthropologist Mead points out, the members of a social group are linked to each other in intricately various ways: while they have multitudes of common social interests, in many other aspects, they have conflicting interests to varying degrees.[28] Within the immigrant "ethnic niche", just as there are good moments of co-operation and harmony, so there are bad times of conflicts, ruptures, exploitation and even hatred. Home natives in a foreign land are necessarily trapped within the cycle of co-operation and rupture – a cycle common to all human organisations and societies.

In this age of intense mobility, both human and material resources are placed within a process of constant circuitry. Our immigrant entrepreneurs have one thing in common, that is, their businesses are diversely located, and most have chosen their native home as one of their business bases. On the one hand this is because in traditional Chinese society, the family is a clan-based "extended entrepreneurial community" in which an entrepreneur can mobilise not only his own personal network, but also the totality of the family's networks that have grown out of geographical and blood relations. On the other hand, fear comes with strangeness and security with familiarity. Closeness with the native place gives our immigrant entrepreneurs a relative sense of security, and their familiarity with the language, customs and business culture back home is also expected to clear the way for their business. Their return is, of course, also the result of their emotional attachment to the native soil and the motivation of government policies and propaganda. Once they are back, they come to assume dual identities as "patriotic home-comers" and as "outside" investors. The interchangeability of these two identities, or labels of similarity and difference, enables the entrepreneur to obtain double recognition: they come to possess, in the words of Peter Blau, "intrinsic" as well as "extrinsic" attractions.[29] But the return is sometimes accompanied by mixed feelings. Not all

---

[28] George Herbert Mead, *Mind, Self, and Society: From the Standpoint of a Social Behaviorist.*

[29] Peter Blau, *Exchange and Power in Social Life.*

home-comers have fared well. Many have fallen during their investment adventure in their native home. The native folks can be destroyers as well as helpers, a stumbling block as much as a stepping stone. These otherwise trustworthy people can turn out to be a dangerous gang who feast upon the home-comers' resources and do nothing but "begrudge and rebel" once something bad comes up. In the reality of our everyday life, each of us is putting on a show, but not all internally identify with the roles they are playing. Current research generally concentrates on the positive functions the native place has performed for the emigrant entrepreneurial management, but what kind of show, or game, is actually going on between the home-coming entrepreneur and his native folks at home? This is a question that invites further exploration.

The native home, Hong Kong, as well as other workplaces, forms a spatial triangle in which the immigrant entrepreneur circuits. Years ago, they were still hankering to find a place for themselves in the promised land of Hong Kong. Today they feel an urge to leave, to be out of this place where all their hope was anchored, so their achievements can extend into the future. Indeed, in this globalised world of ours, Hong Kong is losing its edge as a middleman in international trade. For our immigrant entrepreneurs, the exit is largely for the sake of "identity rearrangement" – they need the new identity of a "Chinese factory" so as to eliminate the suspicion of trying to cash in as a middleman. In dealing with different clients, however, one has to advertise different identities. While the label of a "Hong Kong company" is to be avoided with overseas clients, it needs to be highlighted when one deals with mainland factories, because the label has taken on certain symbolic significance of commercial value and come to stand for efficiency, credibility and repute, institutional and legal solidity, which are all important in commercial interactions. For the enterprise to survive in intense competition, it is now a trend to leave Hong Kong and at the same time remain partly stationed in the territory- a strategy that Goffman calls "impression management".[30] Thus, our entrepreneurs have become a "border people" living in the "border city" of Hong Kong. And to live across the border means a division of one's life between Hong Kong and the mainland of China. While emotionally most of them are more inclined towards the former, life's realities, as well as the restrictions of time and space, have immensely limited Hong Kong's share in our entrepreneurs' lives. As they stay in one place while their hearts hanker after another, they feel like an "emotional island" where a price is being paid for their intensely mobile mode of existence, where all pain goes unnoticed by the nonchalant, unsympathetic outsider that is also their family.

[30] Erving Goffman, *The Presentation of Self in Everyday Life*.

Associations: Mediating Self-Identities

Network Institutionalisation and the Formation of Ethnic Groups

Collective memory and self-identity

The "leftist patriotic schools", which catered largely to new immigrant children, have formed, in effect, an invisible inner city that closes in an identity, an experience and an ideology entirely different from those on the outside. A common school life and a common identity label imposed upon them from the outside have resulted in a particular draw between these immigrant children so that each becomes "one of us". Since it is built upon the less sophisticated rapport of former schoolmates, their friendships have lasted relatively longer. The distance in time and space has always been an arch-nemesis of relationships: the passage of time reduces mellowness to insipidity, while the widening of space alienates the originally familiar. There are exceptions, of course, but the psychological closeness that new immigrants once felt for one another as "one of us", and the friendships they built among themselves as former schoolmates, could never have endured and grown and continued to play a positive role in immigrant entrepreneurship had it not been for the existence of intermediary organisations.

The sustenance of immigrant identity is largely dependent on the active operation of intermediary organisations, which fall into different types. There are those based on blood relations or geographical relations, e.g., "clan associations" (*zongqin hui*) and "native place associations" (*tongxiang hui*), as well as those based on schools attended, such as "alumni associations". By regularly holding a variety of activities or ceremonies, these institutionalised intermediary organisations have managed to set up various opportunity platforms to organise and unite the diverse groups with certain attributes, thus enhancing their self-identity.

Many of the immigrant entrepreneurs we interviewed are enthusiastic participants in community activities. Compared with other kinds of organisations, alumni associations have generally had a stronger appeal for our informants, most of whom have

Chan Kwok-bun and Chan Wai-wan, *Mobile Chinese Entrepreneurs*,
International Series on Consumer Science, DOI 10.1007/978-1-4419-9643-5_6,

assumed important positions on alumni boards. That alumni associations have had a stronger appeal than "clan" and "native" associations is, as we see it, due to the different bases on which they have been built. "Clan" and "native" associations are built on blood or geographical relations, but both are only clan-relations broadly defined, given China's vast territory and large distances between even neighbouring towns. While the majority of our informants are Fujianese, they have come from towns and villages of such disparate customs and traditions that they may still feel distant from one another. Even when they have come from a clan with the same family name, the connections are so remote that there is little emotional involvement left. Alumni associations, however, are built on different foundations, for the kind of identity one finds among the alumni stems from the schoolmates' individual and collective memories:

> My friends in Hong Kong are mainly my former high school mates... We have known each other for more than ten years and have formed a solid relationship... We got to know each other in high school, when there were hardly any conflicts of interest. We never had problems between us. When there are no problems, our relations can naturally hold out. (Yee)

> My friends in Hong Kong are mostly Fukien schoolmates. Secondary school friendships generally last longer, because we were still simple in school. There was more room to develop a certain rapport... We usually had the same desk mate throughout the year. We would help each other with our homework. That's how our friendships grew stronger. (Chiu)

Both Yee and Chiu believe that friendship between schoolmates endures because they stayed together for a long time in school and their friendships grew out of the absence of "conflicts of interest" at a time of "purity". The hardworking days in class, the happy hours on the sports field and the carefree teenage friendships are one's most lasting memories. Precisely because identity among former school friends is built upon such remembered "purity", the "alumni" status has come to assume positive, symbolic significance in people's social interactions and in the judgment of their relationships with one another. It has also been effective in pulling together an "imaginary community" of mutual trust, which has proved helpful in future business developments.

In addition, alumni associations have more of a school atmosphere to them, rather than the more unrefined "gang" flavour of "clan associations" and "native place associations" that are built on blood or geographical relations. Places for the expansion of knowledge, schools are supposed to be the patrons of cultivation and refinement. Thus alumni associations, which have schools as their emotional anchorage, generally have a stronger appeal. Irrespective of their years of graduation, they have their common crumbs of *madeleine* that promise to trigger familiar memories. It could be either the sports ground and classrooms they once shared, or the same teachers and headmasters they once had, which combined to form an alumni association more accommodating than other such organisations. With such substantial common emotional anchorage (on people and things alike), there is inevitably more involvement of personal feelings and commitment.

Institutionalised role expectations and identity enhancement

No interpersonal relationship can survive the ravage of time if sustained solely on emotion. While emotion, admittedly, lays the foundation for identity, action is what actualizes identity,[1] and action has to be induced by what society expects of the individual's role. Institutionalised associations assign a specific role to the individual, and society's expectations of that role make possible the practical presentation of individual identity. In other words, it is emotion plus role that sustains and fosters an interpersonal network. In what follows, we will provide a detailed analysis of the bylaws and activities of the Fukien Secondary School Alumni Association (FSSAA), of which most of our informants are members, and examine how institutionalised organisations help to construct and foster individual identity and ethnic networks.

FSSAA bylaws state that the purposes of the association are "to foster mutually beneficial relationships among its alumni; to enhance general alumni welfare through the use of educational and entertainment programmes and activities; to raise the visibility and reputation of Fukien Secondary School; and to participate in social services". We can see that fostering "mutually beneficial relationships among its alumni" is one of the association's major purposes, and it seeks to achieve this goal through two prominent means or arrangements. First, they provide occasions that allow alumni to get together on a regular basis so as to keep them in touch. That is why each year they host large activities and ceremonies such as school anniversaries, alumni board inauguration, banquets celebrating Hong Kong's return to China, alumni mahjong and basketball competitions, business inspection tours, Chinese New Year dinner parties, etc. All these occasions have helped maintain friendships among the Fukien alumni and served as a reminder and enhancement of their identity. Many local people, on hearing the name "Fukien Secondary School", think it is a school in Fujian, mainland China; and knowledge of the full name, "Hong Kong Fukien Secondary School", immediately reminds them it is in fact a school for new immigrant children. All in all, the name "Fukien Secondary School" evokes a series of symbols such as "Fujianese", "new immigrant", "patriotic school", to name just a few. The FSSAA as an institutionalised organisation provides a role for the alumni and conveys, on various occasions, the Association's expectations (in accordance with the Bylaws purposes) for that role. In this way, the Association manages to build up a sense of identity among the alumni and internalises it as its own requirements for their individual roles.

Structurally, the FSSAA has sought to foster and expand the alumni network as well as enhance the sense of identity among the alumni. Eleven departments are set up under the President and the Vice-president including Secretary, Liaison, Publicity, Leisure and Cultural Services, General Management and Welfare, Treasury, Information Technology Services, Current Alumni Affairs, Youth Affairs, Social Affairs as well as Business Department. We have paid particular attention to the work of the Business Department. The Department is mainly responsible for contacting members in the business field and organising business activities. In fact, the important positions of the FSSAA (consultants, honorary presidents, chairman of the board) and the positions of Director and Deputy

---

[1] Peter Berger, *Invitation to Sociology: A Humanistic Perspective* (Garden City, New York: Doubleday & Company, 1963).

Director in the Business Department are primarily taken up by those in business as well as those in charge at the School. The Department organises business inspection tours to the factories of Fukien alumni, thus creating a platform for exchanging information among those in business, most of whom run factories and businesses on the mainland and whose practical experience is an invaluable kind of "local knowledge". Such exchanges of information, sometimes of internal news that is not yet circulating on the market, have enabled our immigrant entrepreneurs to obtain valuable market information and evade possible pitfalls or seize opportunities and seek new projects.

At the same time, in the relatively utilitarian Hong Kong society, money and fame are closely linked to each other. The Business Department's inspection tours constitute an effective, free advertising platform for accomplished alumni in business as well as for the Association. On one hand, the tours can be seen as a kind of commendation for the alumni's accomplishments. On the other, the tours are capable of transforming the alumni's individual charms (which are directly related to the amount of money they have donated to the Association as well as to the size of their businesses) into the charms of the Association. In other words, the more celebrated and wealthy members it has, the more honoured the Association will be and the more pride the members will take in the association. As a result, the members will be more willing to highlight the roles assigned by the Association as well as the identity it gives them. In the past, new immigrants (especially those from places other than Shanghai) were generally considered to be poor, unskilled people who could only do menial jobs in Hong Kong. Today, through the Business Department's activities and publicity, they are seeking to ditch such labels, imposed on them by the social mainstream, in favour of a positive, active image so that their fellow members will not only refuse to be ashamed of being an immigrant but also be able to claim: "Look, the 'Ah Tsan',[2] the mainlander you used to look down upon, has made it"!

Ceremonial rituals: Dramatising identity symbols

Apart from enhancing alumni identity and the Association's cohesive power by publicising alumni achievements in business, the FSSAA also organises various ceremonious events of celebration and seeks, through the repeated articulation of certain symbols, to strengthen the sense of identity among the alumni. During our visit to the "School Anniversary and Alumni Association Celebrations cum Inauguration Ceremony of the Ninth Alumni Board", we noticed that, throughout the ceremony, a series of different programmes served to bring together elements of sense and sensibility – their common identity was established not only in institutional terms, but also in emotional terms. Here, we shall go on to give a fuller account of certain aspects of the ceremony.

---

[2] Ah Tsan', originally a character in the TV series "The Good, The Bad and the Ugly" (1970), was a popular derogatory term for uneducated and "uncouth" new immigrants from mainland China until recent years.

(a) National and school anthems

The ceremony was held at a restaurant with a long-standing history in North Point. The restaurant was virtually Fukien's "official" restaurant, having hosted all of its important events. More than 50 tables were set, each seating more than ten people, totalling about 500 participants altogether. During the first two programmes, the national and school anthems were played. The master of ceremonies required all participants to rise to their feet when the two anthems were played, with the impassioned words, "Arise! All who refuse to be slaves"! sung out in an atmosphere of prevailing patriotism. It is commonplace to play the national anthem at national day banquets, but it was rather unusual, particularly among the local schools, for "School Anniversary and Alumni Association Celebrations" to open with the national anthem. That both the national and school anthems should be played at a ceremony must have particular significance in itself.

In the colonial days, the national anthem was never played at any official, semi-official or local community activities and ceremonies. But in the organisations, and schools in particular, funded and founded by early Chinese immigrant businessmen, playing the national anthem has been a set feature of large activities. At a time when the Union Jack was still fluttering above the territory of Hong Kong, playing the Chinese national anthem was undoubtedly intentional – it was a vicarious expression of the participants' identification with the motherland. To play the national anthem at an alumni ceremonial gathering was a clear reminder that it was "tied" to the mother country and its ancestor would not be forgotten, even when living under colonial rule.

Most Fukien alumni were immigrants from the mainland. While they had been away from their native place for a long time, they kept reminding themselves, on various occasions and through different channels in their new home, of their own identity as "mainland compatriots", a deliberate construction that differentiated them from the surrounding social mainstream and fostered their social network, which was built on their emotional attachment to the native soil. After Hong Kong's handover, the tradition of playing the national anthem at various ceremonial events and banquets continues. The purpose is to perpetuate, with the help of national sentiment, people's memory of history in their transitory social life, so that their original sense of themselves as well as their original interpersonal network will be sustained, even with the lapse of time and changes of space.

(b) Inauguration and toasting ceremonies

The Alumni Board inauguration was a major event at the banquet. The 60 people in different positions under the Board went on the podium and, supervised by an officer from the Liaison Office of the Central People's Government in Hong Kong, raised their right hands as they swore, in *putonghua*, to serve the Association wholeheartedly. After the oath-taking was completed, each of them received a certificate or letter of appointment from the Liaison Officer. In the course of the banquet, the newly appointed Board members were led by the Chairman to drink to every table the way newlyweds traditionally do at a wedding banquet, led by their respective parents. At that point, they must have felt like the host of the banquet, the "head" of the family which is the Alumni Association.

The oath-taking ceremony has symbolic significance. On the level of organisational regulations, it rationalises the status of the Board in a public and formal setting. On the level of self-consciousness, it internalises, and is witnessed by more than 500 people, the obligations and duties imposed by the Association as the members' expectations of their own roles. Sense and sensibility combined makes an effective cohesive power that draws together the alumni, shaping, at the same time, their identity through such frequent public expression.

Fukien is a school with a very strong geographical boundary. It is representative of the "new immigrant groups" in the broad sense. As an intermediary organisation, the FSSAA is fundamentally an identity "broker" that sustains and fosters immigrant identity. It gives the immigrants a role that is closely related to their immigrant experiences, and creates settings in which the role and personal feelings blend in the construction of a powerful ethnic identity. This not only strengthens the alumni network, it also sustains the Association.

You and Me: Personal Feelings and Ethics

The futurity of self-identity

Fei Xiaotong summarises interpersonal relations in China as operating on a "differential mode of association" (*chaxu geju*) where each individual is claimed to be surrounded by a series of concentric circles of social relationships, produced by one's own social influence. Attached to each nodal point is an ethical factor characterised by what the Confucian school has called *renlun* (human relationships).[3] As an intermediary organisation, the Alumni association has transformed, on the institutional level, the relationship between the members to varying degrees and in such a way that the sustenance of that relationship is no longer merely dependent on the individual moral character of "self-restraint" or "control of oneself". Rather, the existence of an "association" serves to supervise and balance this relationship. In each association, there are written regulations that govern its members' behaviour and unwritten "norms" that can be equally effective. These written or unwritten "rules of the game" provide norms to follow – norms that can be internalised by individual members as a self-regulating power. Such a regulating power extending from the presence of an association is what bolsters trust and co-operation among the members, so much so that business conflicts can normally be held in check when the parties involved wish to stay in the association for future co-operation opportunities:

> Then I said I was quitting… I felt I wasn't being treated in equal terms and decided to withdraw. I got exactly what I had invested, not a buck more. It wasn't in proportion to my shares in the company. I accepted it because I felt we were still friends, being former schoolmates… I withdrew because I didn't want us to end up in arguments. We might be partners again in the future, who knows? So I didn't say a word [about the division of profits].

---

[3] Fei Xiaotong, *Xiangtu Zhongguo* [From the Soil: The Foundations of Chinese Society] (Beijing: Sanlian shudian, 1985).

> I was satisfied just to get back what I had invested. It was settled and it would not get in our way when we worked together again. (Wing)

Wing was originally doing advertising with two former schoolmates, to whom the business had belonged. When Wing joined, the company was in deficit. After 2 years' work, it started to make good money, with a cash deposit of over HK$100,000, which was a handsome amount in the 1980s. Now that the company was making a profit, Wing asked to draw a bonus in the Chinese New Year but his partners simply refused his request. Moreover, despite being one of the major shareholders, Wing was denied access to all the company accounts. Feeling that he was not being treated in equal terms, he decided to withdraw in order not to ruin their relationship in case conflicts arose. He gave up what he was really entitled to, as most Chinese businessmen would have, to maintain the relationship, because he was well aware that in China, where personal relations lasted, there would be business. A Chinese proverb says: "As long as the green mountains stand, one need not worry about firewood". In addition, "dignity" as such is not something to be proud of in the world of business people. For in the world of business, there are "no permanent enemies". True to the common Chinese saying "Feng Shui rotates, fortunes go up and down" (*fengshui lunliu zhuan*), as those in business are aware that, the relative equilibrium of life is constantly shifting. In business in particular, one can become a millionaire or turn flat broke overnight. No one ever knows when one will need to be rescued by another. The importance of keeping ties is buried in the minds of business people, who would probably not say it.

As Wing has shown, when business people try to hold a conflict in check, they are invariably more concerned about their relationship with each other and its future than the situation at hand. People's positioning of themselves from each other is essentially a matter of identity. In other words, how a business person identifies with another's future will determine the attitude with which they will solve the conflict. This process of envisaging the futurity of a relationship comes under the influence of a variety of factors, of which an intermediary organisation like the alumni association is one of the most important, particularly to those immigrant entrepreneurs arriving in Hong Kong before the 1980s.

Emotional interventions

We may have entirely different reactions to what a friend does and what a stranger does to us, much as they are the same thing. We may, for instance, feel indignant about the stranger and simply let it pass with a friend. The difference is largely dependent on whether there is "emotional intervention" in our relationship. A relationship without "emotional intervention" is largely free of complications so that once conflicts arise and the two parties have to break up, it will not entail much social cost. With "emotional intervention", one has to weigh one's moral responsibilities and conscience, and much social cost will follow when the relationship is ruined. The alumni association not only sets the "rules" for interaction among its members, but more importantly, it ensures that, apart from such disciplinary supervision, there is a certain degree of emotional intervention – the involvement, that is, of "personal feelings" and "ethics":

> I was taken care of by some native folks when I first arrived in Hong Kong. This is why I want to do something for my native folks... All of my board members were Fujianese...

> Are my friends mostly Fujianese? They certainly are. And they're mainly fellow members in my alumni association and native association. (Yue)

Yue runs printing factories. Most of his board members are Fujianese and are friends as well as former schoolmates. As the person in charge of a number of organisations, Yue spends a great deal of his time on community services. He is, for example, Director of Development at his Native Fujianese Association, Associate President of the Alumni Association, Deputy Council Member of the Hong Kong Eastern District Community Association, Vice-Chair and Secretary General of the Co-ordination and Promotion of Eastern District Limited, and President of the North Point Residents' Association. He is concerned about everything related to his Fujianese natives. Such an attachment, or rather commitment, to his native fellows and alumni has stemmed from his gratitude for being "taken care of by some native folks" in his earlier days in Hong Kong. Many of these native folks were Fukien graduates. Wing got his first job as a teacher in Fukien. His later jobs were all recommended by his former school friends. In school and at work, he has been living among Fujianese people. Schoolmates, friends, native folks – this is a mixture of different identities and diverse feelings. One of the outstanding characteristics of our immigrant entrepreneurs is precisely this intricate overlapping of relationships with business partners. Within a network like this, they tend to be tolerant or even "get out of the kitchen" to avoid the heat of conflict in order to retain the "goodwill" in the original relationship. Such a problem-solving strategy is, in the final analysis, targeted at some future saleable asset that will arise from the well-being of business relations. Indeed, once pared down to its core, people's behaviour will often reveal the utmost human selfishness, which many of us find repugnant and refuse to accept or admit. "Ethics" and "personal feelings" are, therefore, nothing but a public camouflage that covers up the undercurrent in our behaviour by conforming to the social expectations for our conscience – a comforting strategy indeed, for all.

This strong emotional intervention in alumni bonding is closely related to immigrant experience. The negative labelling as "new immigrants" in the early years was an important "revelation" in itself. The discrimination from mainstream society stood in stark contrast to the goodwill among the teachers and friends in the leftist schools. And comfort in adversity is often the source of lasting gratitude. As Georg Simmel puts it, "Although [gratitude] is a purely personal affect, or (if one will) a lyrical affect, its 1,000-fold ramifications throughout society make it one of the most powerful means of social cohesion".[4] When there is gratitude in our heart for someone, we often feel "indebted" with a certain moral obligation towards that person. What we call "personal feelings" and "ethics" are in fact more formal phraseology denoting "indebtedness". "In everyone's heart", as the Chinese say, "there is a steelyard" – a steelyard, that is, with which to weigh their relationship with others according to their closeness to each other. Our immigrant entrepreneurs' multi-layered relationships with their school friends, and with their alumni business partners in particular,

---

[4] Georg Simmel, "Faithfulness and Gratitude" in Kurt Wolff ed. and trans. *The Sociology of Georg Simmel* (Glencoe, Illinois: The Free Press, 1950), pp. 388–389.

dictates that they should adopt different attitudes and approaches (compared with those of the ordinary businessman) to solving business conflicts, when these attitudes and approaches are intrinsically related to their identification with their partners.

For gratitude to last, however, it cannot feed on a past alone. A variety of arrangements is needed that will enable the friendship between schoolmates and between generations to continue. Apart from the various activities of the alumni association, monetary support has proved effective in achieving this end. Each year, during FSSAA's anniversary celebrations, there is always a Scholarship Awards Ceremony for outstanding current students. Some scholarships are awarded specifically to former alumni's children studying at Fukien. Of the latter, some are awarded to those who excel at the year's Certificate of Education Examination[5]; others are awarded to former alumni's children who excel at their school work. As we can see, not all students are eligible for these two awards, since they are available only to the children of former alumni. Such scholarships are a clear invitation to the former alumni to send their children back to their alma mater, although these children were all born and bred in Hong Kong and stand fair chances of enrolling in the mainstream schools. If the children go to the same school as their parents, it will not only enhance the former alumni's emotional attachment to their alma mater but will also push it into the next generation. This circular perpetuation of emotional attachment is not, however, an entirely personal choice on the alumni's part, but is conditioned by a certain interpersonal network. Alumni associations, especially those of "leftist" schools founded by immigrant business people, have provided various settings for socialising as well as substantial monetary support, both being conducive to a social network that builds upon ethnic identity, and that brims with personal and ethical feelings.

Officialdom and Business

Associations: Bridging government and business

"You're in charge of the money", says one of our informants, "when you're in charge of the official chop". Officialdom is generally equated with power and power with money among those doing business on the mainland. In Chinese society, where *guanxi* dominates, one's success in business is primarily dependent on one's connections in the government. To pull the government "strings", however, one needs specific strategies and channels. During our interviews, we discovered that the many so-called "associations" have had an important role to play in bridging business and the government not only on a local scale but in cross-region business as well.

Whether "associations" are effective in bridging business and government are dependent on a number of factors. The first is what we call "group effect". In traditional Chinese society, government officials are the "Eminent" (*daren*) and

[5] The Hong Kong Certificate of Education Examination is a standardised examination which most local students sit for at the end of their 5-year secondary education. The equivalent in the United Kingdom is the GCSE exams.

common people belong to the "Humble" (*xiaoren*). It is difficult for the "Humble" to have any *guanxi* ("personal connections") with the "Eminent". Similarly, unless a business person is well established or enjoys a good social reputation, it is unlikely that he or she will have any dealings with the "big men" in the government. As individuals, ordinary business people cannot even invite high government officials to social occasions. But it can be quite another story if the invitation is sent out in the name of an "association", especially when the people in charge have considerable social influence. At an alumni association anniversary ceremony, we noticed that, as well as the school principal and the head teachers, representatives from the Hong Kong government and officials from the Liaison Office of the Central People's Government were seated at the host table alongside the association president and other people in charge, all established business people. During the banquet, people came to drink toasts to those at the host table, got introduced to one other, and exchanged greetings and name cards. All such occasions undoubtedly help extend the social networks of the alumni in business. Their connection with government officials, once activated, can be a significant addition to their social resources.

Convergence of public welfare and individual good

Another important function that such associations perform is providing a setting for role-switching. While the collusion of government and business is much "carpeted" in society, such practice is most common among Chinese business people. To tone down the interaction between the government and the business sector, one needs the packaging of a neutral setting. Social functions or occasions held in the name of an intermediary organisation can often allow the kind of social interactions targeted at the pursuit of individual good to be camouflaged behind the balloons and bombast of "public service".

The majority of the immigrant entrepreneurs we interviewed have participated in community functions and assumed important positions in community organisations. They have different name cards. Some are for their business positions, some for their community services, others a mixture of the two. To different people they give different cards, presenting different aspects of themselves. Shin, for instance, has had more than 20 public titles listed on his name card, such as the Political Consultative Conference, his native association, commercial chambers, education foundations and so on, in which he has assumed positions such as president, chair, and honorary president. Now the chair and general manager of a corporate group of six companies and factories, Shin is already occupied with his business, circuiting between his companies and factories in Hong Kong as well as in four mainland provinces. In spite of this, he sets aside a considerable amount of time, either in Hong Kong or on the mainland, tending to community matters and performing public duties. Talking about his commitment to public service, Shin says, "I'm happy to do all this. Society has made me what I am, and I'm just trying to do something in return. It's always good to be able to help others when we can. I'm just trying my best".

Shin admits he is truly devoted to public service. When asked why they commit themselves to the public good, our interviewees almost immediately expressed their wish to "do something in return" for the community. Nevertheless, "...individual personality", as Li Qiang observes, "is divided into the public persona that is to be presented and the secret, private persona that is to be kept from the public".[6] The practice of putting public titles on business name cards conforms exactly to an analysis that Coughlin and others have made of overseas Chinese business people, that is, various community organisations, charity organisations in particular, constitute a platform on which Chinese entrepreneurs provide outstanding charity work so as to draw favourable attention from the local government. This, the studies show, is conducive to creating a positive corporate image that proves helpful in sorting out "official channels".[7] Our case studies have also evidenced that business people's commitment to public service is not a purely charitable deed: they wish, rather, to make use of the good reputation they gain from public work to acquire such resources as positive corporate image, fine personal reputation, desirable social renown, and so on. All these resources are helpful in opening up "official channels" that are ultimately favourable for corporate sustenance and development. As far as we understand it, the entrepreneurs' enthusiasm in public service is in fact a managerial strategy to "have the cake and eat it", achieving moral and ethical gratification as well as economic fulfilment at the same time. The strategy has to be implemented, however, with the help of influential "associations". This explains why business people try their best to join these associations and, preferably, take up a position or two even if it means sacrificing a great deal of their personal time and even less time with their families, or donate large sums of money.

Associations: Hybridity and singularity

"Associations" as clearly delineated organisations are open only to the eligible or to the properly "identified". The more associations a businessman has joined, the more identities, of course, he is able to exhibit or perform. The immigrant entrepreneurs we interviewed, particularly the multi-regional business people, are invariably possessors of diverse identities who exhibit different identities when dealing with different people in different places. The switching of identities is quite often a matter of how effectively it will facilitate the opening of "government channels" as well as "business channels":

> I've joined various organisations and associations where I'm doing business. In Jiujiang of Jiangxi, for example, I've joined the Fujian Commercial Chamber; in Yingtan, another city in Jiangxi, I'm a member of the 'Political Consultative Conference' (PCC). These organisations have helped a lot in extending my [social] network... As a PPC member, all you have to do is write up a few proposals and get attention from the government, who in turn provide you with protection and support. Another good thing about this is the government reports

---

[6] Li Qiang, "'Xinli erchong quyu' yu zhongguo de wenjuan diaocha" ["'Double Psychological Spheres' and Opinion Surveys in China"], *Shehuixue Yanjiu* [Sociological Research], No. 1, 2000, p. 40.

[7] Richard J. Coughlin, *Double Identity: The Chinese in Modern Thailand* (Hong Kong: Hong Kong University Press, 1960); Edmund Terence Gomez and Michael Hsiao Hsin-Huang, "Chinese Business Research in Southeast Asia", in *Chinese Business Research in Southeast Asia: Contesting Cultural Explanations, Researching Entrepreneurship*, eds., Edmund Terence Gomez and Michael Hsiao Hsin-Huang (Surrey, U.K.: Curzon Press, 2001), pp. 1–37.

> that you get to read [before others] each year during the PCC meetings. This is where you get first-hand access to information on the city's development as well as government policies... I joined the PPC as a Hong Kong entrepreneur. Most of the PCC members are business people, bosses of state-owned or private enterprises. There are people from other sectors as well. Through them, I've come to know a lot of government people. (Chuk)

As a real estate dealer, Chuk has to go wherever there are projects. Doing real estate business on the mainland, one has to have frequent dealings with the government. After all these years, Chuk feels that *guanxi* and "government recognition" are particularly important for a company's development. For Chuk, the establishment of social connections needs "government support" and the facilitation of certain "organisations". Therefore, he has joined various organisations with different identities. In Jiujiang, he made use of his native place connections and joined the Fujian Commercial Chamber; in Yingtan, he became a PCC member as a Hong Kong entrepreneur.

Chuk's ultimate goal in joining all these organisations with different identities is to pluralize his interpersonal network. Take the "Fujian Commercial Chamber". Its specific geographical delineation shows that it is "singular" by nature. The flocking together of Fujianese people or, on a larger scale, the union of people from the same provinces, means that the more "monogenic" these associations are, the more "exclusive" they become. As Wong has pointed out in his study of Shanghai textiles industrialists in Hong Kong, entrepreneurs of similar attributes (being, for instance, Shanghainese by origin), in order to create a semi-closed competitive environment or even blockage, will form a group for the monopoly of specific economic opportunities.[8] The Fujian Commercial Chamber in Jiujiang is essentially a special group of people who make substantial use of their geographical relations. Chuk started as a construction manager. Construction teams from Fujian are active not only in their home province but in neighbouring provinces like Jiangxi. In such cases, it is important, Chuk stresses, to have good *guanxi* when one works away from home, on the land of *others*. And the organisation of the Fujian Commercial Chamber was aimed precisely at self-protection as well as further development. Such a union, therefore, has its practical functions. That is why Chuk started to look for the local Fujianese Native Association immediately after moving his company headquarters to Shenzhen. He was even willing to donate an amount of money for a position in the Association. The union of home natives in a land of strangers is actually a union of strengths to maximise the so-called "group effect". Through various functions and activities (some of which are organised on various pretexts), people can establish government connections, access "internal" information, and thus get ahead of their competitors.

However, the monogeny of group members can turn out to be a disadvantage. As Mark Granovetter has observed, people with strong ties, family members for instance, who are in frequent contact, often end up receiving pretty much the same

---

[8] Wong Siu Lun, *Emigrant Entrepreneurs: Shanghai Industrialists in Hong Kong* (Hong Kong: Oxford University Press, 1988).

information because similar information is being circulated among the group. Conversely, people who are only weakly tied, those belonging in different groups, for example, whose contact is less frequent, can have better access to information that one does not already have, thanks to their more pluralized sources of information. This demonstrates the strength of weak ties, since the non-overlapping of information is in itself an important part of one's social resources.[9] It also explains why Chuk has, in another city of the same province, made himself a member of the so-called "Political Consultative Conference", which is a highly hybridised governmental organisation. For those in business, a government organisation such as the PCC represents not so much a promise of social eminence (for many, it promises no eminent social status whatsoever) as an assurance of access to certain "exclusive" occasions. Chuk, as a PCC member, has got to know many government officials as well as bosses of state-owned and private enterprises. Indeed, one's ties with eminent figures in the government and business are no less than a shortcut to wealth – a shortcut that promises access to a variety of information through different channels. We once attended, in Chuk's company, two important ceremonies under his business: the launching ceremony of his Shenzhen headquarters and the signing ceremony for one of his largest investment projects. Although different in nature, these two occasions had several common features:

(a) Presence of government officials
Many of the guests in the two ceremonies were government officials. At the one held in the corporate headquarters, ordinary guests and government guests were seated separately, with the latter accommodated in a separate room. Chuk spent the first half of the ceremony with the officials, amongst a spirited exchange of toasts and thanks and brotherly embraces.

(b) Dominance of male guests
The two ceremonies were respectively held in Shenzhen and Hong Kong. On both occasions, the majority of the guests were men, government officials or business people; none of whom had brought along their families. Before the ceremony started, the guests sat together and indulged themselves in a smoking spree that soon filled the room with fumes, as the men exchanged name cards and discussed their business projects. When a chat hinted at the prospect of co-operation, they would make appointments for further discussion, while among those close to one another, the humming chat would sometimes digress from the seriousness of business and turn into a clamouring banter on the subject of "women" and "mistresses", when the names of the protagonists were withheld in a roar of knowing laughter. It appears that within this circle, there is a culture – or a set of rules and norms – that is all its own.

---

[9] Mark Granovetter, "The Strength of Weak Ties", *American Journal of Sociology*, 78 (1973), pp. 1360–1380. Granovetter measures the strengths and weaknesses of interpersonal ties in four aspects: amount of time for interaction, emotional intensity, intimacy and reciprocal services.

As Gomez and Hsiao have pointed out in their study of Chinese businesses in Southeast Asia, Chinese businessmen's affiliation with the local political elite or influential government officials has been one of the major factors underlying entrepreneurial prosperity.[10] The same phenomenon has also revealed itself in our studies. In the world of our entrepreneurs, men take the lead. For the individual, as Berger observes, to be located in society means to be at the intersection point of specific social forces.[11] Within the inner-community of an "association", especially among the Chinese business people in China and Southeast Asia, business is essentially a wrestle of power among the male sex. For this reason, businessmen in general have enjoyed easier entry into the business world than business women do. This tendency is obvious among our 16 informants, of whom only three are women.

Officialdom, they say, is all about putting on shows; and the multitudes of different "associations" manage the stage. On stage, government officials and business people, in their exits and entrances, dramatise their lives. Backstage, they engage themselves in a series of negotiations and "deals" that, though sometimes not entirely gratifying, are conducive to certain exchanges and co-operation.

Conclusion

Current studies of immigrant associations have generally focused on their utilitarian functions, such as the provision of capital and labour, as well as the facilitation of government connections. Another important function of these associations, however, goes largely unnoticed. This function lies in their efforts to re-present, dramatise and intensify the sense of "ethnicity" and "identity" among immigrants through the use of vivid and even exaggerated totemic symbols on a variety of ceremonial occasions.[12] The majority of the immigrant entrepreneurs we interviewed are enthusiastic participants of community and public activities. Of all the community organisations, alumni associations have had the most extensive and lasting appeal. Tung's survey of overseas Chinese[13] has also demonstrated from another aspect that individual or collective identity hinges not so much on history and shared experiences as on the deliberate and recurrent dramatisation by some external forces at a later time. To a very large extent, the various associations serve as brokers for individual or collective identity. Their job is precisely to intensify the originally feeble sense of

[10] Edmund Terence Gomez and Michael Hsiao Hsin-Huang, "Chinese Business Research in Southeast Asia".

[11] Peter Berger, *Invitation to Sociology*.

[12] Tung Yuan-chao, "Guding de tianye yu youyi de zhoubian: Yi Daxidi Huaren wei li" ["Stable Fields and Moving Boundaries: The Chinese in Tahiti as an Illustration"], in W.T. Chen and Y.K. Huang, eds., *Shequn yanjiu de xingsi* [Reflections on Community Studies] (Taipei: Institute of Ethnology, Academia Sinica, 2002), pp. 303–329.

[13] Ibid.

identity among the new immigrants by whipping their existing and ever-accumulating collective memory into a potent cohesive power that will in turn enhance the associations' continuity.

While they have generally labelled themselves charity groups, such associations are often involved in business.[14] The devotion of time and money was not, of course, a purely charitable deed. It was performed with a hope to create a "win-win" situation for one's ethical as well as economic enterprises. Precisely because "associations" provide them with a stage to perform their different social identities, business people will try their best to become part, if not an important part, of as many associations as possible. They may hold their conflicts in check just to stay in an association and retain access to the potential business opportunities in its hoard. A businessman's vision of his future relationship with others and what he expects of his future identity will largely determine his commitment to the organisation and the attitude with which he will solve a conflict. The future is now.

Indeed, what these associations represent is a mixture of hard functionality and soft emotionality, a convergence point of public welfare and individual good. Politics and competition will arise with the pursuit of profit; and pain will come along with happiness where emotions are involved. Many such associations are in fact clearly delineated factional communities, with entangled relations within and without. One of the prominent challenges we encountered during our interviews was a general reluctance to discuss conflicts within an organisation. Those still "wading" through the troubled waters of business are particularly reticent about their "internal issues" when interviewed by an "outsider". As a result, the few of the informants who were actually willing to talk about these problems gave very skimpy accounts that skipped the major details. In spite of this lack of resources, however, we are fully aware that light and darkness are twin brothers. Under the peaceful waters of altruism and harmony, selfishness and conflicts surge in irrepressible undercurrents.

[14] Richard J. Coughlin, *Double Identity*; Edmund Terence Gomez and Michael Hsiao Hsin-Huang, "Chinese Business Research in Southeast Asia".

The Double-Edged Sword: Mobility and Entrepreneurship

So it is that whenever Heaven honours a person with great responsibilities, it first tries his resolve, exhausts his muscles and bones, starves his body, leaves him destitute, and confounds his every endeavour. In this way his patience and endurance are developed, and his weaknesses are overcome.

– Mencius (Master Kao)[1]

Mobility and Entrepreneurial Spirit

New immigrants: Battling for success

Immigrant entrepreneurs were not born miracle makers. From "Ah Tsan" to "taipan", they have toiled and suffered their way to success. They carried so much hope in their hearts as they arrived in this city, leaving their native homes behind, in such energetic anticipation. But the reality of life, especially during the early days, was a far cry from what they had expected. In the face of discrimination and exclusion, their lives were full of frustration and bitterness. Yet discrimination, hostility, frustration and despair tempered the will of these people as much as they all tormented them. Immigrant experience "tried their resolve" and "exhausted their muscles and bones" in such a way that transformation had to, and gradually did, take place within these people. Some of them eventually acquired the qualities that make the best business personality – resolve, a practical mind and confidence:

> For three years I was a part-time cycle delivery boy, and it taught me to persevere. I was going to a so-called 'leftist patriotic' school. While I didn't have much of an education, at least I didn't keep bad company. And I've always believed you'll never make it unless you keep at it. New immigrants are the hardest-working people. We worked 15, 16 hours a day, all of us. Difficult life. (Shin)

[1] David Hinton (trans.), *Mencius* (Berkeley, CA: Counterpoint, 1998), p. 230.

Chan Kwok-bun and Chan Wai-wan, *Mobile Chinese Entrepreneurs*, International Series on Consumer Science, DOI 10.1007/978-1-4419-9643-5_7,

> Looking back at the various things I went through over the past decades, I think Hong Kong is truly a good place to temper one's mind ... It was a difficult, painful trip, what I went through and how my mind changed ... It wasn't all success along the way, but I think every step was worth it, because it taught me to appreciate what others don't. Today, wherever I go, people say that I'm a tough woman. I think it's the confidence I show in business. (Siu)

Shin is now president, chair of the board and general manager of his corporation, which consists of six factories and companies in Hong Kong, Shenzhen, Fujian, Jiangsu and Shanghai. Shin has "toiled and suffered" his way to success. He came to Hong Kong when he was eight or nine years old. His father, who was in the Philippines, died when Shin was ten, and he and his mother had to depend on each other. As a young boy, he had to put the family's livelihood on his own shoulders, working part-time doing deliveries on his bicycle every day after school. But the hardships, far from crushing Shin, simply strengthened his will. Shin's boss, satisfied with his hard work, eventually offered to go into business with him. The collaboration started small. As soon as he arrived home in the evening after a day's work, Shin would start work on his business, "toiling" with his wife, and would not stop until one or two in the morning. Each day there were 15 or 16 hours of work. Shin accepted this difficult life and has stressed that, as a "new immigrant", he was ready to suffer. That "new immigrants" had to suffer stemmed from two reasons. First, discrimination was still prevalent in Hong Kong against these newcomers. Second, it was difficult in the 1970 for "new immigrant" children to make a name for themselves like what the local children could do with a good education in this "elitist" society. Resigning himself, like those who had come before him, to such inequality, Shin was convinced he would never make it if he was not ready to "toil and moil". While he could never change his identity as an "immigrant", he was certain that if he was to keep at it, working harder than other people, one day he would stand out among the ordinary millions in this city.

Siu is a health products franchiser, with distribution stores in a few cities in China. A former national martial arts champion, she had taught physical education at a Chinese university before coming to Hong Kong. Back home, Siu was a big name, a much- respected figure. She had lived, in her own words, with "a halo over my head". But the move to Hong Kong shoved all that into the past tense. Due to the differences in the two education systems, Siu's education was not recognised in Hong Kong, which ultimately made it impossible for her to find a teaching job at the same level. Because of her accent, she was neglected and disrespected. A high-spirited woman, Siu had been so confident of herself. Now the move to Hong Kong forced her to face the realities of life and reflect on herself, asking her to "accept it with grace". There were, however, good moments as well as bad moments in her experience as an immigrant. A life of mobility means one must experience culture clashes and transform oneself amid a new series of unpleasant social interactions. All the setbacks Siu encountered in her new home led her to develop a totally different outlook on life. Crushed by the drastic change in social status, Siu tried to change herself in order to get recognised and accepted. Yet the changes, far from boosting her confidence, only served to shed her "true colours" and turned her into a caricature of herself. After tempering herself for a period of time, Siu came to realise that "hardship increases stature" (*Chi de ku zhong ku, fang wei ren shang ren*). The hardship of immigrant life gave Siu and her fellow entrepreneurs a resourceful and resilient character, which was exactly what has sustained them over the years, making them appear "invincible".

Shame and courage

In examining multifarious social phenomena, C. Wright Mills introduces the notion of "sociological imagination" and contends that " ... the individual can understand his own experience and gauge his own fate only by locating himself within his period, that he can know his own chances in life only by becoming aware of those of all individuals in his circumstances".[2] In other words, the lives of individuals cannot be truly understood until we put them within larger historical and social contexts. To examine the changes that have taken place within individual contexts, we must look to the outside for the underlying causes, making use of our "sociological imagination" to understand not only the social structure that encompasses the individual, but also the relationship between them. Why is it that so many Jews became outstanding merchants after leaving their national homeland? If a tendency is noticeable not just among a few individuals, but among an entire specific group of people throughout history, then we might safely conclude that there are factors at work that transcend the boundaries of the individual microcosm, factors which we can trace back to institutional and opportunity structures in society. While each of our immigrant entrepreneurs has his or her unique story to tell, they have one thing in common: underlying their growth and success is a series of battles against unfair treatment from mainstream society as well as against opportunity limitations imposed upon them by predominating vested interests. Theirs is a silent rebellion. Their road to business has been a road to dignity, where they refuse to submit themselves to fate:

> I went to Fukien Secondary School in Hong Kong. I started at primary six and stayed there until form six. Form six was preparatory for undergraduate studies. I could not, of course, go to a local university. So I decided to try my luck back on the mainland. But unfortunately, the 'Cultural Revolution' had just started in China and [at a time of tense xenophobia] no 'outside' applicant was to be admitted. That was how my education was terminated. (Yue)

> The social climate at the time was rather antagonistic to the so-called 'leftist patriotic schools'. Society tended to exclude leftist schools ... I thought, if I continued to be a teacher, I wouldn't be able to go very far without a university diploma. Young people like to dream about the future, and so I left ... Then I started work in an insurance company ... In the insurance business English was very often used, and I soon became aware that my English wasn't 'up to par' ... And I quit again and started to trade in medium- and low-rate jewellery. (Wing)

Yue came to Hong Kong in 1958 at the age of 13. Wing came in 1961 at the age of 11. Both arrived during their school days and both were denied, like those who came before or after them, access to a proper education that would have put them on

[2] C. Wright Mills, *The Sociological Imagination* (New York. Oxford University Press, 1959), p. 5.

the professional track. That the same ethnic group should have had the same opportunity structure at different periods of time is testament to the fact that fate is not entirely determined by individual capability but by the social institution. Although these immigrant entrepreneurs' move from the mainland to Hong Kong was nothing more than a move from one Chinese community to another, a move to another social group that, like them, had yellow skin and dark hair, they were still labelled "outsiders" and "strangers" in their new home. Although a similar story repeats itself throughout history, the "new immigrants" react differently to the changes in their lives: some never managed to walk out of the shadows of adversity and remained full of remorse throughout their lives; others surrendered themselves to reality and never tried to fight back; still others, exemplified by the immigrant entrepreneurs we interviewed, successfully transformed the negative factors into a positive dynamic that led to their making a name for themselves.

Confucius said, "To possess the feeling of shame is to be near to energy".[3] Others have written about pre-modern Chinese people who "failed in school and went into business all around the country".[4] The "shame" brought about by their accents, their "leftist" education, and their "new immigrant" identity threw these people into a pandemonium of mixed feelings. "We (new immigrants) were never to become professionals": having "failed in school", they were acutely aware that "new immigrants" were at the bottom of the scale of power. How, then, were they supposed to reverse this situation? As Stuart Hall points out in his analyses of the abstract concept of "personal identity", the formation of an individual's or a group's identity is in fact the outcome of a negotiation between the individual and society, between specific groups and the social mainstream.[5] As long as the "new immigrant" identity is disadvantaged during this negotiation, the only way to break free from the fetters of this identity is to assume another identity, that of a "boss" or an "entrepreneur", for example. In a society where "big bucks" is the name of the game, such an identity is certainly something to be marvelled at:

> Under those circumstances, under the elitist colonial rule, there was no way we [new immigrants] could become professionals. We could never become a lawyer, or an architect, or an accountant ... I may have lost the game in this, having failed to be a professional. But one day, I'll overtake you all, elsewhere in life ... I'm doing business with Westerners. I want to affect them, conquer them with my commercial techniques. It's kind of a mission for me now, a mission that keeps me going. (Yam)

Yam came to Hong Kong with his family at the age of 12. Because of the differences between the local and mainland Chinese educational systems, he was put back, like many other new immigrant children, to a lower grade. He realised that in school

---

[3] Confucius is quoted as saying this in *The Doctrine of the Mean*. See James Legge, *The Chinese Classics with a Translation, Critical and Exegetical Notes, Prologomena, and Copious Indexes* (Taipei: Wenxing Shudian, 1966), Vol.1, p. 407

[4] He Qiaoyuan (1558–1632), 'Fengsu Zhi' ['Records of Customs'] in He Qiaoyuan, ed. *Min Shu* [Fujian Provincial Gazetteer, 1630], vol. 38 (Fuzhou: Fujian renmin chubanshe, 1994).

[5] Stuart Hall, 'Cultural Identity and Diaspora' in Jonathan Rutherford, ed. *Identity: Community, Culture, Difference* (London: Lawrence and Wishart, 1990), pp. 222–237.

he "never held any particular edge over the others" and that he was the one to "lose". Young as he was, Yam knew he would have to excel in some other way. As he saw it, apart from professional fields, the only way to "excellence" was to start his own business. The ultimate motivation behind an entrepreneurial adventure is the desire to assume an identity free of "shame" and full of power. Even if the road ahead is still a long and arduous one, the new immigrants were willing to go against all odds and "go decent". Their hard work and perseverance were to become their future corporate spirit – a major component of their corporate culture – which is what has sustained their enterprise, from the inside, through all the adversity and challenges.

The Shuttling Nomads: One Face, Many Masks

Chan Kwok-bun, co-author of this book, and Tong Chee-kiong have pointed out that the Singaporean Chinese are in possession of "one face" (in consanguineous and ethnic terms) which bears "many masks" (in their cultural traits), and that the Chinese, though unable to change their ethnicity, are able to choose what constitutes their ethnic traits.[6] Relating to this, Chan has drawn attention to the "multiple rootedness" that immigrant Chinese identity displays. The word "multiple" as Chan used it has three-fold connotations: first, it refers to a manifold and non-singular heterogeneity; second, it denotes a "renewed existence" as of a "rebirth"; third, it implies regard for one's "roots", as the polyphonic Chinese character "chong" ("multiple") does in its other pronunciation "zhong" ("cherish"). While overseas Chinese have retained some of the essentially Chinese sense of value and identity, they are in possession of a new identity that displays multiple emotional attachments and accommodative cultures and life experiences. Precisely because of this feature, overseas Chinese people tend to change their identities as the occasion or the "audience" varies.[7] This portrayal of Chinese emigrant identity applies neatly to the problem of personal identity among the immigrant entrepreneurs discussed in this book. The trait of having "one face, many masks" comes with the mobile nature of their life. Their experiences in business show that there is a certain connection between one's success in business and how one is identified with. The ability to shift identities constitutes some latent and yet substantial managerial resource for these immigrant entrepreneurs, which has a curiously ingenious function to perform in cross-regional corporate management. In the early days of an enterprise, when business had to be accumulated bit by bit through individual visits to potential clients, such identity alteration or alternation was practically important in shortening the psychological distance between each other.

---

[6] Chan Kwok-bun and Tong Chee-kiong, 'Yi zhang liankong, duo ge mianju: Xinjiapo huaren de shenfen rentong wenti' ['One Face, Many Masks: Singaporean Chinese Identities'] in *Mingbao Yuekan* [Mingpao Monthly], September (1999), pp. 20–123.

[7] Chan Kwok-bun, 'Shi gen, xun gen, chong gen: Fansi haiwai Huaren shijie zhuyi xin shenfen' ['Unrootedness, Root-Searching, and Multiple-Rootedness: Reflections on Overseas Chinese Identity and Cosmopolitism'], *Mingpao Monthly*, September (1999), p. 19.

Business bit by bit

> In mainland China, you need to go from shop to shop promoting your business. (Ngai)

> Half of my clients in Shenzhen came through my assistant's contacts. I got the other half by making cold visits. (Lok)

> We first managed to obtain addresses of toy factories from the local Commercial Management Bureau. Then we went on individual visits to those factories with our cloth samples, door to door … you had to pay individual visits. (Chiu)

> My problem was that I didn't have my own network. Then I'd have to build my own. I did that in two ways: on the Internet or by cold visits. Both take time and patience. (Kei)

The function of "interpersonal networks" has been much flaunted and even exaggerated in many studies of corporate management. Yet, apart from exploring the benefit it brings, studies of a corporate manager's social network must also pay attention to its actual daily operation. Our informants' businesses vary in size, with their staff ranging from a handful to thousands. They have come from a medley of different fields that range from computer fittings, pesticide services to toy and garment manufacturing. All of them, however, have stressed "door-to-door promotions" and "individual cold visits" as an important access to business opportunities, especially in the early days when one had to depend on hard work to survive. These "door-to-door" visits were to our entrepreneurs what field research is to anthropologists in the sense that these business people needed to analyse, like an anthropologist with his scientific seriousness, their objects, trying to understand their needs and fathom out their "humanness", so as to come up with effective communication strategies:

> If in any way I was to be thought of as 'successful', it would be because I can talk to anybody. I learned to talk in life. I like to 'read' people's minds, whoever they are. I like to think, but not in a bad way. I just enjoy knowing more about a person. (Siu)

> The most powerful network as I see it must be the computer network, because in this network you can transcend different boundaries. You can, for instance, get into contact any time with buyers from all over the world … But the computer network is only a platform where you get to know more about someone. So first impressions are very important. In cyberspace, people no longer care where you're from as long as you can get along. In this case, you need to be special. (Kei)

Self-complacent in her own way, Siu is considered by her friends to be the sociable kind. She calls herself a "mind-reader" and says she can talk to anybody, which has helped secure many business opportunities. Kei, before he set up his own business, was a computer technician. In the early days of his adventure, he had no business network of his own. This, coupled with his limited money, made things worse for this new starter. Kei is well aware that in this age of global cybernation, the computer network has become the most efficient cross-national and cross-regional communication platform. Yet business, Kei realises, is always done with human beings rather than with machines. So to establish business relations with a client thousands of miles away, the two parties must first of all get to know each other as "human beings" and show what is "special" about themselves as "human beings". It is not until they become friends that a business relationship can be properly established.

Having the "right people"

An old Chinese saying says that success has to depend on "right timing, right places, and right people" (*tian shi, di li, ren he*). This, we believe, applies to business. While "time" and "place" are quite often beyond human control, the "right people", in business, is a factor that can be "put together" through human work. The immigrant entrepreneurs that we interviewed, compared to those without immigrant experiences, are generally more capable of pulling together the "right people" to their own advantage. The diversity of their business locations has allowed them to access social networks in different places, as they travel in and out of different spatial configurations, circuiting between their birth place, their business locations and their new home. Such are our informants, valiant wayfarers whose life, time and energy are "sectionalised" into various localities. Their actual life experiences in all these places have enabled them to invoke and assume sets of "shared local symbols" – speaking the same dialects, having common identities, experiences or memories, etc. – as they interact with people in different places and on different occasions. These local symbols, being pleasurable traits of belonging, constitute a kind of intrinsic attraction that is conducive to the construction of congenial social networks for corporate management:

> Whenever I'm in Beijing, people always ask whether I've lived there for a long time, because I speak Putonghua just like the locals. In Hong Kong, my clients normally don't believe that I'm a mainlander, because I don't speak Cantonese with a typical mainlander's accent. When I talked with my former Fukien teachers, they were amazed at my fluent Hokkien. I've been living in different places, assuming different identities and mastering different languages and dialects – all this has made it easy for me to communicate with different people ... My knowledge of different dialects has given me a great competitive edge, because good relations quite often come with a shared language. (Yam)

> The government of my home town sent a delegation to Hong Kong a while ago, dropping by at our native place association. There were the local Communist Party secretary and other VIPs, lots of people. We sat together and started to chatter ... We treated these people to dinner, including the Secretary and the town bailiff; and they treated us in return. The chat over food covered diverse topics. We got introduced to one another, identifying the villages that we each were from, the schools we attended. We talked about the problems back home. We talked about what was happening here in Hong Kong. It was an endless exchange. Though we had come from the same town, each of us had so much to say about ourselves. (Yue)

Yam is a glass trader, having to travel extensively on the Chinese mainland, entertaining suppliers in different places. In contrast to other business people from Hong Kong, his language competence has proved to be an absolute advantage. Born in Indonesia, Yam grew up in Fujian to be a fluent Hokkien speaker. In Hong Kong, he attended a so-called "leftist school", where the major enrolment was new immigrant children and most of the teaching staff were from the mainland. When Putonghua was virtually extinct in other local schools, Yam improved his with the help of the teachers from the mainland, and he also managed to pick up Cantonese. In addition, being in the glass business, Yam has to travel frequently to the north of China, where glass factories are concentrated. On his visits to more than 600 factories, he came to know so much about the northern character and the northern ways of communication that he is able to assume the identity of a native Beijinger when he encounters one, or a Fujianese, or a Hongkonger for that matter. Yam's language abilities have been an important source of capital. Compared to other Hong Kong business people who barely speak Putonghua, Yam's proficiency in Putonghua and other dialects has proved to be a great advantage when dealing with the local authorities – a common tongue works its magic in enhancing business partnerships.

Yue runs his printing factories. As an active member of the Fujian Native Association, which has funded the building of a large of number of schools at home, Yue has to travel back to Fujian on a regular basis to attend various activities. Because of this, he is able to keep himself updated with the latest happenings in Fujian, although tremendous changes have swept across both urban and rural China since he moved to Hong Kong at the age of 13. These frequent trips home have enabled Yue to come up with authentic "local" topics when dealing with local government officials. In Hong Kong, he talks with visiting officials from his native place about "our village", about "the schools we attended" and about "what was happening in our town". Chitchat of this kind undoubtedly draws the two sides closer in a psychological sense, helping them to position themselves in relation to each other. In a society like China where *guanxi* plays a central role in social life, *guanxi* largely determines how one is going to be associated with another, since people tend to treat others differently as their *guanxi* differs. If the *guanxi* is oriented such that the two sides view each other as "one of us", they will feel more obliged to help when needed. Many of the important people in the Fujian Native Association have returned to their native place to invest, facilitated by the local government, setting up factories, trading companies and farms. Like other immigrant entrepreneurs, Yue has acquired, in his constantly mobile life, an assortment of local knowledge which has greatly enriched his conversations with others and helped in constructing various local networks that are beneficial to corporate management.

To mask oneself as an "insider" in the establishment of a business relationship, one needs to construct certain discursive contexts. This can be the shifting of language, from Cantonese to a shared native tongue, for example. It could also be a change in the form of address, *Dage* or *Xiaodi* (lit. "Big Brother" or "Little Brother", with more of a touch of fraternal affection) while they are by no means related; or *Laoshi* (lit. "teacher", a respectful title for any senior) when there is no teacher-student relationship between them. An identity such as this, that comes with the shift in discursive contexts, is intended to transform and enhance an existing, general relationship which one deems usable. The utilitarianism manifest in this kind of self-identity bespeaks a hope to incorporate an unrelated "other" into one's emotional composition. From this amalgamation of utilitarianism and emotion emerges a heterogeneous relationship[8] which, once established, serves to stabilise and perpetuate the existing rapports with the help of such "emergent properties" as trust and commitment that come from the two parties' joint actions.[9]

---

[8] K.K. Huang, 'Renqing yu mianzi: Zhongguoren de quanli youxi' ['Feelings and Faces: Power Games Among the Chinese'], in K.S. Yang, ed. *Zhongguoren de xinli* [The Chinese Psychology] (Taipei: Laureate, 1989), p. 289–317.

[9] Peter Blau, *Exhange and Power in Social Life* (New York: Wiley, 1964).

Mobility and local wisdom

The immigrant entrepreneurial enterprise is essentially an "adventure" in its truest sense. In embarking on this difficult adventure into different business terrains, they cast their lives adrift in a state of unpredictable mobility and assume "one face" and "many masks". This attribute has made them highly adaptable masters of various cultures and local dialects, capable of shifting among languages, mannerisms and even appearances as their objects of interaction vary. They are like "cultural chameleons"[10] that can modify their behaviour to fit in wherever they are by quickly obtaining recognition from those around.

With a diversity of authentic life experiences, these "mobile" immigrant entrepreneurs are more acutely sensitive than others to certain local cultures and local ways of life. This penetrative understanding constitutes what Pollock and Van Reken call a "3-D view of the world"[11] that enables these entrepreneurs to better communicate with clients from different countries. This is precisely what gives them a competitive edge over the less-than-mobile business people:

> Our neighbouring factories had offered similar quotes, but one of the reasons why the client eventually decided to stay with us was that, as clients, they were more concerned about whether their requirements were understood and whether they themselves were understood. This is very important ... I think we could talk because I had stayed in their place for some time and I could look at things from their perspective. In other words, there wasn't much of a cultural gap between us. After I started this business, I came to realise that people from different places can have totally different views of a product ... As I lived there before, it's easier for me to understand what they really are talking about so that I can avoid misunderstandings. (Chai)
>
> Each time I go on a work trip I take along a pair of sneakers. When the day's work is finished I will change to casual wear and the sneakers and walk around. I'm curious about things. I like to see and experience the local things. That's why I don't normally eat Chinese food when I go abroad. You won't do well in business until you have experienced the local ways of life and understood the local needs. A lot of people in China are trying to do business with Britons, when they themselves have never been to the UK. How can you establish a long-term relationship with someone, anyone, without knowing about their life ... As business people, we need to travel around more. This will give access to more market information and to the local wisdom. We can become less biased and more tolerant when we know more about others. (Yam)

Chai and Yam are engaged in totally different businesses. One a garment manufacturer, the other a trader of glass products. Both, however, have stayed in the UK for a period of time, an experience which has served to minimise the cultural differences between them and their overseas clients. In Chai's case, while not offering a competitive quote, she proved better at communicating with clients thanks to her overseas experience, which made her aware of "what the client was looking for", thus "making things easier". Each time Yam goes abroad to visit his clients, he takes time to walk around, getting to know the local ways, experiencing the local cultures.

---

[10] David Pollock and Ruth Van Reken, *Third Culture Kids: The Experience of Growing Up Among Worlds* (Nicholas Brealey: Intercultural Press Inc., 2001). 'Intercultural kids' refers to those children or young people who accompany their parents on foreign assignments.

[11] David Pollock and Ruth Van Reken, *Third Culture Kids*, p. 84.

As Yam sees it, in order to sustain a long-term cooperative relationship with a client, one needs to acquire some "local knowledge" of the community in which the clients live. Such "local knowledge" is essential for the construction of a multi-layered sense of identity that will help shorten the psychological distance between one's client and oneself, thus making the operation possible.

A Double-edged sword: The pain and frustration of nomads

(a) Weariness

On a theoretical level, studies of mobility have shed light on and reconstructed the positive relationship between the mobility of people and their interpersonal networks. The cases of our informants have provided us with detailed life materials to "flesh out" that theoretical framework. The existing studies, however, have fundamentally focused on the advantages of mobility and largely ignored its negative sides, which persist nevertheless and bring about all kinds of pain and frustration:

> You feel weary when you travel around too much. Not in the physical sense. Mentally you feel even more burdened, since you're always in a hurry … You feel like, gosh, I'm burnt out. Are you really that tired, though? You're just sitting there, waiting to go through customs. But you feel truly exhausted in the mental sense … You didn't really feel that way when you started, but the weariness has accumulated, as you do the same thing day in, day out, year in, year out. Then you feel mentally exhausted. (Chin)

> A life like this [circuiting between Hong Kong and the Fujian factories] is tiring enough. The weariness was most intense in the early days. But I knew I had to travel like this. Each time I came back from a trip, it would take a week for my life to go back to normal. The trips totally messed up the regular pattern of my life. All kinds of stuff would have heaped up at home. On top of the accumulated housework and laundry, there would be what was left undone at work, which was now very difficult to follow after you had left it aside for a while. It would take a week for me to get everything back to normal, before I could do shopping and lunch with my friends. I felt really bad those days. The mere idea of it just put me off. (Chai)

There is an age difference of 30 years between Chin and Chai. Yet their perennial shuttling among different places has left both the younger Chai and the older Chin feeling "wearied" and "exhausted". Such a back-and-forth way of life is by no means easy for these business people, whose energy is not inexhaustible. This life may appear easy because it is basically about "going through customs" and "taking a few trains or buses or aeroplanes", but the mental stress it brings is not readily comprehensible for the onlooker. Toiling around various business locations, these circuit entrepreneurs are seldom found unloading this stress onto others.

(b) Self-estrangement

The instability of our immigrant entrepreneurs' "nomadic roaming" inevitably disrupts their daily lives, which instead of displaying a linear continuity are punctuated with inconsistencies. In the words of Chai, the regular pattern of her life is entirely "messed up". Indeed, for these tenders of multi-regional businesses, life is unavoidably torn between different places. The disruption of life's regularity is not only a source of immense mental and physical stress, but also induces in these "shuttling nomads" a sense of self-estrangement:

> There is not so much of a home in my heart. It's alright as long as my family is doing well. My native place, Hong Kong, and my work places all have their respective emotional appeals, but none has had as much of a draw on me as home. Deep down, I feel 'rootless'. The native place now appears so distant, because I have been away for so many years; the work places haven't had much of a grip on my heart either. I'm ready to settle for where my family can enjoy themselves. (Chuk)

> I don't feel I have a home. Where is my home? I come back to Hong Kong to my 'house', but that is not home. It's only my house. Home should be a cosy place ... Hong Kong is no home. So where is home? ... A home should consist of not only you, but all those around you. The house where my grandparents lived was my ancestral home. The whole village knew each other. But now, when I go back, the home folks know me but I know nothing about them. Would you still call it home? I used to be so familiar with each of its trees, each of its lanes. But now I get lost in it. (Ngai)

These business people, who spend most of their time travelling, have learned to make themselves at home wherever they are while feeling "both there and not there". They circuit from place to place, knowing a great deal about each one, but none has a particular draw and they simply feel estranged. For the folks back home, these returning natives seem to be "one of us" yet at the same time are different. The difference alienates them. Perpetually suspended between being "inside" and "outside", these mobile business people are frustrated by their rootlessness.

Immigrant entrepreneurs are also often perplexed and plagued by a sense of self-estrangement. In an age of convenient, efficient and speedy transport, they may still be among the metropolitan hustle and bustle of Hong Kong in the morning and find themselves in an industrial city on the mainland of China in the afternoon. Such a mobile mode of life requires them to shift between languages and ways of speaking, and even change the way they look:

> At this very moment, I feel like I'm a Hongkonger. It depends, of course, on who you're talking with. (Lok)

> When we work together we mainly speak Putonghua. They (the partners on the mainland) will not speak Hokkien to me. I like to think I'm one of them, being fellow Fujianese people. Plus, we got to know each other through some relatives of mine. But they don't think this way. They tend to treat me as a Hong Konger ... In fact, when I was negotiating with them, I also considered myself a Hong Kong businessman ... You gotta identify yourself differently in different places so as to develop more trust for each other ... It all depends on what you need. (Kam)

Like a chameleon who plays to a gallery, an immigrant entrepreneur can be a Hongkonger, a Fujianese, or anybody else at different times as they come into contact with different people. As immigrant entrepreneurs change their masks, they are allowed no transition period, which means they have to adapt themselves instantly to the new persona. This power of swift adaptation inevitably makes those around them suspicious of their sincerity. David Pollock and Ruth Van Reken's study of children who accompany their parents on foreign assignments (referred to as "third culture kids") shows that this particular group has in a similar way aroused the suspicion of others: as they swiftly change their masks, their cultural value is increasingly being labelled as ambiguous, so much so that whatever they do or say is seen as dubious, underlined with no personal faith.[12] Immigrant entrepreneurs, in their frequent changes of personal style as they travel in and out of various cultural practices and modes of behaviour, are often objects of dual suspicion. On the one hand, their authenticity is often suspected by those around them, who doubt whether outwardly they are just putting up a facade. On the other hand, immigrant entrepreneurs themselves are growing unsure and skeptical about their own system of values. They feel they are losing themselves, not knowing who they are. This kind of self-estrangement, or sense of being a stranger to oneself, is the source of their deep-rooted distress, which is not readily perceptible by others, neither understood nor sympathised with, even by their families. To overcome the distress, they put all of their energy and strength into their businesses, the very light of their life. The businessman in his most "ambitious" mood is possibly the most alienated from himself, when he is divorced from his own personal emotions.

(c) Strangers

In relation to their families, immigrant entrepreneurs cannot but live in alternate reunion and separation. Their family life is never "complete" in the ordinary sense. The ever-intense market competition is quite often a competition against time, when the days scurry past and family life turns out to be mere luxury:

> My mom came with us to Hong Kong, stayed here for some time and returned to the mainland to continue her business ... They [my parents] had thus been separated for a long time, living their own lives ... For me, the result of such a family life in separation is that I came to feel less close to my mom ... We no longer have much to talk about. It's not that we're not getting along. We do. It's just that we no longer talk as much. We no longer confide in each other, we no longer go shopping together, we no longer give each other advice on make-up or anything. We no longer do the usual stuff that other moms and daughters do together. I don't even talk to her about my relationships, and she never gets to know any of my friends. This is a real pity. I've always envied others having their mothers cook for them, take care of them. They may find their moms annoying, but I just wish I had my mom living with me. (Chai)

> On average, I stay in Hong Kong for one or two days each week. Sometimes more, sometimes less ... When I'm back, I usually stay with my family. My time is just that little. I have to see my kid and my husband, for as long as possible and then I need to go again. That's it ... I've been too busy. (Lee)

Hustling to different places as they try to take care of their businesses and their family, our immigrant entrepreneurs often feel helpless. For most of the year, husbands and wives, parents and children, like in the case of Chai, are forced apart, "living their own lives", getting together only for as long as business allows. Lee's child is only two. She has to hire a domestic worker to take care of the housework. Each Saturday she tries her best to come back from Dongguan, where her factory is, to see her husband and child. But sometimes problems in the business keep her from coming home. On the day of our interview she had just arrived home, but then a

[12] David Pollock and Ruth Van Reken, *Third Culture Kids*.

factory emergency forced her to leave again. The next day, after spending some time with her child, she went straight back to the factory.

Separation is involuntary and lonely. Yet when they finally get together, reunion can be no happier than separation. In the minds of the children who have been living away from their parents, the image of the absent parent is often a blur. This somehow estranges the children and their parents, "not that we're not getting along. We do. It's just that we no longer talk as much". These business people fight against all odds, coping with all sorts of stress and distress, toiling and straining themselves, just to "make life better for their family". In fact, when they come home from work, it occurs to them that what their children actually want is their mother at home cooking their favourite food and their father there playing with them in the park. The spouses of business people (mostly men) are often frustrated to find themselves sharing their bed with a stranger. Separation has kept their spouses ignorant of the adversities in business or of the reality of their daily life. The widespread reportage in the media of Hong Kong businessmen having mistresses on the mainland has made their spouses generally suspicious of their husbands. While we were not able to conduct interviews with our entrepreneurs' wives, conversations in private have found the ladies distinctly resentful at and suspicious of their men. Some of the women suspect their men are already having an affair and feel they have to treat it as if nothing has happened, as long as no evidence surfaces.

The children find their dad a stranger as he is always away. The wife finds her husband a stranger because he seems to have given himself solely to the struggles in business. The local people find their boss a mere businessman who has come for money, because business people, a group supposedly with no genuine sense of belonging, are expected to be where money is. The businessman, being a stranger in the eyes of others, will also find the others inscrutably distant. Between himself and them, there are gaps of varying sizes. What this sense of estrangement brings is an inexplicable fear that comes with the unease and frustration of being rejected. We have seen the glorious side of successful business people, but there is a price to pay, we are reminded, for that glory at the cost of personal feelings which are as unredeemable as they are invaluable. But have these business people ever had sympathisers?

Encountering the un/real

The business field is a battlefield, where business people are tempered in deception and dishonesty. As a result, they are always instinctively following opportunities, so much so that they never come to fully enjoy the pleasure of interacting with the so-called "insiders" (*ziji ren*). Instead, they are always in search of opportunities, trying to see who could make the best partner in business:

> It's most lucrative selling paintings and calligraphy works. I made handsome money out of that. My sister knew of some Hong Kong companies that demanded paintings and calligrapy. So I began to collect such works on the mainland and then have these works sold to Hong Kong. This brought a substantial middleman margin, ranging from tens to hundreds of thousands ... These items had largely come from my connections in Chinese artistic circles, some of whom were well-known painters and calligraphers. These people would

often let her have their works for very little money or even for free. These friends were my invisible capital … My latest business was introduced to me by a former classmate at university … The first social network I mobilised was Guangzhou and around Shenzhen. I had many of the people around me buy our products. Only three of my Hong Kong connections became my clients, after they agreed to visit me in Shenzhen. Now I'm trying to mobilise my connections in Xi'an. (Siu)

You need to always be on the alert when you're doing business on the mainland. Many of these people won't tell you anything about their personal background. When asked, they'll simply gloss over it. Doing business is basically about mutual deception … To mince no words, it's all about making use of each other. It's like that in every business. Say this guy's got all the source suppliers and construction teams, but I've got the orders. Then he'll feel that he won't get his hands on greater profits or that his business won't be secured in any way, unless he has established a special relationship with me. Now you see that it's all about resources sharing and exchange. (Yee)

Siu's most lucrative business was in paintings and calligraphy works. She would acquire works from her connections on the mainland for very little money and then sell them to Hong Kong companies at fairly high prices. Such a substantial middleman margin came as a result of making use of people as "friends". Through his own experiences, Yee has realised that doing business is basically about "mutual deception", about "making use of each other"; that the ultimate incentive behind a business relationship is to strike a good deal. A businessman's job is round the clock, meaning that unlike the ordinary employee they must have their business on their mind every moment of the day. For the businessman, life and work are intermingled. Driven by his professional instinct, the businessman is always consciously or unconsciously seeking to mobilise his connections, be they family members, relatives, friends, former schoolmates, native folks or colleagues, in order to attain his goals, thus turning purely emotional bonds to utilitarian calculations. He has utilised his relationships to such an extent that it becomes difficult to tell whether what he does is out of purely personal feelings or out of calculations of profit. There are often merciless consequences to this non-distinction of the real and the unreal: people come to have a great mistrust or dislike for the businessman and some even deliberately distance themselves from him.

It is generally believed that the friends one makes in business are not real friends since there are no emotional ties. A businessman quite often feels isolated from his old friends. "Who are my real friends?" he wonders on one solitary night, as he is seized by fits of loneliness and helplessness. In the media, however, business people are often portrayed as "resolute, staunch, unwavering and self-composed" professionals, when in fact they are internally and externally stressed as they brave the challenges and cope with the deceptions of dishonesty in business:

My family has been running this business for decades. But things and people are rather different now from before. I know this because I've been at the front line. No one knows this better than me. I'll try what I feel is right. This has given me quite a lot of pressure … We're all emotional beings! When you feel dejected, you gotta hide yourself. You must appear energetic, not only to cheer yourself up, but also cheer up the others. At any rate, you need to boost the morale. Then I'll hide up in my room and cry the bad mood away. (Chai)

While her family has been in the garment business for years with a solid base of clients, Chai is still particularly cautious, especially in such an ever-changing market, as she seeks to develop the business to which her parents have devoted their whole lives. Like other business people, Chai is far more stressed than the men she hires. Walking at the forefront of her business, she has to take care of her overseas clients while assisting her family in managing the factories. As a boss, she has to conceal all her concerns, worries and anxiety in front of her clients or staff. Her family, living away from her, are never able to offer timely comfort and consolation as problems arise. The pain that accompanies the inability to express oneself is unbearable. The professional that clients see, the leader that employers look up to, and the philanthropist that the public respect, are roles performed and sustained under tremendous stress. Such personal sacrifices the businessman considers worthwhile because his sole concern is for his family to "live better".

Family and Work: Sentiments and Swords

Personal emotions: Building and destroying

The role of the family or the extended family has been widely valued in studies of Chinese enterprises. In corporate management, the family as a major support for the entrepreneur, as the first source of capital and as a provider of inexpensive labour, has attracted the most attention for its practical function, which was emphasised lot aduring our interviews:

> I didn't start from all naught; I got all this from my father ... I mean, my father didn't start the company himself, but he gave me the money to start with ... Father's help in our businesses was mainly financial. It played a crucial role, especially during the hard times. (Chiu)

> My mom has been a tremendous help in my career. At each stage when there was a lack of money, she would offer to help. She's always there when I need help. (Lee)

Chiu's ten factories are now quite sizable, employing more than 4,000 people. Chiu gives the credit to his father, whose assistance "played a crucial role". The father has offered the most timely support in the hardest of times, which ultimately put the business back on track and enabled it to develop further. The shoe factory that Lee manages was founded by herself alone, and it now hires about 150 workers. As early as 1988, when she had just finished high school, she was already doing business with her mother. In 1994, Lee left Jilin for Guangdong, where she was to establish the shoe factory she is still running today. After more than 10 years, Lee feels the most challenging part of her business is the factory's management, of which the biggest headache has been the problem of capital turnover. Fortunately, at each stage "when there was a lack of money", her mother was there to help.

The practical and economic function of the family and the extended family has been repeatedly highlighted in studies of Chinese enterprises. They have commonly adopted a functionalist approach to the family, whose powerful economic function is built upon the blood-based identity of being "one of us" (*ziji ren*), a identity that is being constantly constructed and strengthened by society to such an extent that a strong sense of ethical responsibility is internalised, urging family members to offer financial assistance when "one of them" is having a problem in business. Few studies, however, have analysed the function of the family from the perspective of "feelings". Organisations based on blood relations or geographical relations, such as "native place associations" (*tongxiang hui*) and "clan associations" (*zongqin hui*), are to a certain extent important sources of financial support. The family, apart from functioning as an automatic teller machine, is more significantly a source of positive emotional support. Indeed, the rapports between families, between the family and the individual, have often evolved around personal "feelings". The family is where individual feelings are found most intensely concentrated; and individual feelings, in turn, constitute the core of the family structure. To truly understand the "family", whether on the individual or the corporate level, one must not neglect the influence of "feelings". During the interviews, our informants made as much mention of their family's "emotional" support as their financial assistance:

> I don't usually talk to others about my problems except to my mother. That's because she's been a great help all along … She has given me tremendous support, whether in my personal feelings or in work. She's been standing behind me since I was very small. (Lee)

> My wife is fluent in a number of foreign languages. She's very smart. Now I'm doing business with her. She's been so unstintingly supportive. Emotionally she's been an important support. (Yam)

> I wouldn't have made it had it not been for my wife's support. (Yue)

> Since I started my business, my family's support has been the only reason I held out till now. (Kei)

Invincible as they appear, these business people, being flesh and blood, when faced with the hardship and challenges in business, do sometimes feel bogged down and helpless – there are, moments of vulnerability. The stress can be particularly huge in the early days of their business. In such cases, whether a business can survive the challenges and difficulties is largely dependent on the entrepreneur's will power and how he manages his own emotions:

> The failure of a business is often the result of the boss's inability to cope with stress. As a boss, one has to bear an awful lot of pressure. So EQ management is very important. If you have a poor EQ, then it's most likely that you'll sulk every minute of the day. You may easily get provoked or feel pressurised by the most trivial matters, which can turn out to be disastrous. (Chai)

> Since I started this business, there have been few times that I felt truly anxious. But since the future is never certain, you never feel assured. In those beginning days, the company was still very small in size and there was little management work to do. Then you'd have to take everything on your own shoulders. (Lok)

Indeed, as a boss, one bears tremendous pressure; one is daily anxious about the development of one's business; and one jitters over "what might be looming ahead". As Chai sees it, the success of a business is directly related to one's ability to cope with stress. The Chinese say, "One never fails but collapses" (*bing bai ru shan dao*). If one fails in coping with stress and in managing one's mood, one collapses like a soldier in war because one's will has failed. In the face of stress, the family's support and consolation play a particularly positive role in helping one adjust one's mood, telling one to persist. In addition, in contrast to the deception and dishonesty that one finds in business, the family's loyalty undoubtedly gives a sense of security. While this does not mean there is always harmony and understanding in the house, there is at least one reason to hold out – one cannot collapse, because of the loved ones.

Just as the family's emotional support enables one to overcome the difficulties and challenges in business, so is one's emotional input in the management process conducive to corporate success. This is particularly true when the business is still seeking to expand, for in order to motivate the staff to devote themselves to the factory, there must be some kind of emotional commitment between the boss and his men:

> I love my work, and I love the kids (the workers) in my factory … I adore them … I feel blessed because whenever a problem comes up, they're always there to give a hand. This is because I've been willing to help too when they get into problems. Now everybody will take the factory's problems as their own problems and are willing to work hard together for solutions. I think I've been right to have treated them as my own kids … This, I think, is pretty effective management. I call it 'heart-for-heart' management. (Lee)

> For a business to prosper, the boss must take a humanistic approach to management, that is, manage according to human nature. (Wing)

Both transactions and management evolve around "humans". One's success in business is largely related to one's relationship with one's clients, buyers, workers, suppliers, etc. To establish good relationships and to ensure that one's factory is doing well, one has to, in Wing's words, be "humanistic" and "manage according to humanism". Lee's factory currently hires about 150 people. She tends to treat young workers from other places as her own children. Her management philosophy is that one has to give one's heart for the heart of others. Thus, apart from the practical relationship of employment between Lee and her workers, they get along with an emotional commitment to each other. In fact, Lee's proves to be an excellent managerial strategy. Many of her employees have "come for a better life" from the economically deprived provinces. In the reality of the drastic urban-rural differences, rampant discrimination has driven home to these people that, once away from home, they have become "worthless". Being immigrants themselves and having experienced the mental impact of being away from home, immigrant entrepreneurs like Lee are more acutely aware of the psychological demands of being a "home-leaver" than the usual business people. The "emotional" ties are powerful, therefore, that bind them together with their home-leaving workers. Being home-leavers themselves, immigrant entrepreneurs have developed a stronger psychological attachment to the factories they have toiled to sustain, taking their factories as their homes, their workers as their "comrades", or fellow fighters, that share their life as work and work as life. The power of emotion is so great that it internalises the company's expectations as self-imposed demands on the workers themselves, pushing them to work harder and be loyal to their boss and company.

Just as "emotional affiliation" can play a positive role in the management of a business, so can it hamper or even destroy what a businessman has toiled to establish. Current studies of this negative aspect have focused on family businesses. Wong Siu Lun's survey of Hong Kong textile industrialists has shown that, in a family business, the use of one's relatives in the management can put the business in jeopardy.[13] Likewise, studies of overseas Chinese business people have revealed that, within a family business, rivalry and disharmony often arise among different interest groups.[14] Most of the businesses we surveyed are SMEs (small and medium enterprises), which have been the result of years of our immigrant entrepreneurs' work. The survival of these businesses, particularly during the pioneering days, has relied primarily on the exploitation of the so-called "insiders" (*ziji ren*) who ungrudgingly provided low-paid or even free labour. Quite often, when the enterprise came on track, these early "trail-blazers" began to lag behind the times and, failing to follow the enterprise's development, became less competent managers. Even if they are not performing up to par, however, these family members and relatives stay in the company because their early contributions made their boss feel obliged to keep them. Feelings have got in the way of decisions:

> Most of the people in management are friends and relatives. We decided who to hire, of course, but the decision was often related to [the company's] history ... By all means, this has proved to be a managerial challenge ... Once these friends and relatives were hired, they would only be re-located to other departments if they were later found unsuitable, unlike the openly employed staff, who will be fired instead ... Now we don't normally hire people from the home town. There are only a couple of them still working in our factory. They have been here since the 1980s, when we just started. So we have kept them all along. (Chiu)

> In the early days, most of the workers were from the home town. But as they worked on, they just couldn't keep up. These native folks were not very competent in general. Not educated. Most of them have turned 40, 50 now ... But we don't normally lay them off even if they are less competent ... There is no way that you cannot make use of a person; it all depends on how you use him. (Chuk)

---

[13] Wong Siu Lun, *Emigrant Entrepreneurs: Shanghai Industrialists in Hong Kong* (Hong Kong: Oxford University Press, 1988).

[14] Wong Siu Lun, 'The Chinese Family Firm: A Model', *British Journal of Sociology*, 36 No.1 (1985), p. 58–72; Mary B. Rose, 'Beyond Buddenbrooks: The Family Firm and the Management of Succession in Nineteenth-Century Britain', in *Entrepreneurship, Networks and Modern Business*, eds., J. Brown and M.B. Rose (Manchester: Manchester University Press, 1993), p. 127–143; Edmund Terence Gomez and Michael Hsiao Hsin-Huang, 'Chinese Business Research in Southeast Asia', in *Chinese Business Research in Southeast Asia: Contesting Cultural Explanations, Researching Entrepreneurship*, eds., Edmund Terence Gomez and Michael Hsiao Hsin-Huang (Surrey, U.K.: Curzon Press, 2001), p. 1–37; S. Gordon Redding, *The Spirit of Chinese Capitalism* (Berlin: Walter de Gruyter, 1990).

If a relative is fired for incompetence, one has to bear a great deal of social pressure and could be denounced by other family members. The only option is to "keep the men and save the feelings". When the relatives fail to do their job in one department, they are usually re-located to another. About the inadequate performance of these "fellow fighters" who blazed the trail with him, Chuk explains, "There is no way you cannot make use of a person; it all depends on how you use him". For a businessman who struggles in a world fraught with deception, the "loyalty" of those on his side is irreplaceable. But this emotional value judgment not only prevents the enterprise from becoming standardised and systematised, it hampers its overall development:

> I have no idea about their (my business partners') backgrounds ... Our good fellowship has made up for all that's missing between us. I never really assessed our partnership or investigated the market situation ... We are all from Fujian after all, and we got introduced to each other by relatives. So we felt like we were in the same boat and had trust in each other. (Kam)

> I got conned quite a number of times ... Later (in 1999) I got conned again ... It was a really bad experience. About HK$400,000 were swindled from us ... I had trusted this guy so much because he was friends with a friend of mine ... I had trusted him because he was also from Fujian ... We were put in a very embarrassing situation, because we got to know him through some very close friends ... We were just not cautious enough. (Wing)

Through his uncle on the mainland, Kam got to know two local "upstarts". While Kam did not know much about these people, he believed his uncle's contacts were reliable, as he was on very good terms with this uncle. He became partners with them, without knowing much about them, and started a company, which got into various problems after operating for just six months. Then Kam realised that, because he was seldom in Fujian, he was not able to supervise the company's operations, nor was he aware of the company's fiscal situation, so much so that the business was running entirely outside his control, despite the fact that he had invested all of his savings in it. When the problems became more serious, he decided to quit without even negotiating with his partners, giving up all the money he had invested. Kam felt that "money was a small issue" and it was more important to maintain his fellowship with these people, as they had been introduced by his uncle. Through a former schoolmate, Wing got to know a businessman from the mainland. He was a fellow Fujianese who had been introduced by an old friend, and Wing came to have total trust in him. He delegated him to take orders and develop business in the name of Wing's company. But the man worked against him, secretly selling the goods that other factories had left with them to offset payments, and embezzling all the proceeds.

Just as "water can both sustain and sink a ship", as the Chinese say, so the complication of personal feelings can both sustain and sink a business. On the Chinese market, where the business system is far from mature, business people, always on guard against possible fraud *out there*, are generally more willing to work with friends and relatives from the *inside*. Such an inclination exists, as James Coleman has observed, due to the existence of an intermediary entity which facilitates interactions between two parties who both trust this third party. The "trusted third party" as a mediator gives both parties the psychological assurance that helps to establish a successful partnership.[15] The involvement of personal feelings and the complication of interpersonal relationships in the management process can create relatively strong internal ethical restrictions, reminding one of the high social price one has to pay if one goes astray. Business partnerships among the Chinese are built not so much upon restrictive legal agreement as on this consensual ethical bonding, which has often led to a lack of supervision and control. Thus, the overdose of trust often results in the abuse of trust. Much as one values "credibility" between partners, in reality the most trustworthy can turn out to be the least reliable. In an age of intense mobility, as they circuit among their various business locations, travelling entrepreneurs have actually grown more dependent on their local partners than the single-location businessman. In such cases, travelling entrepreneurs will have to take immense risks if the partner's "credibility" is the only thing they can rely on when other supervisory organisms are absent.

On the other hand, the mobility of the day has invested more "mobile" qualities in our travelling entrepreneurs than in the ordinary businessman. They have diverse interpersonal networks in different places. In each place, they have an identity, a mask, that helps them break into the local business circle. For these "nomads", their highly mobile lifestyle decides that they cannot put all their time into one place and that their energy and emotions are bound to be divided. In the past, when life was far less mobile, people tended to have a strong emotional attachment and sense of belonging to the place where they were "born and bred". In this most mobile of times, however, business people may feel somewhat attached to each of their work-places but the emotions are never strong. This will weaken their affective and ethical bonding with the local people and local things, as compared with the previous, less mobile generations. The dispersal of affection has also made the immigrant business people relatively "callous". In the past, when people's emotional attachment and social networks were so concentrated, they would have an immense price to pay if they failed to live up to the expectations of their community. But now, with the multiple passports of their multiple identities, people can change their place of residence whenever they like. Under such circumstances, one's "ethical credibility", which is based on affection, may be easily abused. This has unavoidably put our travelling business people in a dilemma: while they are perfectly aware of the importance of "credibility" and are actually trying hard to build up their own, their lifestyle in this specific age has forged their personality in such a way that they are practically destroying the "credibility" they are working so hard to establish. The intensity of mobility has caused their affections and emotions to fade, making their "ethical credibility" brittle.

Travellers and non-travellers

At any rate, one needs to be positioned within one's times. In an age of intense mobility, the problems that individual business people encounter may speak very well of society as a whole. As we have shown, considerable research has been done by others

---

[15] James S. Coleman, *Foundations of Social Theory* (Cambridge, Mass.: Belknap Press of Harvard University Press, 1990).

on the inappropriate use of personnel as well as the rivalry and disharmony among different interest groups within family businesses. While the same problems, as our study shows, have extended into the Chinese family business in the new millennium, another outstanding issue has largely been neglected in existing literature, that is, the disagreement and conflicts between the family's travellers and non-travellers:

> From my perspective, if we are to continue with the business, we will have to take some risks as everybody does. But for my father, the stakes appear just too high. You didn't even meet your partner in person, he says, you just phoned each other and sent each other facsimiles and now you're gonna sign the contract and wire them the money. He feels it's too much of a risk. But I think the other way. How else can we go about it? This is business! We all take risks! (Chai)

In the family's division of labour, Chai "walks at the forefront" and takes care of their overseas clients' requests. While her family stay in Fujian taking care of the factory, Chai is basically stationed in Hong Kong, taking charge of the local office and having to travel between Hong Kong, Fujian, where their factory is, and other countries, where she is to visit their clients. Conflicts have often occurred between Chai and her parents during the course of managing this business. On the one hand, Chai tends to "go about it as others do" and thinks that as long as the risk is predictable, it will be worth taking. Her parents, on the other hand, consider this way of doing business "too risky" and not worth a try. But having lived and worked in many places and seen much of the world, Chai knows that there are other ways, and widely practiced ways, of doing business which may not be used by the Fujianese people nor even among Chinese companies in general. Her multi-regional experiences have undoubtedly widened her horizons and activated in her a pluralised mode of thinking, so much so that some of her ideas have struck her parents, who do not have overseas experience, as incomprehensible and even unacceptable. Indeed, the older generation of managers, intent on the "Chinese way of doing business", the older growth and management strategies that they believe have been proved effective over the decades, become defensive when their original beliefs are challenged:

> These [disputes over growth and management strategies] are not disputes that can be diluted in time. They will stay there until the older generation steps down. As long as they're involved, their influence is there. So it's essentially a question of whether they're willing to let their children take over. Now, everything has to be done with their consent. They will never say yes to what they think is risky ... So you don't really have much decision-making power. (Chai)

With her master's degree, Chai is the best-educated member of her family. Having lived abroad, she speaks fluent English and is familiar with the English culture, which has helped to reassure her clients. In fact, many of the company's new clients were found by Chai and their Hong Kong staff. Yet in a family business, authority, rather than coming down to one's competence, still lies in one's status in the family. The older generation, unless they "step down" or "let their children take over", will continue to hold control over the company, when "everything has to be exercised with their consent".

The family, just like any other social organisation, is fraught with politics and power struggles that involve many factors. While much eulogised as a harmonious cosy nest, the family, the Chinese family in particular, is in fact the most stratified social unit. Far from being free of discord and conflict as it is idealistically portrayed, the Chinese family operates on a clearly differentiated power structure, in which each member is required to stay within his or her specific role. Having experienced diverse cultures, ideologies and values in their roaming lives, the younger generation of managers' sense of value, their faith and dreams have experienced tectonic changes. As they travel to different places, these modern nomads have their own culture clashes and conflicts. Consequently they let go some of their old ideas and borrow new ones:

> I was a traditionalist in the way I viewed things. Now I'm beginning to unfetter myself. I feel I don't have to stay in this tradition, which is full of [undue] responsibilities and pressures. (Chai)

Looking back at her schooldays in the UK, Chai feels the experience was actually a tremendous shock. At the time, she was the only Asian student in her university dormitory, when all the others were Anglo-Europeans. Living and studying within this interracial community, Chai began to reflect on her own values and beliefs as she came to have more in-depth exchanges of ideas with students from different countries. When she finished her studies, she had also transformed herself and came out with entirely new ideas and expectations. Her family, however, remained in the original mode of thinking. Hence the conflicts:

> I was struggling a bit: Should I live up to the expectations of the folks back in Fujian or should I live my own life like Hongkongers do? The fact is: Once I'm back in Fujian in the company of my family, these questions will keep coming back to me. But when I'm back in Hong Kong, they'll be all gone. (Chai)

Quite often, tension develops between the traveller and the non-traveller, between change and fixedness. Whose expectations should one live up to? Should one be loyal to oneself or, putting on a mask, play the part expected by others? Such struggles are excruciating, but one cannot give vent to one's exasperation as it is, because in that case, disagreement and conflicts will arise:

> At that time, I was thinking to myself: now if my dream was to make my family happy, I was doing exactly the opposite. I just made them worry. There were so many things to tackle in our business, and that gave rise to a lot of conflicts between us … Consequently I was so perplexed: why am I doing all this? It really wasn't worth all this trouble. I was lost: what on earth have I done? Maybe I just couldn't find where my true values were. (Chai)

Originally she had wished to do something in return for her family and "make them happy", but once they had to work together, Chai discovered that what she was doing could actually go against what she was hoping for. Chai was perplexed and began to wonder where her "true values" were. She toiled every day for the family business, only to discover it did not seem to be worth it. More frustrating was that, when conflict erupted, there was never a sound mechanism for negotiation with her family. The only solution, it seemed, was to compromise:

> Now I've given up the idea of growing it (the family business). I'll only try to retain its clients, preserve its business, and stabilise its staff. I've given up the idea of expansion altogether. I no longer think about enlarging our recruitment or launching any plan to grow the business. (Chai)

A sensible mechanism is basically lacking for negotiation within a family when conflicts arise. The family business is a tyrannical business in which authority and status will have their sway. The only way Chai can cope with the frustration of such inherent conflicts is to settle for reality, adjust herself, compromise for the business's "stable" development, and give up any hope of expansion. Each family drama seems to have the same theme, "All for the good of the family". As society sets up role expectations for each of its members, the individual within a family internalises such social expectations as self-imposed ethical restrictions. As a result, the afflictions one suffers – exploitation, struggles, unfairness, agony, frustration and despair – all get dwarfed when compared with the "largeness" of the family's good. But what is "the good of the family"? According to whom? Who says? This is neither negotiated nor substantiated. Rather, only the *de facto* trustee of the business will be in a position to define it.

Life in anticipation

Faced with the restrictions of the family business, one only hopes to "break away" and establish one's own career. The future is now, and all the trouble taken today should pave the way to success. In anticipation of a better future, one learns to look at the present as a temporary drilling session that equips one for the days to come:

> Personally, I would like to do something I'd really like to do after this business has been stabilised. That is to say, when I can be away (from this family business), that is, when it can operate with no problem without me here, I will take time to develop my interest in other things. Or I might start another business. This is what I have in mind now. (Chai)

> When the company has made a fair amount of money, I'll start my own business … But I'd like to build a farm of my own in the future, to have everything in my charge. Now I'm helping my sister manage the company. I see this as a kind of training. I've learned a lot during my stay here on the mainland. Now I know everything about this business. (Ngai)

Both Chai and Ngai are running their family businesses, and both feel that their talents are being restricted. They feel ambivalent about their status. In front of their clients, they are the "bosses", and make decisions. At home, they are the juniors of the house, "fledglings" who have yet to grow. They have been forced to postpone their ambitions and plans and hold out until they can "break away" to develop their "interest in other things" or even to "start another business". They are convinced these dreams will come true and that the family business is giving them the kind of training important for their future "identity". Hope gives them power and lets them turn negative factors into positive ones.

A life of mobility gives the circuit entrepreneur access to more diverse information than it does the non-traveller. The comparison and contrast between places allow our traveller to develop better insight into the advantages of each place. For our travelling businessman, each place is lovely and ugly in its own way, each fulfilling him in some way and yet leaving him dissatisfied in others. His is a life in anticipation. And the hope for a better tomorrow is what motivates him to go further:

> I feel that I'll step beyond Asia and find a world of my own. I don't know where that world will be. It will have to depend on where my business takes me. (Ngai)

> My goal is to spread Chinese martial arts overseas with the help of Tian Hu (alias of a certain health product) … I'm hoping to take the Xi'an martial arts team to other countries. Tian Hu is a truly big platform, and I'm determined. (Siu)

Having experienced a multitude of cultures in such constant to-and-fro manuoeuvres, immigrant entrepreneurs, compared with ordinary people, are generally more imaginative and harbour more splendid dreams and expectations for the future. They are not satisfied about their current identity but are instead looking forward to their future selves. Ngai, for example, is not happy about his current identity and is seeking to find a world of his own, which, he envisages, will be the best place to develop his own career. Siu, on the other hand, aims to spread Chinese martial arts, of which she is an aficionado, to the rest of the world. Through co-operating with other companies, she seeks in particular to take the martial arts team of her hometown to other countries with the help of powerful corporations. The present, it appears to them, is never enough and always in want of something. It is precisely such anticipation of the future, of what will come next, that allows our immigrant entrepreneurs to be so fluid, that gives them a force putting them ever on the move. They are aware that all dreams lie in the future, when the future lies in the present – this is the very dynamo that pushes immigrant entrepreneurs to develop their business in multiple areas, not only in China, but beyond Asia, in the rest of the world. This is one of the fountainheads of globalisation, the very impetus to humanity's ceaseless exchanges and progress.

Summary

Mobility is vividly polymorphous. There is an intriguing story behind each incident of human mobility. Yet just as it brings us joy and pleasure, mobility also turns upon us with its woes and challenges. We have seen in our immigrant entrepreneurs an energetically positive relationship between mobility and entrepreneurship. These "new immigrants", having come from economically backward parts of China, carried so much hope in their hearts as they arrived in their new home. But their identity as "mainlanders" was always a negative label. On one hand, the prejudice and contempt from mainstream society brought them a great deal of frustration and bitterness. On the other hand, as "outsiders" to be excluded, they were confronted with a disadvantaged opportunity structure. With their English lagging behind and themselves being restricted to the much stigmatised "leftist schools", "new immigrant" kids were never able to make a name for themselves like the local children could do with a good education in this "elitist" society. Underlying their growth and success is a series of battles against unfair treatment from mainstream society: on one hand, they came to realise that, as "new immigrants", they would have to suffer more than others; on the other, they were ready to fight back, knowing they would never make it unless they went all out. So these new immigrants, having "failed" in school, decided to go into business, as the Chinese have done since pre-modern times. The "shame" imposed upon them by their "new immigrant" identity became what motivated them in life.

Various studies have praised the "diligent" and "hardworking" character of new immigrants, but they were not born with such a character, it was shaped by life's adversity. The "shame" they felt was exactly what goaded them into the pursuit of a new identity which would not be looked down upon, and that of a "boss" or an "entrepreneur", for example, is certainly something to be marvelled at.

The road to entrepreneurship is rugged. The personality transformations that come with early immigrant experience became a kind of essential cultural capital for corporate management. Their resolve, practicality and confidence have enabled immigrant entrepreneurs to persevere. Their shuttling lifestyle has also familiarised them with local wisdoms. Their mastery of local dialects/languages, knowledge of local customs and understanding of the local ways of business have transformed them into "cultural chameleons" that can invoke and assume different "shared local symbols" as they come to interact with different people. In so doing, they manage to shorten the psychological distance between each other, thus extending their interpersonal networks to facilitate corporate management and development. Having "one face" and "many masks" has proved to be an asset. In their to-and-fro movement between various clashes, exchanges and interactions, immigrant entrepreneurs have come to appreciate Lu Xun's quintessential "grabbism".[16] Their life and work experiences in different places have given them a pluralised mind and driven home to them that there are in fact diverse ways of tackling a problem. Indeed, by pluralising their solutions, entrepreneurs have successfully overcome different difficulties and challenges during the course of management. "The range of an individual person", Peter Berger aptly observes, "can be measured by the number of roles he is capable of playing".[17] And the range of performance for immigrant entrepreneurs understandably extends wider than the non-traveller, as they skillfully shift among their many identities and roles in multi-regional business operations.

Mobility, however, is a double-edged sword. Their intense mobility makes immigrant entrepreneurs the spokesmen of this nomadic lifestyle; what they have gone through and experienced in person testifies to the joys and agonies, fortunes and misadventures, of life. In this intense fluid mode of existence and perennial back-and-forth manoeuvres across space, immigrant entrepreneurs are not only fatigued but also plagued by a sense of self-estrangement and defamiliarisation. For these people, who are trapped in an intermittent circularity of coming and going, "home is everywhere and nowhere"; the places where they live and work, the people they see every day, are all familiar and yet distant. Perpetually suspended between being "inside" and "outside", they are afflicted with a sense of being a stranger to oneself, a rootless frustration which is not always perceptible to others, not understood nor sympathised with, even by their families.

---

[16] Lu Xun coined the term "grabbism" (*nalai zhuyi*) to encourage the appropriation of anything useful from the West (advanced thoughts and means of production, for instance), or the appropriation of best of any other countries for that matter, to develop China.

[17] Peter Berger, *Invitation to Sociology: A Humanistic Perspective* (Garden City, New York: Doubleday & Company, 1963), p. 105.

With their businesses and lives scattered about different places, immigrant entrepreneurs have found themselves racing against time and being torn between business and family. In their fight against time, in the ceaseless shuttling and selfless devotion to work, they lose control of themselves and temporarily forget that, emotionally, they are in limbo. Here, we see the ultimate conflation of life and work. "It is alright as long as my family is doing well" and "I'm only trying to make life better for my family" become the most often heard refrains in this intense mobility.[18] These are decent excuses indeed that rationalise all the indecent and inadequate – absence from parent meetings, birthday celebrations, lack of time for one's wife and children – because even debauchery can be counted as "courtesy" carried out "for the sake of the business, the company, and for the good of the family".

There is a price to pay for this frequency of social and business engagement, be it for the business, for the company, for the family's good, for better or worse. The absent husband/father gets marginalised in emotional terms: with the children distancing themselves and the wife growing suspicious, he becomes the stranger in the family. Our immigrant entrepreneur toils every day "for the good of the family" but may not be aware of the discrepancy between what he is trying to give and what his family truly want. The disruption of family life is the result of an endless see-saw between life and work, a battle which he both wins and losses. Torn and perplexed, he can only hope that concentrating on work will help drown their sorrows and worries.

In fact, the businessman not only feels distanced from his family for their lack of understanding and sympathy, but finds in himself a stranger as well, due to the "false self" that lurks inside him. Just as business practitioners are trained to keep their emotions in check in front of clients, so we are requested, in the course of socialisation, to act and speak in public according to the roles that are expected of us by society. Our feelings are, in other words, "managed feelings".[19] As he tends his business in different places, the immigrant entrepreneur's social networks become increasingly complicated, so much so that every day in and out of various social structures, he is living in a sophisticated fabric of affirmations and negations. Confronted by different social environments and power structures, he is compelled to make prompt judgements and evaluations of his object of interaction so as to assume the right identity, use the appropriate communication strategies, or even to change the way he communicates altogether. Because of the instabilities of this nomadic existence, the immigrant entrepreneur's authenticity often baffles and even appears dubious to those around him. As Arlie Russel Hochschild has pointed out, a professional actor will sometimes find it difficult to come out of the role he is playing and eventually the role becomes part of him without his even knowing it.[20] By the

---

[18] Chan Kwok-bun and Seet Chia-sing, 'Migration Family Drama Revisited: Mainland Chinese Immigrants in Singapore'. *Sojourn: Journal of Social Issues in Southeast Asia*, 18, No.2 (2003), pp. 171–200.

[19] Arlie Russel Hochschild, *The Managed Heart: Commercialization of Human Feeling* (Berkeley: University of California Press, 1983).

[20] *Ibid.*, p. 195.

same token, when day in and day out the businessman has to change his masks to different settings, like an actor who plays to a gallery, the "mask-changing" will become part of his life and character to such an extent that he confuses his true self and the role he plays, and he ultimately fails to "come out" of his camouflage even when he is with his family, his loved ones. As one is being plagued by one's sense of self-estrangement/defamiliarisation and baffled by one's very own inauthenticity, we come to realise that the price one has to pay for mobility is unquantifiable.

Home and work take up a large portion of one's life. We have given much credit to the positive functions of the businessman's family, and yet an understanding of its darker sides is yet to be achieved. For a researcher who seeks to explore the family's functions from the outside, what he can glean from the businessman's account will be nothing other than a glossed tale haunted by the storyteller's cautious attention to his own image. This is because people are inclined to portray theirs according to the "model family" flaunted by our social culture; and businessmen, not being an exception, will try their best to play R. D. Laing's "happy family game".[21] But behind the closed doors, in total contrast to the warmth and harmony that one feels from the outside, there may be a repertoire of conflicts, power struggles, even violence and pain.

Current studies of the family business have generally focused on the practical economic function of the family, and have largely neglected its emotional functions and even dysfunctions. For one thing, the immigrant entrepreneurs we interviewed have unanimously stressed the family's emotional support. The family as an individual's emotional anchorage differs from other social units for its significant involvement of personal sentiments. The complication of personal feelings into the management process, as we have shown, can both sustain and sink a business; and there is a fine line between growth and destruction. As far as the family business is concerned, while the family's dreams are what goads one to work and the family's good is what one strives for, the family could ironically be the first place one wishes to flee. In an age of intense mobility, conflicts within the family become ever more pluralised and complicated. In the past, the family used to live together, but in this most mobile of times, the family is forced to live apart. The gulf between the traveller and non-traveller is not only in space, but in ideology, emotions, and in the value system. As the traveller in his nomadic roaming lets go of some of his older self and incorporates new elements, he extends and enriches his own social imagination in this pursuit of new identities. Yet such self-transformation may not be readily understood, recognised or accepted by the people around him, hence the conflicts. While much eulogised in current studies as a model location of "self-sacrifice" and "infinite love", the family is in fact fraught with gender and generation politics, and shot through with the inevitable tension between the traveller (businessman) and the non-traveller (his or her family), between kindred sentiments and business analyses. When conflict erupts, there is no other solution than to compromise, "all for the good

[21] R. D. Laing, *The Politics of the Family and Other Essays* (New York: Vintage Books, 1972).

of the family".[22] Under the mammoth banner of the family, the dreams of the young are to give way to the authority of the old, and the wishes to grow the business have to yield to conservatism within the family. Such conflicts are, however, not altogether negative, as "all revolutions begin in the transformation of consciousness".[23] The minds of the travellers and non-travellers, younger and older generations, are undergoing a gradual transformation as the clashes spark a quiet revolution.

Man as an emotional animal cannot feel good when he comes into conflicts and clashes with others. In such circumstances, one can only hope for a better future, hoping that one day one will eventually break away from the family business, and from its "patronisation". The future is now, and the trouble one takes today should pave one's way to some splendid success tomorrow. The anticipation of a better future, the pursuit of a future identity, is what moves one ahead.

[22] Chan Kwok-bun and Seet Chia-sing, 'Migration Family Drama Revisited: Mainland Chinese Immigrants in Singapore'.

[23] Peter Berger, *Invitation to Sociology*, p. 136.

Conclusion

> *Sociology is the scientific study of the changes and transformations of a given society so as to know its whence and predict its whither. This study applies this specific discipline's principles to an exploration of the ebbs and flows of society to reveal the laws that govern its development.*
>
> – Yan Fu[1]

In the twenty-first century, we live in an intensely mobile and globalised world. The rapid advances in science, technology and mass transport have greatly compressed time and space, the dual dimensions of existence. The physical distance from city to city and from country to country has drastically diminished, extending the scope of people's movement and casting them adrift in a state of ever more frequent mobility. Such an intensely mobile life has become a global trend. Since ancient times, for entertainment, work and life, people have been shuttling between different places. Today, such centuries-old topics as "mobility" and "migrancy" are of renewed interest, and are now given a multitude of new meanings by historians, geographers, sociologists, psychologists, economists and political scientists alike. Each attempts to portray, understand and illuminate various social phenomena and facts, having examined their own social lives along with their respective traditions and through their respective professional lenses. Yet each of their lenses can scrutinise but a portion, not the whole, of reality. This explains the presence of all the myths and perplexities that complicate accounts of mobility and migrancy.

---

[1] Yan Fu, 'Yi "Qunxue siyan" xu' ['Preface to the Translation of *The Study of Sociology*'] in Herbert Spencer (trans. Yan Fu), *Qunxue siyan* [The Study of Sociology] (Shanghai: Commercial Press, 1925). C.f. Herbert Spencer, *The Study of Sociology* (London: Routledge/Thoemmes, 1996).

Chan Kwok-bun and Chan Wai-wan, *Mobile Chinese Entrepreneurs*,
International Series on Consumer Science, DOI 10.1007/978-1-4419-9643-5_8,

What is New?

Circuit entrepreneurs

In Chinese, *yimin* is a term that broadly encompasses the three types of people denoted by the English words "immigrant", "emigrant" and "migrant". Past studies have referred to overseas Chinese business people as "immigrant entrepreneurs", who migrated to other countries (Southeast and Euro-American countries for instance), settled down and started their own businesses (small, family-run shops in Chinatowns, for example) in their new homes. What is implied in the word "immigrant" here is in fact a kind of "disengagement". At least in theoretical terms, there are two aspects to such "disengagement": first, as these people left their original homes and moved to another country, they cut their ties to China; second, through a variety of administrative means and emotional pressure in their new home, they were quickly assimilated into the local society. The businessmen we studied and wrote about in this book, however, should perhaps not be called "immigrant entrepreneurs". It is not that they left China, immigrated to Hong Kong and stayed permanently here after having cut all ties to China and been assimilated into Hong Kong society. It is not that they did not cut ties: on the contrary, they have actively maintained and nurtured them – since or even before their departure from China. In fact, they went back to China, usually first to their hometown (or their parents' hometown), and then to other parts of China to set up factories and offices for different functions of their businesses. While in China, they set their sights on elsewhere in the world. They should instead be called "migrant entrepreneurs", with migrancy as a lifestyle, a personal preference, a psychological propensity – or perpetual mobility as a condition of post-modernity which bestows on the individual a personal advantage, a competency.

Migrant entrepreneurial experience is not a story with a definite ending. What migrant entrepreneurs go through is not a one-way process of being "uprooted" and "re-rooted". Rather, their migrant experiences are always in progress, manifest in their daily lives as a mobile, "to-and-fro" circuiting movement. In a world of "typical mobile, roaming hybrids", the migrant entrepreneur's life, instead of being bound to a certain land, is thrust into a shuttling mode of existence that accompanies the forward movement of globalisation. In this light, we would want to call these people "circuit entrepreneurs" who typically engage in the act of moving around in a world orbit. A circuit entrepreneur is reminiscent of a circuit judge, the sort that once presided over a British or American circuit court that sat at multiple places. The reach of these circuit entrepreneurs will be phenomenal as the globalisation and internationalisation of Chinese entrepreneurship, which seem to go hand in hand, accelerate and run their courses.

Circuiting within the triangle of birthplace (ancestral home on the mainland), home (Hong Kong) and workplace (mainland China), migrant entrepreneurs travel freely in and out of different spatial configurations. Their mobile life experiences have given them wider access, compared with non-travellers, to diverse cultural resources and international knowledge. Indeed, it was the advent of globalisation that occasioned the emergence of migrant entrepreneurs, whose unprecedented mobility in turn accelerated globalisation. In the post-post-modern world of the twenty-first century, migrant entrepreneurs' cross-boundary movement has extended time and space to a far greater extent than ever, making the world more and more a "global village". The study of migrant entrepreneurs is, therefore, a subject of periodical urgency.

Back to the macro: The chain reaction between cross-boundary enterprise development and globalisation

A conceptual distinction has been made in the field of entrepreneurship between internal and external factors associated with it. For a long time, studies of Chinese entrepreneurship, particularly of overseas Chinese entrepreneurship, have largely focused on internal factors such as an entrepreneur's personality traits, traditional Chinese cultural values, unique ethnic networks and interpersonal relations. The most recent literature in the field, however, tends to relate the processes and outcomes of Chinese entrepreneurship to broader, global socio-economic factors and forces of globalisation and transnationalism. Some of the latest studies, for example, have sought to examine overseas Chinese entrepreneurial interactions with the world against the larger backdrop of globalisation, in an attempt to renew people's understanding of the influence of "external" factors.[2] This is indeed a new trend of study – a clear departure from the traditional gaze at factors internal to the personality, culture, values, ethos, community or even civilisation – that places analyses of entrepreneurship within a broader, now global context. This is a turn away from the ethnic microcosm to the global macroclimate, a link between the individual and society, internal and external, local and global, domestic and foreign.

Our study aims to understand and explain Hong Kong migrant entrepreneurial experiences in a global context. Though geographically and politically an exiguous city, Hong Kong has undoubtedly been a forerunner and a window on the world for the Chinese mainland, whose doors were kept closed until as late as 1978. In terms of its stages of economic development, Hong Kong's economic function has followed a complicated trajectory: once a frontier town, then a "town at the frontier", and now it is forced to reposition itself in the context of globalisation. Hong Kong's experience is invaluable for the fast-developing market economy on the mainland of China. In order to establish itself in this globalised age where speed is everything that matters, Chinese enterprises must cease to grope about all on their own. Not only do they have to obtain local knowledge in the shortest possible time, they also need to have a good command of the universal sciences that will link them to the rest of the world. The migrant entrepreneurs surveyed in this study are already running different factories and companies in Hong Kong and their native homes as well as

[2] Eric Fong and Chiu Luk, 'Introduction: Chinese Ethnic Business and Globalisation', in *Chinese Ethnic Business: Global and Local Perspectives*, eds., Eric Fong and Chiu Luk (London: Routledge, 2007); Chiu Luk and Eric Fong, 'Conclusion', in *Chinese Ethnic Business*; Ivan H. Light, 'Globalisation, Transnationalism, and Chinese Transnationalism', in *Chinese Ethnic Business*.

other places in mainland China. Yet they are not ready to stop, and some of them are gearing up for transnational developments beyond China and Asia. Yam, a glass dealer who has companies in Hong Kong, mainland China and Germany, is seeking to set up joint-ventures in Portugal and Greece; Ngai, an established farm owner and fresh vegetable exporter in Hong Kong and the mainland, is opening a new branch in South Korea. The experiences of Hong Hong migrant entrepreneurs, such as those exemplified in this study, will prove substantially invaluable for Chinese mainland entrepreneurial development.

Divided in Union: The family business goes International

As Chinese thought has traditionally centred around the ideas of the family and the country, leaving one's home/country or having to wander around homeless is generally considered the worst of life's misfortunes. During the course of our research, we have come to realise that Chinese entrepreneurs are often wanderers between tradition and modernity, embracing and yet forsaking part of each. This is particularly the case with family businesses. The preservation, or renouncement, of traditional ideas, however, is not decided by the entrepreneur's individual inclinations, but is the result of the individual's interactions with the outer environment. For example, we have discovered that, in multi-regional corporate management, "loyalty" to the family, an important part of traditional Chinese thought, has been repeatedly stressed, while the ideas of "home-leaving" and "separation" have been invested with new and positive meanings.

"Nepotism" is rampant among Chinese enterprises. Our case studies too have reflected this deep-rooted character of Chinese society. To be "family-oriented" means to have most of the management occupied by family members or relatives that one trusts. The involvement of blood relations is a guarantee of the management's loyalty to the boss and to the enterprise. Such an emphasis on the "loyalty" of family members is related to the larger business environment on the Chinese mainland. While the country introduced its "reform and opening-up" policy 30 years ago, in business one still faces problems such as institutional defectiveness, "rule of man", ill-implementation of regulations, etc. It has therefore been an important corporate managerial strategy to retain elements of traditional culture that are protective of the enterprise.

On the other hand, when time and space are being largely compressed in the face of globalisation, the exchange of cultures and ideas as well as cross-boundary communication are becoming increasingly frequent. In order to stand firm amidst tense international competition, enterprises will need to adjust their managerial strategies according to the changing international climate. One important move is to diversify investment portfolios in various geographic sites and to internationalise, globalise themselves while responding to or taking advantage of globalisation. As they "break out", however, Chinese entrepreneurs are not entirely confident of their management systems. In fact, their attempts at internationalisation would not have been as easy if it were not for their transnationalism, their capacity to create and nurture ties, connections and networks that have long transcended geographic and political boundaries. In one case, the business family has eloquently worked out a geographic division of labour such that the father is in one site, the mother is in another, and a son and daughter are in yet others. Family dispersal has become a conscious, intentional business strategy. Divided, they are strong as a family conglomerate. Or, paradoxically: the family business is strongest when it is divided, separated, scattered, dispersed – being diasporic. It is exciting to continue to look at the development of Chinese business in the context of globalisation and transnationalism. External forces will attract considerable future analysis from researchers in the field. It is the way to go.

Rethinking "cultural factors"

Such an analytical gaze at the external (to the ethnic enterprise) forces and dynamics of globalisation and transnationlism, however exciting they may be, should not blind us to the so-called supply, or internal, side of Chinese entrepreneurship. In a recent, most insightful essay,[3] Ivan H. Light wonders aloud, in the midst of considerable literature which challenges attempts at cultural essentialisation and their attendant fallacies and mythologies, if culture matters in our understanding of Chinese entrepreneurship, or if there is something about Chinese entrepreneurs that is uniquely Chinese. The answer, Light writes, is affirmative, and he goes on to urge future studies of Chinese entrepreneurship to "bring culture back in".

We have discovered in our study that, while migrant entrepreneurs have consciously made use of international capital managerial practices and strategies such as seeking potential clients by going to international expos and getting publicity through global business channels, there are many things Chinese about them which are akin to worldly Confucianism, especially when it comes to interpersonal communication, partnership and coping with crises. Wing, for example, told us he didn't want to make enemies with his business partner who was once his high-school classmate and who repeatedly cheated on him, his reasoning being that he may encounter him on another occasion in a small "moral community" where everybody seems to have something to do with everybody else and which functions on the basis of a "custom of cooperation" and mutual aid: Let's forgive and not hold grudges for too long. There is an unbreakable sense of collectivity among the Chinese, where identification with the "insider" has an overwhelming part to play. These are elements unique to Chinese culture, which we have to take into consideration in any account of Chinese entrepreneurship.

Another respondent, Shin, spoke about the importance of contributing to the reconstruction of his hometown – building schools, roads, bridges, factories, temples – a sort of "paying back" to the community after having "taken so much" from it. The Chinese entrepreneurs have a long-standing discourse on repaying their community and society, on acknowledging their gratitude, their indebtedness, to others – by engaging in charity work. Yet another entrepreneur, Chiu, told us a good Chinese boss will never fire an incompetent staff, he just relocates him or her elsewhere to suit his or her competency. Consequently, one continues to put one's ageing or aged

[3] Ivan H. Light, 'Globalisation, Transnationalism, and Chinese Transnationalism'.

employees on the payroll because they were the trail-blazers or pioneers when the boss first got started. The business, now successful, has a moral responsibility to its ageing staff and their families. All these examples manifest emotional inclinations which are typically Chinese. They often baffle researchers who, without prior knowledge of deep-rooted Chinese values, beliefs, ethos, traditions and norms, approach Chinese entrepreneurship solely from the perspective offered in MBA classes in business schools in the West.

Live and learn

The migrant entrepreneur's social field is one that crosses geographical, cultural and political boundaries. Mobility has made him an active cultural carrier who, circuiting between different places and acquiring diverse cultural elements in his business practice, integrates and amalgamates what he has learned with what is already *within* himself into a hybrid culture. In fact, the theme of learning the necessary "tricks of the trade", the socialisation into the merchant/entrepreneur type, has been a significant finding in our study. As Chinese enterprises try to diversify and even globalise themselves, they need not only "establish themselves on a local scale" but "look out into the whole world". As the entrepreneur roams in and out of different cities, countries and cultures, taking care of their diversely located businesses, they need to keep a balance between the local and the global, traditional Chinese culture and modern Western values, embracing and yet forsaking part of each. Thus, these are the questions which deserve more future analytical attention: What do migrant entrepreneurs need to borrow and let go of in the process of globalisation and their daily mobile lives? What have Chinese enterprises "taken" from the international market and what have they "given"?

The migrant entrepreneurs presented in this study are to a very large extent walkers at the business forefront. Through their own life experiences, they have laid bare the importance of learning the necessary "tricks of the trade". They have become acutely aware of the important balance between corporate management and the mastery of local dialects/languages, policies and regulations, regional symbols, local knowledge, unwritten rules of business, ways of life, and so on. In an age of globalised competition in particular, language competency,[4] local knowledge "about foreign lands, knowledge about business globalisation (international markets, modern techniques of accounting, banking, trading, international business norms and etiquette, etc.) are all key to Chinese entrepreneurial success in the international business scenario. Fully aware of this, our migrant entrepreneurs, family business people in particular, have sent their children to overseas MBA and accounting programmes, hoping that the younger generation can "learn" the Western business way and integrate into the mainstream of international trends.

On the other hand, as they roam amidst different cultures, migrant entrepreneurs become well aware that while "grabbism" plays an important role, it will never work to be completely "Westernised" when one is doing business in China. As a result, we see an intentional re-learning, or re-socialisation into, the traditional Chinese culture

---

[4] *Ibid.*

amongst twenty-first century Chinese entrepreneurs, when some of their flawed cultural characteristics (*liegen xing*) are gradually worn away as they clash with the Western way. In this way, while Chinese business culture has undergone tremendous changes in the course of globalisation, many of the traditional values have stayed largely untroubled so that what the "mother" culture expects of the businessman still works its way into what he expects of himself. Our respondents were generally intent on becoming a much-respected "Confucian merchant", who conforms to the Confucian ethics of self-cultivation, control of greed, frugality, diligence, trustworthiness, interpersonal harmony, forgiveness, honesty, altruism – the list continues.[5] The making of the "Confucian merchant", however, makes hard demands on the individual, calling for self-discipline and self-control, which requires life-long learning. The soft culture, or soft power of Confucianism, or Chinese culture, is hard and harsh on the self, but it is an important part of the occupational socialisation of the Chinese entrepreneur. This theme runs through almost all literature on Chinese businessmen, merchants and businessmen. Our study just adds another piece of evidence to it – and the tradition and its legacy continues. This is precisely what is significant about Light's urge to "bring culture back in", when he attempts to re-invoke "the best of culture" amidst outcries against attempts at so-called "cultural essentialisms".

Apparently culture matters, especially in a modern world where alienation and estrangement tend to predominate as both a social condition and as a personal dilemma. Indeed, social modernisation is accompanied by very strange bedfellows like darkness and opportunity. Technological advancement and global economic integration have created a large number of opportunities as well as exposed darker sides of society that were previously unknown, or at most, less known. In this light, the Durkheimian call for a moral order, a moral community, has now become all the more urgent. If alienation is a typical modern condition, we need to find strategies of de-alienation, of community building, quickly or social and personal disorganisation will set in. Both the sociologist and the merchant may then have to turn to some form of religion or worldly ethics to construct a new moral order.

Ethical and economic enterprises: What's "confucian" about a "confucian merchant"?

"Credibility" and "reputation" are often considered to be an important kind of capital in the Chinese business world. Interpersonal relations are usually portrayed as bound together by morality.[6] Traditional Chinese businessmen are always chasing the good name that comes with being a "Confucian-merchant". Studies of overseas Chinese entrepreneurs have revealed that Chinese business people will gain good social renown with the help of different community associations, charity

[5] Chan Kwok-bun and Claire Chiang, *Stepping Out: The Making of Chinese Entrepreneurs* (Singapore: Prentice Hall, 1994).

[6] Fei Xiaotong, *Xiangtu Zhongguo* [From the Soil: The Foundations of Chinese Society] (Beijing: Sanlian shudian, 1985); Y.C. King, *Zhongguo shehui yu wenhua* [Chinese Society and Culture] (Hong Kong: Oxford University Press, 1992); S. Gordon Redding, *The Spirit of Chinese Capitalism* (Berlin: Walter de Gruyter, 1990).

work and community service in order to create a fine personal and corporate image that is ultimately favourable for corporate sustenance and development.[7] Abundant and detailed research has been done to probe into the motives and functions of such "charitable deeds", especially when it comes to big entrepreneurs; but hardly enough has been done to survey their "unethical" (non-Confucian) or even unlawful behaviour. And yet it is difficult to access information in this respect, because there is a general reluctance among business people to talk about how they will use whatever methods are necessary to achieve their business goals, which is often seen as business secrets and a taboo even among business people themselves. Rather, they stress the importance of "paying back" to the community after having "taken so much" from it, hoping to gain the good reputation of being a "Confucian-merchant". However, as the present study reveals, there are common deviations from their self-proclaimed "Confucian" merits. Such deviations seldom occur between business people and their suppliers or clients because credibility is after all an important factor that sustains their business. What we have noticed as "deviations" from "Confucian" merits refer to some of the phenomena that have already been explored in past studies, including the exchange of interests between business people and government officials and, more surprisingly, fraudulence between business partners and between friends as well as suspicion and dishonesty between family members.

In fact, the collusion of government and business has been a common, international social phenomenon. The exchange of money and power takes place in developed as well as developing legal systems, the only difference being degree. The migrant entrepreneurs that we have studied are generally aware that, to set up factories in mainland China, the key problem is to establish good *guanxi* with local governments, especially when it comes to issues concerning land, taxes, approval documents and other policy-related matters. They understand that they have to do whatever they can to sort out "official channels" before they can stand out amidst intense competition. One of the most effective ways to go, as they have realised, is to join, and assume important positions in, different community organisations, a platform on which public welfare and individual good converge. The common practice of putting public titles on business name cards as a manifestation of one's business achievements, as well as charity work, is an apt illustration of how Chinese entrepreneurs manage to "have their cake and eat it", achieving moral and ethical gratification as well economic fulfilment at the same time.

Beneath the glossy surface of an entrepreneur's "moral enterprise", however, one may resort to deception and fraudulence, dirty tricks and murky plots, which are a complete contrast to the public image one has created. Through their own

[7] Chan Kwok-bun and Claire Chiang, *Stepping Out*; Richard J. Coughlin, *Double Identity: The Chinese in Modern Thailand* (Hong Kong: Hong Kong University Press, 1960); Edmund Terence Gomez and Michael Hsiao Hsin-Huang, 'Chinese Business Research in Southeast Asia', in *Chinese Business Research in Southeast Asia: Contesting Cultural Explanations, Researching Entrepreneurship*, eds., Edmund Terence Gomez and Michael Hsiao Hsin-Huang (Surrey, U.K.: Curzon Press, 2001), p. 1–37.

experiences, our migrant entrepreneurs have realised that doing business on the mainland is basically about "mutual deception" and about "making use of each other", so much so that "deception" becomes a means of survival in business. Man, we are reminded, is what he sees and hears around him, and so an entrepreneur may find himself cheated and then cheating, affected by a social ambiance like this. In fact, the first time some of our migrant entrepreneurs got cheated was not by strangers but by friends and even business partners, people who they had thought to be trustworthy. Wing, for instance, first got cheated by a former schoolmate's husband and again by a partner he knew through an old school friend. Are friends really "sheep" or "wolves"? Are business partners really "friends" or "foes"? In fact, "trust" built upon a relationship can be unexpectedly brittle; reliance on "friendship" and "ethics" can turn out to be as tenuous as buying a tank of gas. Just as business co-operation is marked by an oscillation between "trust" and "suspicion", so a businessman works his "way" through a choice between "ethics" and "gain".

Once "deception" becomes a recognised part of one's personality, it enters one's family from the business world. As migrant entrepreneurs shuttle from place to place, "staying most of the time on the mainland", the dark sides of migrancy, its emotional costs, begin to show. The segregation of their living and work space suggests many moments of emotional distress and anxiety which sometimes impacts detrimentally on marriages and families, between husband and wife, and between generations. Marginality as the fate of a stranger in a strange land usually brings a strong desire for consolation. The most direct way out, it seems, is to find someone to share one's life, especially through the loneliest nights. As a result, Hong Kong businessmen are known to keep a second wife and set up a second home in China – a phenomenon that has been accepted as the new "norm" and the "new culture" in business circles. Yet, however unrestrained one is away from home, once back in Hong Kong, one will again don the persona of a caring father and good husband. At work, they live behind masks, and this pretender's life continues at home. There may be nothing "Confucian" about a Confucian-merchant's life but the ultimate "confusion" of the real and the unreal, the ethical and the unethical.

Hong Kong businessmen: Living in the margins

Entrepreneurs are by experience extreme risk-takers. Many of our respondents spoke sorrowfully about setbacks and failures while doing business in China, especially when it comes to business disputes or failures, abrupt policy change, or work injuries. These Hong Kong businesses, mostly SMEs (small-to-medium enterprises), often feel insecure and unprotected, handicapped by their deficient knowledge of the workings of the law and the business environment on the mainland. They also lose out because of a lack of local support, emphasised currently with the absence of legal or institutional assistance from the Hong Kong government. When a uniform policy is enforced (a phenomenon the Chinese call *"yi dao qie"*, literally cutting everything with one slice of the knife) and projects have to be suspended, there is nowhere these Hong Kong SMEs can turn for help, except to appeal to their local contacts. Wing was originally co-operating with a state-run corporation in the petroleum business, but a sudden change in petroleum import policies forced his business to stop immediately. Desperate to preserve the business he had worked so hard to build, Wing mobilised all his contacts, asked for help from the people concerned, appealed to different government departments for exemption, all to no avail.

In the early days of China's "reform and opening-up" campaign, the government used to "give a lot of weight" to Hong Kong SMEs and a variety of preferential policies were introduced. The earlier one entered the Chinese market, as our respondents recalled, the more beneficial it would be. Thirty years later, however, the Chinese government has been more attracted by transnational syndicates with their mammoth potential. Such a shift in attitude was acutely experienced by migrant entrepreneurs running factories on the mainland. Yu, who has printing factories in Dongguan, laments, "Small businesses like us no longer mean anything to the local government. We've become such 'nobodies' that they don't even look at us now. Things were different in the past." The Hong Kong entrepreneurs, once trail-blazers in China's economic reforms, are now in the throes of marginalisation. Admittedly, many of them, taking advantage of the opening-up and reform, had had better days, but they have been put at a disadvantage in competing with transnational corporations. With the Chinese government's change of attitude and the lack of substantial assistance from the Hong Kong government, these businesses are in a passive situation. As the number of Hong Kong entrepreneurs doing business in China increases, the Hong Kong government needs to begin to think about developing measures, policies and institutions to help and support them. Hong Kong businessmen also need to develop, perhaps with the assistance of the Hong Kong government, ways of helping and supporting each other like their overseas counterparts, and of sharing among themselves social as well as business information. The days of a lone Hong Kong entrepreneur trail-blazing in China have long gone.

The Sociological Perspective

Back to the "human"

The emphasis of this book is to bring sociological studies back to the real. Going back to the real, or the human, means that sociological studies must not only probe the outer social structures, institutions or material environment, but concern itself with the "merely human". Talking about the sociologist, Peter Berger observes, "… [the sociologist's] consuming interest remains in the world of men, their institutions, their history, their passions. And since he is interested in men, nothing that men do can be altogether tedious for him. He will naturally be interested in the events that engage men's ultimate beliefs, their moments of tragedy and grandeur and ecstasy. But he will also be fascinated by the commonplace, the everyday".[8]

---

[8] Peter Berger, *Invitation to Sociology: A Humanistic Perspective* (Garden City, New York: Doubleday & Company, 1963), p. 19.

In fact, to understand the human, one need not only look into the everyday, but explore the indistinction between sense and sensibility, spirituality and desire. Current studies of entrepreneurship, however, are too intent on scientific analysis while largely ignoring sentimentality, stressing economics and management rather than the "human" in the businessman. What we know of a businessman is therefore largely his public persona, the easily observable aspects of his life. Biographical accounts tend to trace his road to success, sketching out a hero-figure to be commended at all levels. Yet such portrayals offer no more than a one-sided understanding of the businessman's life: with the "business" side much explored, the other side, the "human" side of him as an emotional animal, is yet to be excavated in all his likes and dislikes, joys and woes. As Jean-Paul Sartre once remarked, "all human existence is a passion": one of the traits of our existence is that we all live with and in emotions. It is a major deficiency in current studies to have largely ignored the emotional worlds of business people, who are often portrayed as determined and dauntless decision-makers. It is high time we took note of their human pains, frustrations, loneliness, fears and despair.

The Dialectical relationship between man and society

The primary task of a sociologist is to define the factors that caused the current anxieties and apathy. C. Wright Mills contends that a kind of "sociological imagination" is needed to understand what the time has left in the individual. He believes it is not until the individual has been placed within his own social position that the significance of his internal as well as external life can be properly understood.[9] During the course of our research, we were also aware that we had to put individual entrepreneurs against a larger backdrop of "mobility" before we could gain some insight into contemporary social structures as well as the interactions between the individual and society. Anthony Giddens has pointed out that an understanding of the world can only be achieved by virtue of a threefold exercise of the sociological imagination that involves a historical, an anthropological, and a critical sensitivity.[10] Historical sensitivity urges us to rediscover our immediate historical past and make out the differences and similarities between the society we lived in and the one we live in, to see how the traditional has masked the modern. Anthropological sensitivity serves to destruct ethnocentrism, asking one not to impose one's social and cultural standards upon another; it tells us to appreciate the various ways of life of different ethnicities so that, by way of understanding the multitude of human societies, we get to know more about our own. These two forms of sensitivity combined enable us to break out from the ideological restrictions and fetters of our times and society. Critical sensitivity makes us aware that human beings refuse to be dictated to by any force of natural inevitability, that the future lies in possibilities and in the roads that we take. Such sociological imagination extends and relates seemingly individual cases to the larger social milieu so that the interactive relationship

---

[9] C. Wright Mills, *The Sociological Imagination*, Fortieth Anniversary Edition (New York. Oxford University Press, 2000).

[10] Anthony Giddens, *Sociology: A Brief but Critical Introduction* (London: Macmillan, 1982), p. 26.

between the individual and society can be brought to light with the help of cautious and deliberate association. Reflected therein are not isolated, individual cases but the characteristics of an era. This is exactly what Yan Fu has identified as the significance and function of sociological studies, that is, to examine "the changes and transformations of a given society so as to know its whence and predict its whither". More importantly, the use of sociological imagination enables us to dismantle some of the myths about migrant entrepreneurship, bring it back to "life" and restore its "human" side.

Current studies of migrancy have often consciously or unconsciously glossed and even "deified" the personality of migrants. The image of the "diligent" and "persevering" newcomer stands out large in accounts of migrant entrepreneurship, particularly in surveys of overseas Chinese emigrants. Such a positive portrayal of the national character is admittedly an oversimplified social imaginary. Indeed, what we experience in our specific milieux, as C. Wright Mills observes, "… is often caused by structural changes. Accordingly, to understand the changes of many personal milieux, we are required to look beyond them".[11] Most of our 16 respondents have confessed that "personality" had not led them onto the road to entrepreneurship. Much as we may claim that character can change one's fate (*xingge gaibian mingyun*), personality is, to start with, not inborn but shaped by circumstances. Our migrant entrepreneurs' initial motivation, as we have shown, came with the sense of personal shame brought about by prejudice and discrimination – on the basis of their lack of English, their birthplace, and even the school they attended – from mainstream society. "To possess the feeling of shame," as Confucius says, "is to be near to energy." Along a similar line, Helen Lynd points out that shame has revelatory, transformative potential.[12] Denied fair opportunities and confronted with disdain, migrant entrepreneurs turned the flame of shame into an emotional impetus and became determined to prove the significance and value of their existence. Being the product of particular social circumstances, they are to a certain extent "reluctant entrepreneurs",[13] meaning many, if not all, of them would have much preferred to incorporate themselves into the mainstream economy by the route of formal education and professional integration and joining the middle-class. Instead, the disadvantages of blocked opportunity engendered a sense of personal shame which gave them the courage to travel a road of no return, a road to self-employment and entrepreneurship. This was also a road to self-esteem, to a place where each hoped to create his own rose garden and assume a decent identity of social significance. That of a "boss" or "entrepreneur" is certainly something to be respected and desired. With this new identity, they turned a structural disadvantage into a personal one, overcoming the sense of personal shame by economic achievement. Just as the literati who try to achieve glory by writing a masterpiece (*li yan*),

---

[11] C. Wright Mills, *The Sociological Imagination*, p. 10.

[12] Helen Lynd, *On Shame and the Search for Identity* (New York: Harcourt Brace, 1958).

[13] Chan Kwok-bun, ed., *Chinese Business Networks: State, Economy and Culture* (Singapore: Prentice Hall, 2000).

so these entrepreneurs tried, in the same pursuit of psychological fulfilment, to establish their own enterprise to be handed down forever.

Such a sociological analytical perspective enables us, in our analyses of particular social groups, to be fully aware of the interactive, dialectical relationship between man and society. On the one hand, the individual as a product of society is restricted by various opportunity structures and powers. On the other, the individual as a constituent of society is never a passive object of its constraints and repressions: rather, his sense of agency and subjectivity ask him to strike back as circumstances dictate. There is an interactive relationship between the individual and society: as much as he is restricted by the environment, man can always react by restructuring his environment. As Peter Berger says, "It would seem, then, that just as there is no total power in society, there is also no total impotence".[14] This is applicable to all human societies and not to overseas Chinese communities alone. Studies and surveys by Light and others of non-Chinese ethnic entrepreneurship in America have shown that ethnic immigrants have met with the common fate of being categorised as "outsiders", who, refusing to yield passively to institutional restrictions or adverse circumstances, decided to create their own capitalism among their own kind. The solidarity of outsiders, as we can see, has been externally created or constructed by insiders' discrimination – a kind of social construction of emotions through blood and geographical relations, which quickly developed into highly homogeneous and united social networks, creating, within a larger uncongenial environment, a congenial inner environment in which these excluded newcomers could survive.[15]

Faced with exploitation and unfair treatment from mainstream society, immigrants as a minority strike back. Being emotional animals of flesh and blood, they battle against exploitation and unfair treatment as well as against prejudice and disdain from predominating local vested interests. As long as resources are limited so that people still vie with each other, as long as there are power differences so that the "outsiders" are still distinguished from the "insiders", new immigrants as "newcomers", as a relatively weak group, are bound to be deprived, excluded and discriminated against, whether they are in the East or the West. The same story is being told in all corners of the world, with just the scripts varying a little. Thus, what the 16 profiles in this study represent is not just a story of Hong Kong or Fujianese people: it is one about "mobility", about the common fate of "migrants" in general. Since mobility and migrancy are now a trend of all humankind, so the explorations of the present study may well be said to have global significance.

Insights from economic sociology and social psychology

It is the burden of researchers in the field of entrepreneurship to do more, deeper theoretical work. To place our analyses in the context of globalisation and

---

[14] Peter Berger, *Invitation to Sociology*, p. 129.

[15] Ivan H. Light, *Ethnic Enterprise in America: Business and Welfare Among Chinese, Japanese, and Blacks* (Berkeley: University of California Press, 1972); Ivan H. Light, 'Immigrant and Ethnic Enterprise in North America', *Ethnic and Racial Studies*, 7 (1984), p. 195–216; Ivan H. Light and Carolyin Rosenstein, *Race, Ethnic, and Entrepreneurship in Urban America* (New York: Walter de Gruyter, Inc., 1995).

transnationalism is a step in the right direction because the latter are at the very forefront of social sciences research, theoretically and empirically speaking. Our own study comprises economic sociology and social psychology by situating the 16 cases of migrant entrepreneurship within the global structure of globalisation and transnationalism, and by relating it to works on identity, self-presentation and social networks, thus opening up some exciting theoretical windows. Our work sees ethnic entrepreneurship as a social dynamic, while identity acts as the vector for symbolic transactions between the host society and foreign communities. Migrant entrepreneurs as a transnational mobile group serve to link their home country with their new home during the course of their cross-boundary activities. Their construction of transnational social networks and ties is integral to transnationalism. When done in this way, our exercise in economic sociology has the promise of insights which have far-reaching implications for social theory, and for the formulation of public policy on migrant/ethnic entrepreneurship – which operate on the premise that businesses and governments have common interests, and both sides should learn to nurture such common interests by co-operation and mutual support, by "doing things together". Without adequate understanding of the structural disadvantages that business people are trapped by, or by some misjudgement of embedded social conflicts under the surface, government policies are not only doomed to fail but may well aggravate the original problems. The age of globalisation is in fact an age of co-operation. It is time that entrepreneurs, sociologists and policy-makers work together to avoid possible pitfalls. But as far as Hong Kong is concerned, such co-operation happens just once in a blue moon, when everyone acts without regard for the general interest.

The expected and the unexpected

The sociological perspective allows us to see "through" the structural issues hidden behind the façade of social phenomena. It is like looking at a building: while most of us see the exterior glass walls and windows, the sociologist examines its concrete and steelwork as well as the interdependent relationship between its deepest groundwork (society) and its piles (individuals). In other words, what the sociologist aims to see is the interactive relationship between the individual and social structure, as he tries to understand how the individual is restricted by society while refusing to be restricted. Sociology also offers a critique of, a reflection upon, this relationship apart from merely gaining insight into it. Robert K. Merton suggests that there are two kinds of functions to the motives behind particular human behaviour: manifest functions, which refers to the intended consequences of an action; and latent functions, which refers to the unintended or unexpected consequences of the action.[16] This Western perspective has a lot in common with the traditional Chinese outlook on the paradox of consequence as expressed in the wisdom of Chinese proverbs and

[16] Robert K. Merton, 'Manifest and Latent Functions', in *Social Theory and Social Structure* (New York: Free Press, 1968), p. 105.

folktales.[17] Such paradoxical two-sidedness, the coexistence of construction and destruction, has made itself felt, though not substantially, throughout our study.

As migrant entrepreneurs left their homes in mainland China for Hong Kong in their early years, they carried much hope, expecting that in this affluent "promised land", all their dreams would come true. Yet immigrant life never abounded in opportunities and happiness as they had expected. They had done so much to get a visa to Hong Kong, but the consequence of migrancy was nowhere near what they had intended: the negative label of being "new immigrants", the prejudice brought by their accents, blocked opportunities, etc., were problems to which they had never given a thought. Unintended consequences are, however, not altogether negative, for in the misfortunes of these newcomers, blessings were in the making. Crisis, according to Chinese wisdom, is often what leads to a way out: blessings and bane are often bound together. As we have seen, discrimination, hostility, frustration and despair have tempered the will of new immigrants as much as they have tormented them: despite its negative effect, their sense of shame has turned into a powerful driving force towards entrepreneurship, pushing them against all odds to "go decent". The external force of prejudice and all its negative effects have transformed into an internal force that serves to create strong ethnic bonds among the immigrants, enabling immigrant entrepreneurs to construct highly homogeneous, consolidated and trustworthy social networks which, once mobilised, prove to be a most important social resource.

After their careers had been established, when they were no longer "new" immigrants, our migrant entrepreneurs decided on a move back to the mainland, hoping to "fare better" and enhance their competitive power via multi-regional operations. They circuit around different places, taking care of all their businesses. Exhausted as they are, they feel that all the pains they take are worth it because they work for the family's good. While this highly mobile life has attained its manifest functions, it has latent dysfunctions as well. On the one hand, multi-regional operation effectively integrates and optimises resources in different places, helping to construct a pluralised corporate image. On the other hand, the migrant

[17] A Chinese proverb says, for example, 'You xin zai hua hua bu fa, wu xin cha liu liu cheng yin' meaning 'when you grow flowers on purpose, they will fail to bloom; when you plant willows at random, they will grow into a shady grove'. In addition, there is the folktale of the 'Lost Horse' ('Sai Weng shi ma') which tells the story of a man living on the northern borders of China who was skilled in interpreting events. One day for no reason, his horse ran away to the tribes across the border. As everyone came to console him, his father said, 'What makes you so sure this isn't a blessing?' Some months later his horse returned, bringing a splendid nomad stallion. Everyone congratulated him, but his father said, 'What makes you so sure this isn't a disaster?' Their household was richer by a fine horse, which the son loved to ride. One day he fell and broke his hip. Everyone tried to console him, but his father said, 'What makes you so sure this isn't a blessing?' A year later the northern tribes came in force across the border, and every able-bodied man took his bow and went into battle. The Chinese frontiersmen lost nine of every ten men. Only because the son was lame did father and son survive to take care of each other. Truly, blessing turns to disaster, and disaster to blessing: the changes have no end, nor can the mystery be fathomed. [Tale adapted from Moss Roberts, ed. *Chinese Fairy Tales and Fantasies* (New York: Pantheon Books, 1980), p. 82.].

entrepreneur has a dear emotional price to pay, which can never be measured in monetary terms. The distanced children, the suspicious spouse and the alienated self are all sources of anxiety and inner torment. Most migrant entrepreneurs experience agonies of this kind, but not all of them know where the pain comes from. Even fewer are aware that their problems are rooted in the mobile nature of their life. Unable to see the dysfunctional and unintended consequences of mobility, they find themselves consciously or unconsciously defending, denying or even justifying their problems in life.

Look and be looked at: The situatedness of self-identity

The individual, as Peter Berger observes, is a repertoire or bundle of roles, and to be located in society means to be at the intersection point of specific social forces.[18] As one plays different roles in the changing scenes on the grand stage of society, one is required to become part of the role. Their nomadic lifestyle has forced our respondents to assume different roles, being, at different times, a "Hong Kong businessman", a "manufacturer from the mainland", a "fellow Fujianese" from the same clan, or an "outsider" with desired economic resources. Thus, as they change their masks, they switch their identities, alternating sameness and difference during the course of their social interactions.

Man is a meaning-making animal. From the perspective of symbolic interactionism, the trait of having "one face, many masks"[19] is in fact the result of the entrepreneur's reading and judgement of, and interactions with, the environment he is in and the people he comes into contact with. In his analysis of the process of human interaction, Herbert Blumer suggests that people are guided in their orientation and action by their understanding of the meaning of the objects around them, when such a meaning is not inherent but engendered in their interaction with one another; and as they inhabit different worlds and come into contact with different people, they guide themselves with different sets of meanings.[20] As migrant entrepreneurs circuit from place to place, tending their business in different social settings, they need to assume the best possible identities for their business by evaluating what others expect of their role and by assigning meaning to neutral symbols to narrow the psychological distance and create trust. In the process of meaning construction, the switching of languages and dialects (such as between Hokkien, Putonghua, Cantonese and English), the crossover of contexts (a change in the form of address, for instance, calling each other "Brother" while not being related; or "Shifu", literally "teacher" or "master", when there is no teacher-student relationship between them) and the assumption of different associate identities (becoming members of "native place associations", based on geographical relations; of "clan associations",

---

[18] Peter Berger, *Invitation to Sociology*.

[19] Chan Kwok-bun and Tong Chee-kiong, 'Yi zhang liankong, duo ge mianju: Xinjiapo huaren de shenfen rentong wenti' ['One Face, Many Masks: Singaporean Chinese Identities'] in *Mingbao Yuekan* [Mingpao Monthly], September (1999), pp. 20-23.

[20] Herbert Blumer, *Symbolic Interactionism: Perspective and Method* (Eaglewood Cliffs, N.J.: Prentice Hall, 1969).

based on a common family name; and of "business chambers", based on a common trade or business), can all be some of the means by which business people can manipulate and appropriate meaningful symbols – a strategy Erving Goffman would call "impression management" or public presentation of self.[21]

To look and to be looked at: the self is constructed in the process of "looking" and "being looked at", and we may as well say that man is partly himself and partly others. Current studies of entrepreneurial identity (studies of identity conducted in Hong Kong are a case in point) have been confined within the closed structure of fixed times and places while largely ignoring the two major features of modern life: its mobile and multi-regional dimensions. It is an extremely challenging and yet glamorous area of study to examine how the individual, placed within different spaces, reads and is read by others. Between his realities, desires and fantasies, between past, present and future, the individual's self-consciousness and sense of identity are ever shuttling among the triple axes of time, space and specific cultural implications. As a result, the understanding of the individual and his innermost feelings is always fraught with limits and limitations. The present study has sought to analyse the inner feelings, emotional lives and identities of migrant entrepreneurs as well as how these three are related to corporate management, a relationship that demands more in-depth practical survey as more and more entrepreneurs operate their businesses in multiple locations.

Theory to Practice: Getting Down to Earth

Changing lives: From life and back to life

What is the practical significance of sociological studies? When Auguste Comte introduced the term "sociology" ("sociologie") as a neologism, he was experiencing a personal as well as social dilemma: the country was plunged into total anarchy, while he was worn out from personal tragedies. Both urged Comte to look into the relationship between science and society, and to find the possibilities of putting society back in order. The idea of "social positivism" reveals Comte's expectations for sociological studies to facilitate our understanding of the problems and needs of man and society to reform and improve current social conditions. Yan Fu, a nineteenth century scholar, was the first to translate the term "sociology" into Chinese, explaining that "sociology", being a kind of scientific study, examines "changes and transformations of a given society so as to know its whence and predict its whither" and "reveal[s] the laws that govern [social] development". Indeed, the ultimate aim of sociological study is not simply to fulfil human understanding in academic terms, but more importantly to apply its findings to real life. It shows us the way we live,

[21] Erving Goffman, *The Presentation of Self in Everyday Life* (Garden City, N.Y.: Anchor Book, 1959).

with the goal of improving the way we live; it changes our lives, as it has come from life and must return to life.

Again as Karl Marx puts it, "The philosophers have only interpreted the world, in various ways; the point is to change it". Émile Durkheim's study of suicide has probed into the wider connections between the individual and the community. He points out that suicidal behaviour is as likely when the individual is weakly integrated into society as when the individual is extremely attached to society, and thus has no life of his own. In the latter case, when individuals are too heavily integrated into a social group or organisation, suicide is more likely if society's will asks for their death.[22] While Durkheim's study dates back to as early as 1897, his insights into suicidal behaviour are still relevant to our times, and his explorations into the root causes of suicide still have a great deal to say to our globalised world. As man's mobility accelerates, his emotional attachment to the community has become a fast-forward blur. A reconsideration of Durkheim's discourse on the interactive connections between man and society is therefore conducive to our understanding of what is wanting in our community life - as far as our migrant entrepreneurs are concerned.

The Cognitive elite and immigration policies

In 1990, some 28 years ago, Waldinger, Aldrich and their associates gave a rather harsh evaluation of the lack of supportiveness and usefulness of the government policies of four countries they had studied (West Germany, the United States, the United Kingdom and the Netherlands) as far as the development of ethnic entrepreneurship was concerned. They pointed out that, other than the US, there have been no programmes or measures to aid ethnic enterprises: in fact, governments acted to impede ethnic business development. Their own theoretical model of immigrant entrepreneurship stresses the interaction between opportunity structure of the host society and the group characteristics and social structure of the immigrant community, warning how quickly the opportunities available would reach their point of saturation when internal competition among co-ethnics intensified.[23] Thirty years later, the opportunity structures in an age of globalisation and transnationalism have vastly multiplied – the sky is the limit, so to speak. As international boundaries crumble under a globalised networking structure, business competition is becoming more startling. With migrant entrepreneurship an important part of socio-economic development, the government, if they are to be of use to ethnic businesses, will have to update their thoughts on migration, transmigration and migrancy, and realise the out-datedness of the classical model of assimilation.

Globalisation paradoxically merges "presence" and "absence" and brings together distant social events and the local scenarios. The emergence of transnationalism has extended time and space in such a way that is unmatched by any previous

---

[22] Émile Durkheim, *Suicide: A Study in Sociology*, trans. John A. Spaulding and George Simpson; edited with an introduction by George Simpson (New York: The Free Press, 1951).

[23] Roger Waldinger and Howard Aldrich, 'Conclusion and Policy Implications', in *Ethnic Entrepreneurs: Immigrant Business in Industrial Societies*, eds., Roger Waldinger, Howard Aldrich and Robin Ward (California: Sage Publications, Inc., 1990).

age. There is an unprecedented interconnectedness between countries and regions, so that an originally local event will come to assume some direct or indirect global bearing. Now, migrants typically do not become immigrants who cut their ties to their countries of departure, and embrace and internalise the cultures of the new world. Instead, their "to-and-fro" mode of migration allows them to stay "attached" while being away: "home-leaving" has not "uprooted" them from their emotional memories, social networks or their local influence in the home country. As mass transport, cross-boundary communication and long-distant travelling become more and more affordable, migrant entrepreneurs can, through frequent visits and cross-boundary investment, maintain and nurture old ties with the folks left behind, thus integrating their social networks in the home country as well as in their adopted country. On a more personal level, migrants can internalise selectively the values and beliefs of both their home culture and their adopted culture. The dual clash with the traditional and the modern serves to catalyse the individual's transformation, allowing him to develop hybrid identities. This hybrid nature gives the immigrant the traits of a chameleon, since he is now capable of evoking different "shared local symbols" as he interacts with different people. In so doing, he manages to narrow the psychological distance between people and break down the regional ethnic barriers.

The age of globalisation and transnationalism is an age of relentless flows of peoples, ideas, capital, identities and goods. Migration no longer presents itself as a one-way linear process; rather, it is becoming more and more pluralised and circuitous, with the social elites walking at the very front of this circulation. Such a continuous "circulation of the elite" is a prominent feature of a modern society. In fact, it has long been occurring in industrial societies, although the circulation was predominantly that between different organisations within the same country. In this globalised age, however, such circulation is no longer confined within a certain country or region, but is occurring on a global scale. The people in question no longer aspire to become the political/economic elite in a local sense, but are a kind of "cognitive elite", highly valued in the international community.

The whole world is competing for such elites, many of whom are the circuit entrepreneurs this book is about. A society's pace of modernisation is in fact closely related to the number and quality of its circuiting elites. It is therefore worth reviewing whether a government is in possession of the kind of "soft power" to retain these mobile elites, or whether a government's immigration policies are capable of making these transnational talents halt and stay. As we see it, there are currently two urgent issues waiting in the way of the Hong Kong government. First, the government needs to learn some new, bold facts about the changing character of international migration, develop a more in-depth understanding of mobility and transnationalism at large, and review the current immigration policies with a renewed evaluation of the social significance of ethnic entrepreneurship. Second, they must keep a keen eye on the ethnic structure of our community, take more careful note of the character of Hong Kong's immigrants and of its ethnic conflicts, bolster its pluralised cultural mind as well as its dedication to tolerance and inclusiveness through education, and rigorously enforce its anti-discrimination ordinances. Of course, the construction of a "tolerant and inclusive" soft culture cannot be achieved single-handedly by one department alone: it must involve cross-departmental and interdisciplinary communications, interactions, discussions and even clashes. Apparently, the Hong Kong Government still has a long way to go, while migrants as risk-takers trail their paths bearing positive and negative consequences. At the moment, various problems are "standing in the way" of boosting ethnic entrepreneurial creativity and attracting international "cognitive elites". Knowledge for the sake of change: the aim of this study is to develop a more humanistic understanding of the growing population of migrant entrepreneurs as well as to acquire a multi-dimensional perspective on the issue of globalisation.

Reading and reflections

Much of the time the sociologist moves in sectors of experience that are familiar to him and to most people in his society. He investigates communities, institutions and activities that one can read about every day in the newspapers. Yet there is another excitement of discovery beckoning in his investigations. It is not the excitement of coming upon the totally unfamiliar, but rather the excitement of finding the familiar becoming transformed in its meaning.[24] Sociological insights and perspectives enable us to look afresh at the things we have taken for granted, and we may turn out to be totally ignorant of them. Sometimes the true character is entirely obscured from us, even though events are taking place just around us. Or we may have been partly cognizant of the truth and remained unaware of the rest, which we may consciously or unconsciously reject and deny. Sociological study not only puts the experiences of a case down on paper, but more importantly it seeks to dissect the case with a scalpel. The process of reading functions as a mirror for the objects of study and their family, as well as for the general reader. We see in this mirror some of our intrinsic traits as well as some truths. The first time, we are probably looking into our own self. The words have not only recorded the surface of life but have also revealed its hidden corners, which prompts us to reflect upon the past, face up to our life, re-evaluate ourselves and, finally, recognise our ultimate concerns – a process that Anthony Giddens refers to as "reflexivity". Sociological portrayals put the reader into events that he did not personally participate in, enabling a dialogue between the reader and the experience of another, thus extending both space and time within the individual.

Beyond the barricades: The resonance of language

Sociological study cultivates new meanings in our language. As the sociologist ventures into people's lives and seeks to approach, comprehend and explain different social phenomena, he takes words from our language and tries to redefine them in clearer terms, investing them with concrete sociological values. Once written down or printed on paper, these words, now reincarnated, will once again be part of people's lives. In fact, if sociological terms can be widely used in daily life (some

[24] Peter Berger, *Invitation to Sociology*, p. 21.

of them are actually already in circulation as part of people's daily vocabulary, for example, "alienation", "peer group", "stratification", "globalisation"), then sociology will be out of its ivory tower and help people to describe their everyday, familiar experiences. From words, sociology can enter people's lives and become embedded in them, affecting them from within. As modern life becomes ever more pluralised and complicated, sociology in its most accessible terms will certainly enable people to go beyond all the psychological barricades that give rise to misunderstandings and other problems in communication, as empathy is usually built upon mutual understanding. In a globalised age, when transnational and cross-cultural communication becomes more frequent, the adoption of sociological terminology in everyday life undoubtedly has its significance. In fact, sociology in the twenty-first century takes upon itself the momentous mission to express itself in contemporary language, to enter people's daily experiences and to provide, at a time when no one can be an island, the kind of urgent knowledge that will give people a much deeper understanding of the society they inhabit as well as their own positions within that society, so they will live on as one world, united and better fulfilled.

Epilogue

The times proceed without let-up. In an age of mobility, it is an inescapable trend for man to get going. With migrants being "the possible pioneers in the evolution of cultures and civilizations",[1] a mobile sociology will become what precedes and leads sociological studies in general. Since "man" is the primary object of study in sociology, any research will become drab and biased if it deviates from man's emotionality. Georg Simmel has stressed that sociology must probe man's inner emotional experience, the best points of departure being our society's aesthetic outlook and our arts.[2] As we advocate the study of mobile sociology in the new century, therefore, we are also in urgent need of a sociology of emotions. Admittedly, there are multiple ways to man's emotional experience, which have been expressed, during the course of history, in literature, music, drama and the fine arts. This prompts us to wonder whether sociological approaches could not be more varied and flexible. For sociology to live a more vigorous and lively existence, the only way forward, as we see it, is probably to move beyond its own confines and become interdisciplinary. Once it manages to transcend the boundaries between disciplines, sociology as a cross-boundary branch of the humanities will have a greater and more global involvement in our understanding of life.

Now we are reminded of Comte's famous dictum, which says, "From knowledge comes prevision; from prevision comes power." (*Savoir pour prévoir, prévoir pour pourvoir.*) For it is the aim of our study to examine, by looking at the life experiences

[1] Chan Kwok-bun, 'From Multiculturalism to Hybridity: The Chinese in Canada', in *Governance in Multicultural Societies*, eds., John Rex and Gurharpal Singh (Aldershot: Ashgate, 2004), p. 242; Chan Kwok-bun, 'Chengshi de neizai hunhe xing: Yi xiang guanyu duoyuanwenhuazhuyi de piping' ['The Intrinsic Hybridity of the Urban Space: A Critique of Multiculturalism'], *Jiangsu Shehui Kexue* [Jiangsu Social Sciences] 3 (2005), p. 197.

[2] Kurt H. Wolff, ed., *Georg Simmel: Essays on Sociology, Philosophy, and Aesthetics* (Ohio: Ohio State University Press, 1958).

Chan Kwok-bun and Chan Wai-wan, *Mobile Chinese Entrepreneurs*,
International Series on Consumer Science, DOI 10.1007/978-1-4419-9643-5,

of migrant entrepreneurs, the intrinsic traits of "mobility", its positive and negative effects on man's everyday life, the joys and agonies it has brought to modern man and woman – and ultimately to provide, in the words of Peter Berger, "a broad, open, emancipated vista on human life".[3]

Now that we have come to the end of our book, if we were to close our eyes for a minute or two, what sort of picture of these circuit entrepreneurs we would form in our heads? It would be a picture of the post- post-modernist "one-dimensional man" who is in a singular, one-track, single-minded, dogged race for cash at the expense of all, everything, his family, his loved ones, even himself. He joins alumni and clan associations not to be nostalgic, or to have fun, but to do "networking", find business partners, and solicit yet more funds for investments. He returns to his hometown in China not to find history, heritage and roots, but to take advantage of *guanxi* embedded in kin relations. He presents himself to his spouse and children behind the mask of a businessman-big boss who has done well in "the jungle out there". He tells himself over and over again that he suffers and toils, sacrifices himself, doing everything, yes everything, "for the family", only to hear their loved ones' complaints and grievances against an absent father and an absent husband. As it happens, he feels misunderstood, grieved, pained, betrayed. He misses all the birthday parties of his children, wife, parents, and siblings because he has a plane to catch. All social relations are business relations. All business relations are social relations. In one cut of a knife, he has severed all his sentimental ties, even those to himself as a human being. He has dehumanised, commodified himself. Sitting in a restaurant over a glass of Chinese wine, he wonders aloud if he were to buy the restaurant this very minute, how much cash he will make in the next. He would murmur the same thing to himself about a cheap hotel, a run-down factory in the countryside, a half-finished apartment block, a boutique whose owner can't pay rent – yes, yes, yet another market to be exploited. The world is his oyster, so to speak. He lives with a suitcase at the door, ready to go any time, any minute--always on call. One might as well say he lives from airport to airport, bus terminal to bus terminal. It is a workaday, even "workanight", life of hypermobility and super-vigilence. As the classical Chinese poet would put it, "In my dream while asleep, I don't know I am a stranger". Where am I? Who am I? What am I? How am I? Or the ultimate question: why am I?

Capitalism premises itself on totalistic excess, mindless accumulation, hoarding, senseless consumption, violence, but it is now a kind of post-capitalism which fears that there may be no tomorrow--as banks, stock markets, economies collapse by the minute, which make mockery of the by-now banal term "risk society". Again, as the ever-anxious Chinese poet has long told us, "The world has unfathomable events, and man has unforseen calamities and blessings". So, the circuit entrepreneur has no time for anything but work, he has no time for himself, for his own pleasure, physical, social, psychological, even sexual. He works as if there is no tomorrow because he does not own his time. Capitalism is no longer something out there, in

[3] Peter Berger, *Invitation to Sociology*, p. 53.

the outside because there is now no outside. No more. It is all inside, capitalism is embodied, he himself is capitalism, his body, his time, is but an instrument of capitalism, oppression, suppression, exploitation. He is not merely in capitalism. Capitalism is also in him. Capitalism is his body, his time, his consciousness, even sub-consciousness. Capitalism is now cosmopolitan as it has abolished the inside/outside divide. The outside is marked by its absence. Capitalism is everywhere. In JG Ballard's novel, *Super-Cannes*, Penrose Wilder, a Nietzschean psychiatrist works in a French business park together with the vanguard of the corporate class which comprises tireless CEOs who are relentless in their business pursuits, forgoing all leisure activities and engaging in non-stop work[4]:

> They've gone beyond leisure....Work is where they find their real fulfilment--running an investment bank, designing an airport…if their work is satisfying people don't need leisure in the old-fashioned sense. No-one ever asks what Newton or Darwin did to relax, or how Bach spent his weekends. At Eden-Olympia, work is the ultimate play, and play the ultimate work.[5]

My office is my rose garden. What is left with is not merely a capitalist's exploitation of others, but his own self-exploitation. Leading a life without affect, pleasure, and play, day in and day out, night in and night out, when capitalism is driven by excess and waste which has no limits, the circuit entrepreneur is now not merely a stranger to others, but also a stranger to himself. It is a violence of self-estrangement and self-destruction. It is not that he does not know pleasure. He must know. After all, pleasure is his business. He specialises in inventing all kinds of alternative life-styles of pleasure which he sells to others. Capitalism thrives on self-denial. Again, as the Chinese say, "those who sell flowers keep only bamboo leaves in their homes". Ballard reminds us, "We're breeding a new race of deracinated people, internal exiles without human ties but with enormous power. Its this new class that runs the planet".[6] He won't cry no more not because he has no tears, but because he is not sentimental anymore. He is now a transhuman setting himself off on a transhumanist voyage — to nowhere, into eternal boredom. As it happens, the rational (capitalism and technology) degenerates into the irrational (excess, waste), thus the distinct possibility of the irrationality of rationality. All work no play makes Tom a dull boy. Dullness and boredom breed violence, against others and self.

Last question: do our circuit entrepreneurs know *about* their condition of existence which we describe in this book, particularly in the above paragraphs? Or is it a matter of "the other false consciousness", meaning capitalism is now so much *in* man, under his skin, in his awareness, that it now controls man from within? You cannot escape from something that is within you. Or can you? Can one exorcise onself of this capitalistic urge, this eagerness to appropriate all that can be appropriated,

---

[4] Chan, Nin, 2009, "Ballard, Bataille and Biopolitics", Unpublished article manuscript, pp. 6.

[5] Ballard, *Super-Cannes*, pp. 94.

[6] Ballard, *Super-Cannes*, pp. 256.

including himself, his time, his body, his emotions–by managing, disciplining them all? Or it is a case of the entrepreneur himself knowing about it, but, to paraphrase the British psychiatrist R D Laing,[7] keeping himself in the dark that he is in the dark that he is in the dark. Indeed a total cover-up. He will then say to himself that he has no choice. At that moment, "the other false consciousness" is conveniently coupled with the Sartrean "bad faith". He is aware of his existential condition, but *not* conscious of it. In the former, he knows about it but cannot and would not do anything about it. In the latter, not only he knows about it, of it, but he believes he can and should do something about it. It is only in the latter condition when the circuit entrepreneur would set himself free and is emancipated. Now he has several options. He can withdraw from his work, he can transform his work into something else, or he can play with it, not seriously, half-heartedly, kind of keeping an inner distance from it, being non-committal, playful, even jovial, like in a carnival.[8] These three options enable the entrepreneur to be dramatic, theatrical, about his life, work, play, and in his dealings with society, capitalistic or not. But then this stepping out, first in mind, then in body, into ecstasy, requires a radical mental transformation only afforded by deep thinking, reflexion, meditation. Sociology, philosophy, art, literature, and religion have this transformative power to engender this cognitive change, this "change of the mind", my mind, your mind, everybody's mind.

[7] Laing, R. D., *The Politics of the Family and Other Essays* (New York: Vintage Books, 1972).
[8] Berger, Peter L., *Invitation to Sociology*.

Index

Kolibri 360 GmbH
Ferdinand-Jühlke-Straße 7
99095 Erfurt, Deutschland
produktsicherheit@kolibri360.de